T0273986

Endorsements for

ANCHORED

I've known Mort for more than fifty years . . . or thought I did; but oh what a rambunctious, emotional, ethical and intellectual food fight has been going on behind that buttoned-down façade. While he has spent a professional lifetime focusing on the most interesting people in a fascinating world, he's done an extraordinary job of concealing one of the most interesting stories of all – his own. Until now. Read on !

—TED KOPPEL, FORMER ANCHOR, ABC NIGHTLINE

In an era where speculation passes for news, thank you for always telling the truth. You left your mark not only in front of the camera, but throughout the community with your tireless efforts to make where we live a better place to be. Thanks for everything, Mort. You were Detroit's answer to Walter Cronkite.

—JEFF DANIELS

The local TV anchor is an American institution. Families like ours find their favorite and stick with him or her for decades. Finally, we get to read the life and spirit of Mort Crim, who the Matthews family regularly and loyally invited into our house back in Philadelphia. For those who enjoyed the satire of "Anchorman" and the reality TV of "The Apprentice," Crim's new book gives us the real-life drama off camera.

—CHRIS MATTHEWS, NBC NEWS

Mort Crim's memoir is far more than a look back at his legendary career and the inspiring story of the personal journey which led him there, although it is surely that. It is also an antidote for the current attacks on the media which engender such cynicism and endanger one of the pillars of our democracy. It is a reminder of how voices in the media like Mort's, with a passion for the facts, can triumph over the voices of discord. It will leave us with a dose of optimism that the power of fact-based reporting will triumph over the centrifugal impacts of the social media.

—CARL LEVIN, U.S. SENATOR, MICHIGAN (RET.)

As fascinating as Mort's professional memoir is, we were gripped by this greater story: the story of a love that would not let (him) go, as this larger-than-life memoir becomes the journey of a man in pursuit of his faith. Or maybe it would be more accurate to say a faith in pursuit of this man.

—BILL & GLORIA GAITHER

For those who believe that the unexamined life is not worth living, Mort Crim's story will strike a responsive chord. His honesty about his life and personal struggles is a breath of fresh air in a society wherein so many of us pretend to believe what we really question and pretend to be what we're not. This book is not only entertaining reading but is a challenge to take a good look at life's journey and what gives it meaning.
—TONY CAMPOLO, PHD, PROFESSOR EMERITIUS, EASTERN UNIVERSITY

Mort Crim's memoir is a remarkable broadcaster's journey, told with heartfelt honesty and humor. Mort tells it like it was: radio, TV, his Second Thoughts series and much more. It's a great trip through a wonderful career.
—BILL DIEHL, ENTERTAINMENT CORRESPONDENT, ABC NEWS RADIO

Mort Crim is one of the pioneers and legends of local broadcasting. His style, wit, tenaciousness, and . . . I'm sorry. I have no idea who Mort Crim is. Umm, but I'm sure he's written a hell of a book that will hopefully go on to sell over 10,000 copies. Is that a lot? Cuz I don't know publishing.
—WILL FERRELL

Mort Crim was a towering inspiration as I considered a career in broadcast journalism. He was the quintessential anchorman - clear, concise, engaging - always in command of the facts, and always trusted. His was an era when facts were not disputed and journalism was at its apex. His story offers a reminder of how essential it is for all of us to rely on honest brokers of information. We sure could use more like him.
—MILES O'BRIEN, NATIONAL SCIENCE CORRESPONDENT, PBS NEWS HOUR

Mort's memoir fascinates, mesmerizes and, most importantly, inspires us to learn and search ourselves for our personal truths.
—DAVID HARTMAN, FORMER HOST, GOOD MORNING AMERICA, ABC

ANCHORED

MORT CRIM
ANCHORED

A Journalist's Search For Truth

BEAUFORT
BOOKS

9780825309441 (hardcover)

9780825308246 (ebook)

For inquiries about volume orders, please contact:

Beaufort Books

27 West 20th Street, Suite 1103

New York, NY 10011

info@beaufortbook.com

Published in the United States by Beaufort Books

Distributed by Independent Publishers Group

www.ipgbook.com

Book designed by Mark Karis

Cover designed by Fisher Design & Advertising

Printed in the United States of America

Dedicated to all my fellow pilgrims who struggle to know truth.

Foreword

THERE IS AN OLD PROVERB that suggests wisdom is not in having the right answers, but in asking the right questions. In this book we find both the power of that path in Mort's life—of moving from right answers to right questions—and a deep wisdom that he not only learns but imparts to all of us on this shared journey.

Mort's quest displays the honesty and vulnerability necessary to move from answers to questions, while also portraying the rich beauty of such a life. His book is an invitation to walk along with him and open ourselves to wisdom; an invitation that all who seek the fullness and beauty of life would do well to accept.

—DR. TOM WALKER, RETIRED PASTOR, PCUSA

Introduction

"HI, WILL. It's such a pleasure for *you* to meet *me*," I said, in my finest Ron Burgundy, faux-anchorman voice.

Will Ferrell smiled and gave me a firm handshake. "Actually, it *is* a pleasure to meet you, Mort." I had been joking. Will was serious.

"And I want to thank you for the way you've dealt with all this," he said.

"All this" referred to Ferrell's revelation that I had been the inspiration for the blow-dried, air-headed, skirt-chasing, irreverent television anchorman character Ron Burgundy. No wonder Will Ferrell thanked me for taking the spoof good-naturedly. Anyone who had followed my career knew that my image was exactly the opposite of Burgundy's.

My real-life role models had been Edward R. Murrow. Walter Cronkite. David Brinkley. Eric Sevareid.

But Ron Burgundy?

Ferrell's disclosure of my unlikely role in the *Anchorman* movies first appeared in *Rolling Stone* magazine. As soon as the issue hit newsstands, I was bombarded with requests for interviews. In the two months leading up to the premiere of *Anchorman II*, I had appeared on ABC's *Good Morning America*; CNN's *Piers Morgan*; *Fox & Friends*; *Kelly & Michael*; *Geraldo;* and scores of local TV and radio stations, as well as in newspapers and magazines around the world. In England, *Esquire* magazine's digital edition featured me on its cover, and Australia's *Today* show interviewed me live via satellite. Paramount's publicity machine had generated a lot of curiosity, here and abroad, about the real anchorman behind the outrageous movie spoof. Interviewers all wanted to know: how does it feel to have your life and career parodied in a major Hollywood movie?

Ferrell was probably surprised that a serious journalist with a solid reputation for news reporting had been so tolerant of the satire, even having some fun with the attention it had generated.

"I've seen several of your interviews," Will said.

"And I appreciate the way you've shown such good humor."

I laughed.

"Well, if you guys had billed this as a documentary, I'd really be pissed," I said. "But I like a good parody as much as anyone."

Ferrell seemed shyer than his Anchorman image, but his look was vintage Ron Burgundy: three-piece navy blue suit,

Meeting Will Ferrell at the Anchorman II premiere

flashy indigo tie, and a squared white handkerchief peeking above the pocket.

Adam McKay, who wrote, produced, and directed the *Anchorman* movies, sat sprawled on a couch nearby, his coat slung over the back and his necktie pulled away from his collar. He was chatting with a couple of movie critics. A few feet from McKay, Fred Willard and Steve Carrell had struck up a conversation with Brooke Shields. It was the kind of party where you couldn't walk to the bar without tripping over at least one Hollywood star.

McKay had grown up in Philadelphia, the city where the late Jessica Savitch and I had co-anchored news on KYW-TV in the 1970s, a decade described in Ferrell's movies as a time when anchormen were beyond legendary. "We were gods," narrator Bill Kurtis intones at the start of the movie.

The *Anchorman* movies were spot-on about the exalted place TV newscasters occupied in those days before Cable and 24-hour news. In most major markets, there were only three television stations competing for the news audience: those affiliated with ABC, CBS, and NBC. With such limited competition, Bill Kurtis was as big a star in Chicago as Michael Jordan, and Jerry Dunphy was more recognizable on Los Angeles streets than Tommy Lasorda.

Salaries for top anchors in big cities rivaled those of many professional athletes, and we were accustomed to limousines, first class airline tickets, invitations to the best parties, and the best tables in restaurants. For the anchormen (and in those days, nearly all of them were men), there was always a gaggle of female admirers or groupies, and we were constantly approached by autograph seekers.

It was a heady time to sit at a big city anchor desk, and occasionally some egos did spin out of control, but most major market anchors were actual journalists who could think, write, and report. Only a handful at all reflected the arrogant buffoon portrayed by Ferrell in the movies.

How I had become a centerpiece for the *Anchorman* movies was detailed in the *Rolling Stone* article; Ferrell told the magazine he got the original idea while watching a *Lifetime* documentary about Jessica Savitch, in which I had been interviewed:

"At one point they were talking to this anchor, Mort Crim,

who was basically saying, 'I was an asshole to her.' What made me laugh was watching him. He still spoke like this"—Ferrell's voice grew gaseous and stentorian; he said he based Ron's inflections on his memory of mine. "He still used his on-camera voice." The *Rolling Stone* article included a photograph of me over the caption *Real-life anchorman Mort Crim, Ferrell's inspiration for Ron Burgundy.*

Will apparently thought I had one voice for doing interviews

Mort and Jessica: the original Ron Burgundy and Veronica Corningstone

or describing space launches, and another for ordering ham sandwiches or reading stories to my grandkids. I have been blessed with a good set of pipes, and Will wasn't the first person to parody my voice. When my current wife Renee and I started dating, her son Randy answered the phone one day and in a mocking basso said, "Mom, the voice of God is on the phone."

Ferrell thought the tension that had initially existed between Jessica and me could be developed into a satire about local TV anchors. McKay then dug up old videotapes of our newscasts on KYW-TV for Ferrell to review. That is how Mort Crim and Jessica Savitch morphed into Ron Burgundy and Veronica Corningstone.

Shortly after the second movie was released, a friend said, "Mort, why don't you write a book and tell the real *Anchorman* story?"

All I can say is, be careful about making such a suggestion to your friends. They might just take you up on it.

Oh, I do want to assure you that all the stories in this book are true, to the best of my recollection, diaries, notes, and day planners. However, I have substituted a few names out of respect for some characters and their families, both living and dead.

Chapter One

THE CALLING

My mother loved children. She would have given anything if I had been one.

—GROUCHO MARX

IT'S OPENING NIGHT and hot as Hell—a place I'm determined to help these sinners avoid.

They stand in front of me, hymnals open, voices loud and whole-hearted.

I am Thine, Oh Lord, I have heard Thy voice, and I know that Thou art mine …

The music and its strong declaration of faith are setting the mood for the powerful and convincing sermon I am about to deliver.

Don Quixote never attacked a windmill with more fury than

I am feeling toward the devil tonight.

The small church has no organ and no choir. There is no carpet on the floor, no padding on the long oak pews, no drape on the unadorned wooden pulpit. You find no carved stone here, no stained glass windows, no statues of saints. Such affectations are for Episcopalians and Catholics. The Church of God in Delavan, Illinois, is simple and austere, and the members are humbly proud of its plainness.

The song director stands behind the pulpit, waving his arms in time to the music as the pianist hammers out the familiar old hymn. A few sweat beads dance on the director's gold rimmed glasses as he works. He is dark-haired, has a slight paunch, is wearing a short-sleeved white shirt and, like most of the men tonight, is tieless.

All the windows in the white frame sanctuary are open, but there's no breeze to offer relief from the July heat. Some women try to keep cool with paper fans donated by a local funeral home, its name imprinted on one side under a green, weeping willow tree logo.

I look over the crowd from my vantage point a few feet behind the pulpit. They are mostly middle-aged men and silver-haired women, with a few younger folks here and there. It's gratifying to see that every pew is filled; why, there must be close to 150 people. Sister Evelyn Barrett, the pastor, had assured me there would be a good turnout on this opening night.

I silently count, because the size of the crowd will affect the size of the offering. My income for these revivals is whatever gets dropped into the collection plate. I'm not doing this for money. I've been called by God to preach the gospel; anointed by the Holy Spirit to evangelize the world. But I do hope there'll be enough to pay for some dry cleaning and for gasoline to get my 1939 Plymouth coupe to the next engagement.

Sister Barrett is a stocky, short woman with cropped, sandy-blond hair and the rich, commanding voice of a prophet—strong but not manly sounding. She probably pushes her voice more than she might today, as this is 1951 and preaching is still mostly a man's world. But the Church of God is ahead of its time and has been ordaining women from the time of its founding in 1880. It's not gender but calling that matters, and Sister Barrett's Bible-waving gestures and earnest declarations tell you she just knows she has been called of God to save souls and spread the Word.

As the congregation sings the final verse, I glance at my King James Bible and review Romans 10:13, the text I've underlined for tonight's sermon: "For whosoever shall call upon the name of the Lord shall be saved."

That's what my revivals are all about: getting people saved and leading them into a new way of life. About keeping them out of Hell. It's clear that most of those here tonight already have accepted Jesus as their Savior. The enthusiastic singing surely is coming from people who know the Lord and who have repented and turned from their sins. My focus now is on those sinners in the crowd who've never accepted Jesus as well as those who may have strayed from the faith, and of course any Catholics or other so-called Christians who have never been born again. (One of our core beliefs is that people who haven't been born again aren't really Christians, no matter what church they belong to.)

How blessed I am to be an evangelist. How fortunate to have grown up in a home and a church where we know the Truth. "God is in this place," I declare as I step up briskly to the pulpit, waving my Bible.

"And he loves you. I can feel the Holy Spirit. Didn't you sense God's presence during those wonderful hymns tonight?"

I am passionate.

I am confident.

I am sixteen.

No wonder the pews are filled.

There has to be a lot of curiosity about a boy—barely old enough to drive, and still dabbing Clearasil on his pimples—who can preach, sing, and play the accordion and piano.

Teen evangelist preaches, prays, and plays

Sister Barrett has pulled out all the stops to advertise my appearance. There are ads in the local paper, interviews on the radio station, and an airplane hired to drop leaflets all over town:

TEENAGE EVANGELIST MORTON CRIM

IN REVIVAL AT THE DELAVAN FIRST CHURCH OF GOD.

HEAR THIS DYNAMIC YOUNG MAN PREACH AND PLAY THE PIANO.

This opening night crowd doesn't know it yet, but during the offering I will be treating them to a jazzy piano version of "When the Saints Go Marching In" while a black cloth covers the keyboard. This has nothing to do with God but is a little showmanship I picked up while watching a piano player on a late-night TV show.

If I got the preaching gift from Dad, my flair for show business probably came from two aunts who had performed on the Vaudeville stage.

REVIVAL

MORTON CRIM, 16 Year Old Evangelist

from Hamilton, Ohio

will speak at the

Church of God

BLUE MOUND, ILLINOIS

AT 7:30 P. M. EACH EVENING

Beginning Mon. Dec. 10

EVERYBODY WELCOME!

H. C. PICKETT, Pastor

Handbill from an Illinois crusade

* * *

"Thank God, the son-of-a-bitch is dead!" my aunt Lillian Morgan shouted gleefully upon hearing the radio bulletin of President Roosevelt's passing. It would be decades later, with the election of Donald Trump, before I could understand how people can feel so passionately about a president.

I should say right up front: The Crim family divided pretty much into two groups—the religious, and the . . . well, not-so-much. Aunt Lillian was part of the not-so-much.

She ran onto the front porch, eager to bellow this wonderful news to the neighborhood. Dressed in a loose-fitting, pale-blue gingham house dress, her gray-streaked auburn hair protruding from under a kerchief tied in the back, the frumpy matron bore scant resemblance to the professional singer and stage darling she once had been.

My father's half-sisters, Lillian Morgan and Vivian Safir, were the show business side of the Crim clan. They had played the Keith Orpheum vaudeville circuit and the Billy Terrell tent shows for several years, along with Aunt Lillian's husband, Jack Woods, a comedian, infamous for painting his protruding ears bright red and performing under the stage name Unconscious.

These aunts regaled my sister Barbara and me with glamorous tales of life on the road. Performing under their maiden name as *The Livesay Sisters*, they claimed to have shared the stage with such Hollywood luminaries as George Burns, Milton Berle, and Red Skelton. We didn't know if it was all true, but there was no Google in those days to check such assertions, so Barbara and I were happy to believe them.

They had also sung and danced at Detroit's famed Fox Theater, where Aunt Vivian caught the eye of a local bail bondsman, Alvin Safir. She and Al married, and when her show business career ended, they settled into a swanky apartment on Detroit's then-prosperous Boston Boulevard. We thought it was neat that Uncle Al played poker and smoked cigars and drove a big Chrysler. He was the first Jewish person we'd ever met.

I was only nine when President Roosevelt died in April 1945, but I vividly remember Aunt Lillian's joyful reaction to the news. FDR was a socialist and a liberal, so in Aunt Lillian's view, his demise was good riddance. It would be many years before I learned the real story about this remarkable president, and how he had led our nation out of the Great Depression and through one of its most terrible wars. But in that moment, when much of America was plunged into mourning, my aunt considered the legendary leader's passing a cause for celebration.

Aunt Lillian wasn't alone. West Frankfort, Illinois, about 50 miles from both the Kentucky and Missouri borders, and culturally more southern than Midwestern, was a bastion of ultra-conservatism and racism. Blacks weren't allowed inside the city limits after dark. That may have been a tradition instead of an actual ordinance, but in West Frankfort it had the force of law.

While the Crim family was as staunchly Republican as anyone in town, they seemed free of the racial bigotry that thrived in the region. I believe this was due to my grandparents' Christian belief that all people are created equal, including "the coloreds" as African-Americans were then called in polite society.

When I was born, America was still reeling from the Great Depression, and I lived with my grandparents so that Dad could attend college in Indiana while Mother worked as a waitress to support him. My sister and I were so close to our grandparents that we called them Mom and Dad, never Grandma or Grandpa, and they were pivotal influences during my growing-up years. In fact, I have no memories of my parents before I was five years old—but vivid memories of Mom and Dad Crim.

Mary Frances Crim was a kind woman, never harsh nor judgmental toward anyone, and ready to hand a sandwich or a piece of leftover chicken to the hard-luck hobos (then called tramps) who showed up at the back door with some regularity. She was blessed with a wonderful sense of humor and had the most charming habit of cupping her hand over her mouth whenever she started to laugh, which was often. Mom Crim's mostly gray hair was always pulled into a bun at the back of her head, and she never wore lipstick nor jewelry—not even a wedding ring—since her church viewed such adornments as worldly and not appropriate for good Christians.

It was a nightly ritual for Mom Crim to read to me from "Egermeier's Bible Story Book," and by the time I was six I knew Noah, Daniel, and Joshua as intimately as any kid today knows Han Solo, Captain Marvel, or Harry Potter. My Bible heroes had superpowers that were just as magical. When I learned that all of them were Jewish, it made me feel much closer to uncle Al.

We had so many clergy in our family, we could have started our own denomination, and because my father and his twin brother were ministers, it was as natural for me to play preacher as it was for other kids to play cops and robbers. Mom Crim said I preached my first sermon at the age of five. By her account, it was a fire-and-brimstone homily delivered to an unsuspecting neighbor boy. I thought he was badly in need of religion because I'd heard him say *damn* and *hell*, and everybody knew that good Christians never said *damn* or *hell*—well, not the ones who went to our church. At least not where we could hear them.

Mom had once taught English and believed that proper grammar was a virtue right up there with Godliness. She must have had me convinced, because pulling up my grandfather's padded radio bench to use as a pulpit, I looked straight at my young friend seated on the floor, shook my finger at him and proclaimed, "If you keep saying *ain't* and other bad words, you're going straight to Hell!" (I should note that it was alright to use Hell as a noun, and our preachers did so regularly as they campaigned to keep people out of it.)

I've often wondered if that dramatic commentary on right and wrong marked the beginning of my brief foray into the ministry and, ultimately, a career at the TV anchor desk.

Dad Crim didn't attend Mom's church. He was an elder in the First Christian Church, founded by his father. He was West Frankfort's only judge and he looked the part: tall, with a dignified bearing, always in a three-piece, dark suit, his white hair and neatly trimmed mustache adding to an air of distinction. Dad's family traced its roots back to Germany, claiming that the first ancestor to arrive in the U.S. was a nephew of the famed Grimm brothers who wrote the fairy tales. A good friend once chided me that with fairy-tale writers as ancestors, it's no wonder I became a TV newsman.

Dad Crim's office was in City Hall, next to the jail and the fire station. Before I was old enough for school, he would take me with him to work and sometimes pretend to lock me up in one of the city's two small cells. I found this delightful. West Frankfort rarely had any real criminals, mostly an occasional disorderly drunk, so the cells were nearly always available. I also enjoyed climbing around on the city's only fire truck. The firemen, like the policemen, didn't have a lot to do.

My grandfather had no secretary, no clerk, and no assistant. He personally typed his own warrants, affidavits, and other legal documents on an old upright Royal typewriter while seated at his plain wooden desk, his unlit pipes standing upright on a small oak stand next to a tin of his favorite tobacco. In the evening, after one of Mom's wonderful home-cooked dinners, Dad would retire to the swing on the front porch with a pipe or cigar and wait for neighbors to drop by for evening chats. He enjoyed telling me stories about his early years as a cowboy in Wyoming, and how, when he was a teenager, he had once met Wild Bill Hickok. He never elaborated, but I knew Hickok was some kind of western hero, and I was impressed.

We didn't have babysitters, but Mom Crim found time to do her housework by looping a clothesline rope around my waist and tying the other end to the big elm tree in our front yard. Occasionally Paul Ramsey, a part-time preacher and full-time cab driver, stopped by in his taxi, untied me, and took me for rides, a special treat since Mom and Dad didn't have a car. Today, leaving me alone and tied to a tree no doubt would get Mom Crim hauled up before Child Protective Services, and Paul Ramsey would be charged with kidnapping.

But it was 1940, West Frankfort was a trusting, Mayberry kind of town where church was a central part of life. Mom's church was appropriately called "the basement church." After the congregation completed the basement, they ran out of money, so they put a roof over it and held services underground until they finally were able to top off the structure years later. The basement church was where we sang, prayed, attended Sunday school and revival meetings, and listened to testimonies and sermons. Lots of sermons. Mom and I were in our pew every

Sunday morning, every Sunday and Wednesday evening, and every night of the week during revivals—which sometimes ran for three weeks. Mom attended quilting bees at the church on Tuesday afternoons and carry-in suppers at least once a month.

Life was pretty simple by today's standards. I was five when my Uncle Alvah installed my grandparents' first indoor toilet. Until then, Dad kept a chamber bucket, which the old timers called a slop jar, tucked under his bed. One of the most memorable evening rituals was my grandmother removing her false teeth and dropping them into a glass of water with baking-soda so they could soak and clean overnight. Maybe Polident hadn't been invented yet, but more likely this was just cheaper.

So that's pretty much the picture of this anchorman's start in life: born into a family where one side forbade cursing while the other called the President of the United States a son-of-a-bitch; where many relatives wouldn't go to movies or wear jewelry, while others danced and sang on the vaudeville stage; where some refused to smoke, drink, or play cards while others freely indulged in all of these sins, and more we probably never knew about.

For me this variety of beliefs and lifestyles was fascinating, and as I grew up, both the power of the pulpit and the excitement of show business captured my imagination.

Working as a teenage evangelist gave me the best of both worlds: I got to perform every night—for the Lord!

How did I learn to preach at such a young age? The same way I learned to do carpentry: by watching Dad do it.

But if it was Dad's preaching that had drawn me to the pulpit, it was his twin brother's crusades that inspired me to hit the road as an evangelist. Before I could become an apostle, I had to work as an intern.

Chapter Two

THE APPRENTICESHIP

You're going to change the world.

—SUPERMAN

THE COUNTRY-FRESH AIR blowing in through the open windows was pungent with the aroma of Oklahoma farmland. Only a few cars in the early fifties had air conditioning. Uncle Alvah's brand new yellow-and-black Buick Special with gleaming white sidewalls was not one of them, but neither of us minded the hot, humid wind. It fluttered our hair and rustled our suits and starched white shirts that hung neatly under filmy plastic on a bar across the back seat. The breeze made it harder to hear the radio, so Uncle Alvah turned up the volume to Benny Goodman's "Swing, Swing, Swing" while tapping out the beat on the steering wheel with his fingers. (Uncle Alvah was a serious fan of all the big bands from the 1940s, and so was my dad, his twin brother.)

As a traveling evangelist, Alvah's income was modest, but with no family to support he was able to buy a new Buick every three years. It was his single luxury.

A few weeks earlier I had left Hamilton, Ohio, as a depressed and frustrated fifteen-year-old. Now, rolling through the Oklahoma hills on our way to Nowata, I had a much better outlook on life. Nowata was the third stop on our revival schedule, and I was relishing my new sense of freedom. Life on the road with an uncle who'd always seemed more like a big brother certainly beat struggling with geometry and being bored to death by geography and history.

My sophomore year in high school had faltered at the start. Boredom, growing agitation with religious restrictions, and the normal angst of adolescence had made me increasingly sullen and withdrawn. It hadn't helped that I'd been sidelined from the football team by a knee injury. Since attending movies and dancing were forbidden by our church, football had been my saving grace. It allowed me to be part of a group, and for a teenager, few things are more important than that. Without football, I had become even more isolated, lost, and angry.

Something else had also been eating away at me: I was madly in love with Naomi Ruth Dale, eighteen months older than me and two years ahead of me at Fairfield High School. Her nickname was Nicki and we had a history; our families had known each other for years, and Uncle Alvah had been the Dales' pastor in Harrisburg, Illinois, before resigning to become an evangelist.

I thought Nicki was beautiful and so did the members of

her senior class who named her "Fairest of Fairfield" in our yearbook. I was only a sophomore, and although we were dating, I had to worry about competition from the older guys. It really bugged me when I would see one of the seniors flirting with her in the halls. There's nothing like teenage love to mess with an adolescent's head, and the mismatch in our ages added to my frustration.

To this day, I find it remarkable that Mother and Dad allowed me to quit school at the age of fifteen. I'm sure they were counting on a few months of travel with Uncle Alvah to pull me out of my depression, and part of the deal with my high school principal was that I would continue my studies through correspondence courses while on the road.

With three years of piano lessons and a good musical ear, I only had to hear a hymn or gospel song in order to play it. I'd also taught myself to play the accordion; I hadn't mastered it, but played it well enough to accompany my uncle when he sang and played his electric guitar at the services. Alvah had promised there would also be chances for me to speak at some youth services along the way, although I had delivered only one sermon in my life. It was a rambling talk in Dad's church during National Youth Week about Adam hiding from God in the garden of Eden. I titled my ten-minute sermon "Adam, Wherefore Art Thou." I should have called it "Adam, Where Are You," but at the time words like *wherefore, art,* and *thou* seemed more churchy.

I loved to perform and probably enjoyed that first sermon more than anyone in the audience did. I'm pretty sure I would have pursued an acting career, but our church believed that Hollywood was the devil's workshop, and the Great

White Way a highway to Hell. Uncle Alvah was a prankster who could fire off one-liners as fast as the late Henny Youngman. He spent his holidays and most of his vacation time with us, so my sister Barbara and I considered him part of our immediate family. He also was athletic and loved to impress us by showing us how many push-ups he could do, or by walking across the room on his hands, perfectly balanced with both feet straight up in the air. Despite his mischie-

In love with Nicki

vous sense of humor, Uncle Alvah was the real deal and totally sincere. What he preached from the pulpit came from heartfelt beliefs. With him there was no pretense and no hypocrisy; he never set a price for his revivals, accepting whatever modest donations were dropped into the offering plates.

"Mort, the Lord knows what we need, and He always provides," was how he looked at it.

I felt incredibly lucky to share this mission with a man I so admired. To be honest, I also relished all the attention, especially from the teenage girls. Maybe their adulation kept me from obsessing about those senior guys back at Fairfield who might be making a play for Nicki. On this sunny day, as we motored our way toward the next crusade to save the lost, I was certain there could be no more important work. We arrived at the home of Brother and Sister Carlton, the couple who would be our hosts, unloaded our luggage, freshened up, and headed for our first night of a new crusade.

* * *

Brother Harcum, the pastor, opens the service with a generous introduction.

"You can't afford to miss a single one of Brother Alvah's dynamic, God-inspired messages, and be sure to bring your *lost* friends to hear this great preacher."

Then the pastor asks me to stand.

"We're doubly blessed this week, Brother Alvah has brought along his nephew to help with the music, and on Sunday night, Brother Morton will be speaking at our youth service."

My pulse quickens and my chest swells.

The congregation stands for an opening song, "I Am Thine, O Lord," on page 195. Like most small churches, this one has no organ, so a middle-aged woman at an upright piano provides the accompaniment.

There is another hymn, some announcements, and then a performance by a local gospel quartet: four men in short-sleeve sport shirts. From various parts of the sanctuary, the singing is punctuated with shouts of "Amen!" and "Praise the Lord!"

When Brother Harcum asks the ushers to collect the offering, Alvah and I step forward, his electric Les Paul cut-away guitar hung around his neck by a red and black woven strap, and my Scandalli accordion attached to me by two black shoulder straps. As ushers pass the plate, we swing into our upbeat arrangement

Making music with Uncle Alvah

of "Mansion over the Hilltop."

Alvah Crim is not a high-powered, stem-winding orator like many evangelists of the day. His preaching style is that of the college professor that he later would become. The congregation is attentive as he lays out in earnest, almost scholarly tones a logical case for committing to Christ and avoiding Hell.

After his sermon, there's the traditional altar call paired with an emotional hymn that is not subtle in its threat:

Why carelessly wait? Your pulse will ere long be still, In death will your blood soon chill; O hasten, obey God's will; Why carelessly wait?

"Listen to those words," Uncle Alvah implores as the pianist continues to play softly in the background.

"Life is uncertain. You don't know that you'll make it home tonight, or that you'll wake up in the morning."

The threat that you might die before you can get saved is a staple on the evangelistic circuit.

Soon, soon in eternity, Poor sinner your soul shall be. What then can atone for thee. Why carelessly wait?

The impassioned appeal works and three people come down the aisle, a middle-aged couple and a younger man, followed by two teenage girls who are practically running. They all drop to their knees at the long wooden railing in front of the pulpit. The girls are sobbing.

I feel their guilt. More than once, under the heavy weight of a convicting sermon and an emotional altar call, I had made the trip forward, tearfully confessing my sins which were difficult to recount since we weren't really allowed to commit any. I always knew I'd had more than a few impure thoughts involving girls, so I would beg for forgiveness. I was no more than eleven years old the first time I went to the altar. The experience always had a cathartic effect, which lasted until the next fervently charged altar call. Then I would hit the aisle for another shot of forgiveness.

Tonight, five sinners kneel at the altar, weeping. The two girls loudly and earnestly pray for God's mercy. Uncle Alvah, Pastor Harcum, and I are now down on our knees huddled around them. A few church members leave their seats to join the cluster, their hands on the penitents' shoulders. Now the entire congregation is praying, and random shouts of encouragement ring out:

"Thank you, Jesus."

"Help them, Lord!"

Souls have been saved. It's been a good night. By ten o'clock, we are sitting around the Carltons' dining room table, along with Pastor Harcum and his wife, enjoying Sister Carlton's homemade apple pie.

The Pastor tells Alvah what a great job he did.

"God really was at work tonight," sister Harcum adds. "And Morton," her husband says, "everybody really enjoyed your music."

By the time we conclude our final revival meeting a few months later in Bedford, Indiana, I'm convinced that this is the life for me.

Besides, what choice do I have? When you feel the call to preach, you have to accept it, or it can end badly.

I was only five when Mom Crim read me that story about Jonah, the prophet who turned down God's invitation to preach and got swallowed by a whale. A kid doesn't forget that kind of thing.

Chapter Three

BUT IS IT TRUE?

It ain't what you don't know that gets you into trouble. It's what you know for sure that just ain't so.

—MARK TWAIN

THE REVIVAL TOUR was over and it was time to return home to Hamilton, Ohio. I had earned enough credits through correspondence courses to qualify for eleventh grade, but Nicki had now graduated so I had no desire to go back to Fairfield High. Instead, I enrolled at the ultra-fundamentalist God's Bible School, a private institution in nearby Cincinnati.

God's Bible School's idea of piety was even more extreme than what I'd grown up with. If the school's goal was to make women look as homely as possible, they were smashingly successful: their formula for snuffing out sex appeal included no makeup, no jewelry or short skirts, and no sweaters or form-fitting dresses. Showing cleavage was unthinkable, although it never kept us boys from thinking about it. The school believed literally in the Apostle Paul's command that women not cut their hair, so most wore theirs tied up in buns pulled to the backs of their heads.

My time at home didn't last long. I was restless and, convinced that I had been called by God to be a minister, I now felt the Holy Spirit was directing me to strike out on my own as an evangelist. (It's amazing how often God's call and divine direction seem to line up exactly with what we've already decided to do.)

With nearly a year's experience as Uncle Alvah's protégé, and two semesters at God's Bible School, I felt completely competent to hit the evangelistic trail as a solo act. It seemed my decision was confirmed by invitations from several ministers to conduct revival meetings in their churches—invitations inspired by the reputation I had gained as Uncle Alvah's sidekick. Of course, the requests further inflated my already exaggerated self-confidence.

I was now sixteen and churches did not hesitate to capitalize on the novelty of my age, sometimes with promotional campaigns that seemed right out of a carnival. Always, they billed me as "The Teenaged Evangelist" in newspaper ads, church bulletins, and printed flyers. Stepping up to the pulpit each night, usually in my three-piece light gray suit, flashy tie, pocket puff, and blue buckskin shoes, I envisioned myself as a future Billy Graham.

On the outside, I wore a façade of unfaltering faith and absolute certainty, but there were plenty of private doubts. There had been one especially disturbing episode while traveling with Uncle Alvah, after a revival service in Nowata, Oklahoma. Because there was no television, my bedtime activities consisted mostly of reading, or working on my correspondence school studies. On this particular night, I had borrowed Uncle Alvah's car and driven to a nearby lake to fish. I didn't yet have a driver's license, but he had taught me to drive and people were a lot more casual about such things in the 1950s.

The air was warm and still, and as soon as my lure hit the water, splashes glistened in the moonlight. I hoped a bass was lurking just beneath the surface. The thrill of fishing is the mystery, the silent, submerged activity. It's a sport of hope, faith, and expectation. I had learned to love it sitting next to my dad on the banks of Midwestern lakes or stocked gravel pits, the two of us with cane poles in our hands.

I will never be able to fully explain what happened to me that night, or why it happened then, in that place. But for the first time, doubts about the church, Jesus, God, the Bible, and my own faith began bubbling to the surface of my mind. Maybe the questions had been there, waiting, for some time. Perhaps those unacknowledged doubts had something to do with the depression, the angst, and the restlessness that I had felt back in Hamilton. For whatever reason, my brain now seemed to fill with disturbing uncertainties:

Is the Bible really God's word?

Was Jesus actually the son of God?

How can we be sure there even is a God?

And is it true that unrepentant sinners are destined to spend eternity in the fiery Hell that Uncle Alvah and Dad preach about?

Like a bass striking a lure, these questions grabbed my thoughts and wouldn't let go. I felt as if I were being pulled under by swift and troubling waters. All of my life, I had been taught that there is only one true path to God—Jesus—and that if you begin to doubt your faith, it's the work of the Devil. But now I wondered, how do we *know* there is a Devil? How do we *know* any of this stuff, for sure? Terrified by these disturbing questions, I did what my parents had taught me over the years to do: I prayed.

Unless a person grew up in a similar religious cocoon of absolute certainty, it may be hard to comprehend the anxiety that comes with a sudden questioning of faith. Until that night, I had never seriously doubted any of it. So complete was my trust in the wisdom and sincerity of my parents, it never entered my mind that they could be wrong. To question their beliefs would risk shaking the very foundation upon which my life, my world, my relationships, and my sense of self had been constructed. Why was I having these doubts now?

To think that Uncle Alvah and I might be scaring people with falsehoods was overwhelming. Besides, how could Dad, my hero and in my mind an intellectual giant, possibly be mistaken?

I have to get rid of these doubts before tomorrow night's service.

On the drive back to Brother and Sister Carlton's house, I continued to pray. Anxious, emotional, with my chest tightening and my heart pounding, tears began to form. *This must be the Devil at work! He's upset because we brought people to Jesus tonight!*

I simply had to look to Jesus, I told myself. He's stronger than the Devil! The Bible says so!

In the midst of my praying, I recalled an old hymn and began to hum it as the words played in my head:

We have a hope within our souls,

Brighter than the perfect day.
God has given us his spirit,
And we want the world to hear it,
All our doubts are passed away.

That last line had always made me feel so confident and serene.

All our doubts are passed away.

What a wonderful, reassuring declaration of certainty! But this night, the words left me feeling hollow.

Empty.

Sad.

By the next morning, I had reached a tentative truce with my doubts. Acknowledging misgivings about my faith had been so terrifying that I quickly retreated into denial, a place I would stay for the next eight years, smothering the quest for truth. Now, being on my own evangelistic circuit and the star of the show helped me gloss over lingering doubts. Most days I was able to convince myself that I really believed every word I said. I'm certain that my preaching contained little substance, and even less logic, but I was an earnest performer. I knew that people who came to revival meetings expected to be entertained as well as saved, and I was quite good at that.

My success so impressed the ministerial assembly in my home state of Illinois that on April 7, 1952, I was officially ordained as a Church of God minister at a ceremony in Chicago. I was one semester short of graduating from high school and three months shy of my eighteenth birthday.

Despite growing self-assurance, I did recognize that an ordained minister probably should at least graduate from high school. By this time, my parents had moved from Ohio to Missouri, where Dad had become pastor of the Church of God in East Prairie. I enrolled in the East Prairie high school to complete my senior year. I did not tell my classmates that I was an ordained minister. Back in Ohio, just being a preacher's kid had been tough enough on my social life.

* * *

Settling into a relatively normal life in East Prairie gave me the opportunity to pursue my love of airplanes, something sparked in Hamilton when a member of our church had taken me for a ride in his two-seat Cessna. I had always been interested in airplanes, and as a kid, built models and read aviation magazines. But that Sunday afternoon flight sparked a passion that would last throughout my life.

I bought a five-year-old Aeronca Chief, a yellow two-seater made of wood and fabric, and powered by a sixty-five horse-power engine. It cost $475—money I had saved mostly from my revival meetings and some summer construction work. The

My first airplane

plane had no battery and no radio. The engine was started by hand-cranking the propeller and, once it started, quickly pulling the chocks out from under the wheels and making a dash for the cockpit before the plane began to move.

Over the next couple of years I engaged in several stupid stunts, any one of which could have gotten me killed, and probably should have: a kamikaze diving pass at a friend's home, a foolish dash under an Ohio River bridge, and a bombing run on a teacher's house in a buddy's borrowed Piper Cub, dropping rolls of toilet paper from the airplane's open door. The rolls unfurled on the way down—the ones that hit their mark dangling for days from willow branches in the teacher's yard like giant icicles on a Christmas tree. Even though I possessed the credential of an ordained minister, I still had the emotional immaturity and underdeveloped judgment of a typical adolescent.

It was one spectacularly silly decision in my Aeronca that came closest to costing me my life as well as that of a friend. My student license permitted me to fly solo while practicing landings and takeoffs but did not authorize me to take passengers.

"Hey, let's go flying and take up some friends," I suggested to my buddy Everett Mitchell one Sunday morning in church.

"How you gonna do that? Your plane only has two seats."

"Well," I replied, "we'll have them go to the farm and I'll take everybody up one at a time."

A family in our church owned a farm just north of town and our youth group had gone there for hayrides. Everett was in. Eventually he had enough brains to become a teacher and a respected school administrator in the community, but in that moment of high exhilaration, he clearly was as crazy and irresponsible as I was.

At the nearby Sikeston airport, I pulled my plane out of the hangar, cranked it up, jumped in, and taxied around to the back side to pick up Everett. That maneuver was to make sure my instructor didn't happen to see me with an illegal passenger strapped into the second seat.

I was not far enough along in my training to know much about navigation, so I followed the roads that led to the farm. As we flew at about eight hundred feet over the house, the barn, and the silo, I could see our three friends leaning on a fence at one side of the pasture. I felt a surge of excitement at the prospect of demonstrating my flying skills.

There was a low fence and a deep ditch at one end of the pasture, and a tall row of trees at the other. Landing over the fence would require flying downwind and, consequently, would bring us in quite fast. But if I approached over the trees, I knew we would arrive at the pasture too high. I opted for the lower fence approach.

As we got closer, the field appeared considerably shorter than it had appeared from the ground. The closer we got, the shorter it got, and rougher it looked.

We came across the fence much too high and too fast and half the field was behind us before our tires hit the pock-marked, clod-filled pasture with a thud and a bounce. We were barreling down that washboard pasture like a terrified sinner running for the altar, and I knew there was no way I could get us stopped before hitting the row of trees. To apply the brakes would send our speeding plane cartwheeling end over end.

Yelling at Everett to hang on, I pushed the throttle full forward. The four-cylinder engine coughed and sputtered and tried to give me everything it had, which proved pathetically inadequate. We bounced a couple of times, then we were flying again with barely enough speed to stay in the air. Everett had never been a preacher, but I could see he was praying with evangelistic fervor as the tall row of trees rapidly approached.

I pulled the yoke back in one final, desperate attempt to clear the trees, but it was too late. The plane stalled, slammed into the highest limbs, spun around on its way to the ground, and nosed into a ditch along the highway.

The plane was totally wrecked, one wing badly crumpled, the landing gear crushed, the door on my side buried in dirt and jammed shut. Gasoline from the ruptured fuel tank in the nose of the plane poured into the cockpit. Neither Everett nor I was hurt. Knowing he wasn't supposed to be in the airplane, I heard him say as he bolted from the badly broken Aeronca, "If anyone asks, I've been fishing all day." With that, he headed down the highway to thumb a ride back to town.

Everett crawls away from the crash

By the time I pulled myself out of the wreckage through the passenger side door, our three friends had disappeared from that fence. After a few minutes sadly surveying the crumpled fabric and splintered wood that had been my airplane, I also hitchhiked home.

My near brush with death had left Mother and Dad more upset than I had ever seen them. At breakfast the next morning, I promised that I would never fly again. Of course, they both knew how totally obsessed I was with flying, and Dad's response was immediate: "Morton, we can't let you make such a promise."

Dad had a fear of heights that bordered on phobia. He did not like airplanes, had never flown in one, and never understood my fascination with them.

"Your mother and I know how important flying is to you. We can't allow our own anxieties to deprive you of something that brings you so much joy."

He was absolutely correct. Flying would be for me a lifelong passion.

It was only after I became a parent that I truly understood the courage and the unselfish love Mother and Dad had shown me in that moment.

Chapter Four

A TASTE OF FREEDOM

You're on your own, and you know what you know. And you are the guy who'll decide where to go.

—DR. SEUSS

THE RADIO STATION was above a bar in downtown Blytheville. A long, steep stairway between grimy yellow walls led up to it, the stairwell reeking of spent cigarettes, cooked onions, and stale beer, which mingled with the mustiness of the building itself.

As I climbed the steps, I heard the twangy sound of Hank Williams and His Drifting Cowboys, Hank's voice working hard to push his hit song "Kaw-Liga" through a small speaker that had all the hi-fidelity of an empty coffee can.

It was June, 1953. I had just graduated from high school and was planning to pursue my ministerial training in the fall at

Anderson College, where both Dad and Uncle Alvah had studied.

What kind of summer job do you look for when you're seventeen and the only experience you can put on your resume is "traveling evangelist?"

Since eighth grade, I had been intrigued by radio announcing. A young disc jockey visited our junior high school in Hamilton one career day, describing what it was like to talk into a microphone and spin records for a living. He made it sound like a lot of fun. He worked for the town's only station, WMOH, and one of my friends said he was sure those call letters stood for "We Morons Of Hamilton."   I had no training or experience in broadcasting, but during my revival engagements I had been occasionally interviewed on local radio stations, and twice I had been invited to deliver brief meditations on the radio.

I was always fascinated by the studio environment with all the dials, switches, turn tables and stacks of records. I was especially intrigued by the performing aspect of being an announcer. Of course, as interesting as it was, I knew I could never allow broadcasting to become an ambition, just as I could never become an actor. I had been called by God to be a minister and couldn't be distracted from that mission.

Television was in its infancy and radio was still king. Some veteran radio announcers would tell you that TV could never become as important as the medium that brought us Lowell Thomas, Walter Winchell, Edward R. Murrow, *Dick Tracy*, *Superman*, *The Lone Ranger*, and *The Shadow*.

There was no radio station in East Prairie, so I drove through all the towns within a hundred miles looking for one that might hire me. Inevitably, I would hear something like, "Sorry, son, we don't hire announcers without experience."

Then how, I wondered, does a person ever get experience?

After at least half a dozen rejections, one station manager told me there might be an opening at KLCN in Blytheville, Arkansas, about an hour from East Prairie. The owner had fired one of his two announcers and the other one quit the same day. I was immediately off to Blytheville.

At the top of the stairs, I looked through the double-plate glass of the control room window. There a man wearing glasses, brown slacks, and a short-sleeved sport shirt appeared to be managing everything going out over the air. He was slightly bald and looked to be in his mid-forties. He motioned for me to come in.

Hank Williams had finished singing and now Kitty Wells was belting out "It Wasn't God Who Made Honky Tonk Angels."

"You must be Crim," he said.

"Yes," I answered, trying to project my best radio voice.

"I'm Harold Sudbury. I own the station."

The fact that the station owner was having to spin his own records, and on a Saturday, suggested that he was a bit desperate to hire someone.

"Have you ever worked in a radio station?" he asked.

"No, sir, but I've listened to a lot of radio, and I've hung out at stations." I realized how pathetic the words sounded as soon as they left my mouth.

Mr. Sudbury sized me up, then turned a loose-leaf book on top of the console to the next page. When Kitty's record ended, he read a commercial. Then he started another record selected from a stack of 78-rpms on the console.

"See these?" he said, pointing to the records. "While one song is playing you cue up another record on the other turntable."

There was a turntable on either side of the console, each big enough to handle the 16-inch discs used for some transcribed programs.

He twisted a large black knob counter-clockwise until it clicked.

"That's the cuing position.

And this book of commercials? When one record ends, you push this mic button, read a commercial, then start the other record. Just keep doing that, alternating between turntables."

With that he pushed back his chair, stood up, and announced, "You're hired, Crim. I'm going downstairs for lunch."

There was no discussion of salary or hours, but I was so excited about becoming an announcer that I would have paid him to do it—if I'd had any money.

During the first few minutes on the job, I felt more stress than when I'd made my first solo flight in an airplane or delivered my first sermon. Trying to remember everything he'd told me, I forgot that I was now in the state of Arkansas.

"You're listening to KLCN, Blytheville, Missouri," I announced on my first station break.

I can only imagine my listeners wondering if the station had moved across the state line.

Minutes later I read my first commercial. It was for a beauty salon, but the word that flew out of my mouth was *saloon*.

Mr. Sudbury came back up to the studio after lunch and I wondered if he had returned to fire me. Apparently, he hadn't heard. He stayed just long enough to say, "The job pays fifty cents an hour." That was about what farm laborers got for picking cotton, but I didn't care.

I didn't know it, but my long and interesting journey to the big-city TV anchor desk had begun.

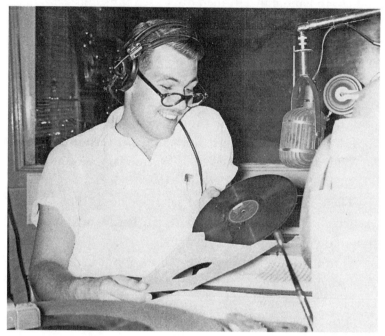

Disc jockey at KLCN, Blytheville, AK

If my travels as a teenaged evangelist had given me a small taste of freedom, the summer in Blytheville would be a smorgasbord. For the first time, I was truly on my own and would face some real choices about my behavior. I was now an ordained minister, but all of that had happened so fast I didn't really feel like one. Besides, how could a teenager possibly know himself well enough to make such a heavy commitment? Isn't adolescence supposed to be the time for figuring out who you are? What you want to do? A time for experimenting?

I could now attend movies. Smoke cigarettes. Drink beer. Play poker or attend a dance. Well, the last two weren't likely to happen since I'd never held a deck of cards in my hand and never learned to dance. Nevertheless, sins that had been totally off limits my entire life would be available to try out in Blytheville. There was no one around to care what I did. Of course there was God, and I had been raised to believe that He sees everything; now, however, I wasn't so sure about that.

It seemed like everybody in radio smoked, and I learned to puff away while a record was playing, then park my cigarette in the ashtray long enough to read a commercial. I tried Kools—they were supposed to be better for you—but didn't like the taste and settled for unfiltered Camels. Cigarettes can't be too harmful, I thought. I mean, even doctors advertise them. I didn't care much for liquor but did learn to enjoy an occasional beer.

A radio announcer was about as close to a celebrity as they had in Blytheville, and a few awestruck girls would sometimes hang around the station. One girl even invited herself over to my apartment, leaving little doubt about her intentions. But sex before marriage was one transgression I would not consider. In our church, premarital sex was the ultimate taboo. You could be a bigot, cheat on your taxes, get drunk, swear, or do any number of things the church considered sins, but the phrase *living in sin* was reserved for that greatest evil of all: sex outside of marriage. My sex education up to that point had come mostly from bull sessions with buddies and sneaking looks into forbidden magazines. As I entered adolescence, I was given one rule and one warning: The rule was, don't do it until you're married. The warning included the dire prediction that masturbation could make you blind. Yes, in those years some parents really did pass along that old wives' tale about the consequences of self-pleasure.

The rule about abstinence from sex with a girl I took seriously, but pretty much ignored the warning about blindness. Whenever I saw any guy in school wearing glasses, I did wonder if he'd been spending too much time in the bathroom or under the covers.

With today's sexual freedom and widely available birth control, it may be difficult for people—especially younger people—to understand my hesitancy to take a willing girl to bed. But anyone reared in a strict religious community like mine knows that such teachings can have an enormous influence on behavior. Also, I had been in love with Nicki from the moment we had met and I'm sure my strong feelings for her helped prevent me from fooling around.

Despite meager pay and long hours, I loved everything about my radio job, even the unglamorous task of emptying waste cans at the end of each shift. Occasionally, I got to use my keyboard skills. Slim Thornton and his *Oklahoma Playboys* were well known in Blytheville as they fiddled and plunked their honkytonk music at a local roadhouse. (A lot of country musicians called themselves "Slim," which is why I adopted the handle Slim Crim for my radio shows).

One morning Slim's piano player failed to show up for the broadcast (my theory is he was suffering from too much honky-tonkin' the previous night). I volunteered to sit in, and after that I became a regular substitute. I would introduce the band from the control room, then rush into the studio while they played the theme song and join them at the piano for the main set. I did have to learn a lot of new songs as my gospel repertoire didn't exactly fit their format.

Blytheville gave me my first real lesson in religious hypocrisy. Each weekday morning, Arvin and Joanne, a husband-and-wife team, performed live gospel music on our station. The two sang duets while Arvin accompanied them on his guitar. Between songs, they offered impassioned and tearful testimonies about what God was doing in their lives. Between these testimonies they hawked their records. But frequently, when they broke for a commercial, God, too, seemed to take a break. I could hear them over the intercom in my control room: "You son-of-a-bitch!" Joanne screamed at Arvin one morning. I hadn't heard what sparked the argument, but apparently it was something that carried over from the night before.

"Shut up, bitch, or I'll stick this guitar up where the sun don't shine," Arvin fired back.

This kind of dialogue went on throughout the commercial break, but the moment I turned their mic on again, they were instantly transformed into messengers of God, praising the Lord, and pleading for donations to support their fine Christian work.

Clearly, not all "Christians" were as genuine as Uncle Alvah.

By the end of summer, my brief hiatus from the pious life was over. I was ready to smoke my last cigarette, chug my last beer, resist the last temptation to lose my virginity, and hop back onto the straight and narrow path to Anderson College.

Chapter Five

LEAVING THE PAST BEHIND

It is when we are in transition that we are most completely alive.
—WILLIAM BRIDGES

MOTHER AND DAD didn't have enough money to send me to college. I would have to work, just as both Dad and Alvah had done. Supporting oneself through school was a family tradition.

In Anderson, I parlayed my three months of experience at KLCN into a part-time job at WCBC, a Christian station owned by an eccentric preacher who showed me another example of hypocrisy. While the reverend ranted from the pulpit against the depravity of television, he would watch his own TV at home through a hidden antenna he had secretly installed in his attic. My broadcast shift included an afternoon country music show under my pseudonym, *Slim Crim, the Arkansas Traveler,* the moniker I'd used in Blytheville. I opened each show with a rousing rendition of "Turkey in the Straw," to which I clapped my hands and sang, "Oh, swing your maw, and uh, swing your paw, and uh, swing that gal from Arkansas... Howdy, neighbors, you're listenin' to your ol' buddy, Slim Crim, the Arkansas Traveler, invitin' you to the best country music in central Indiana."

The "Arkansas Traveler" arrives in Indiana

I had more or less perfected my country twang at KLCN, although I was sure that dropping the "g" from words such as *listening* and *inviting* must have had my English-teaching grandmother turning in her grave.

Anderson had two radio stations, and when I learned that the other one, WHBU, needed a weekend announcer, I applied and got the position. Working at both stations was a big help financially. WHBU was a high-brow CBS affiliate that played a lot of classical music, the programming opposite of Christian-country station WCBC.

The Monday after my first weekend stint, I received a telephone call from WHBU's general manager, John Atkinson. Gee, he must have been impressed, was my immediate thought. I wonder if he wants me to work more days?

"Can you come into the office today?" Mr. Atkinson said.

When I arrived, he did not look like a boss who was about to promote an employee.

"Crim, are you working at WCBC as Slim Crim, the Arkansas Traveler?"

"Yes, sir," I proudly responded, happy to learn that Mr. Atkinson was among my listeners.

He handed me my paycheck.

"We won't be needing you anymore."

Nobody had told me that it's unethical to work for competing radio stations in the same town. I guess you don't learn everything about the business in just three months.

My freshman year at Anderson produced a lifelong friendship with a fellow student, Bill Gaither, who had formed a gospel trio with his brother Danny and sister Mary Ann. They performed at area churches on weekends, where they also sold their recordings. Because WCBC was a Christian station, I was frequently able to play their music on my show. Bill, raised in the Nazarene church, married a Church of God preacher's kid, Gloria Sikle. The two of them went on to become two of the best-known and most-beloved gospel musicians and writers in history. Their Grammy and Dove award-winning songs have been performed by some of the biggest names in the business, including Elvis Presley, and both are in the Gospel Music Hall of Fame. I still like to kid Bill that he and Gloria never would have achieved gospel music stardom if I hadn't plugged their records on WCBC.

Anderson was only a two-hour drive from Hamilton, and I began making weekend trips to see Nicki. We weren't actually dating, but during my senior year in East Prairie we had stayed in touch by letter and occasional phone calls. Since graduating from Fairfield High, Nicki had dated some of those guys who'd

made me insanely jealous, but she was not in any serious relationship. I was still madly in love with her, and by the end of
the year, we were engaged. As I was still in college, wedding
plans had to wait.

The year at Anderson did nothing to give me a clearer sense of
direction. I was still fighting an internal battle between the broadcaster I increasingly wanted to be and the preacher I thought I
had to be. I feared that my growing infatuation with broadcasting
was developing into a dangerous obsession. What had started as a
part-time job at WCBC had become full-time, and juggling work
and studies was becoming increasingly difficult. Maybe getting
back into preaching would remove the radio temptation and help
me settle the matter. Also, it would give me an income that could
speed up the date for Nicki and me to marry.

After one year at Anderson College, I left school to become
pastor of the Church of God in Portageville, Missouri, thirty
miles from East Prairie where I had graduated from high school
only a year earlier. To hire a nineteen-year-old with only one
year of college, the Portageville church must have been about
as desperate for a pastor as Harold Sudbury had been for an
announcer. It hadn't hurt that Dad had put in a good word for
me with the church's trustees.

That same summer, on August 21, 1954, Nicki and I were
married in Hamilton. We had been engaged for seven months.
Dad performed the ceremony and Uncle Alvah was my best man.
I found it ironic that as a nineteen-year-old I needed my parents'
written permission to marry, but as an ordained clergyman I had
already officiated the weddings of several other couples.

Nicki moved into the brick parsonage with me, next door
to the church, but there was hardly time for her to adjust to her

Our wedding Day

new role as a minister's wife. Six months after our wedding, I resigned from the church to build a radio station. Clearly that hasty and ill-informed decision was more evidence of both vocational struggle and emotional immaturity. (It was also another symptom of a deeper issue: unresolved questions about my faith.)

Before resigning from the church, I had convinced Dad and Alvah to invest in the radio station venture. We bought a used FM transmitter and I built the studio mostly from scrounged parts. We included a heavy dose of church programs and religious music in the schedule, no doubt my way of trying to square things with God for having left the pastorate.

FM radio was relatively new and few people in those days

owned FM receivers. But brimming with optimism and self-assurance, I set about to defy the odds. With nearly a year of announcing under my belt plus a year of college, what could go wrong?

Radio stations west of the Mississippi have call letters beginning with K, so I applied for, and was given, the call letters KRIM. We immediately began a campaign to sell advertising. When we couldn't convince a local merchant to buy commercials, we offered to trade advertising for groceries, dry cleaning, haircuts, oil changes—whatever a sponsor had that we needed. We couldn't afford to hire anyone. Nicki and I were the staff, along with Uncle Alvah, who took a break from his crusades to help launch the station.

We each worked an on-air shift and Nicki hosted a one-hour homemaker show, clipping articles from women's magazines and reading them on the air. We never thought about copyrights or who owned those words. We got material for our

KRIM-FM entrepreneurship

newscasts the same way: by stealing it. We had no money for a news wire service, so we "borrowed" news stories from the St. Louis Post Dispatch. We were naively broadcasting material we had no right to use, and by the time it aired, the information was at least a day old.

To fill airtime, we played scratchy classical records checked out from the local library and worn-out jukebox records which we bought for five cents each from the local diner. I had never heard of music licensing organizations such as ASCAP, BMI, or SESAC and didn't realize that we owed them fees for the music we were broadcasting. Thankfully these organizations had never heard of us either.

KRIM had been on the air less than four months when I went into the Piggly Wiggly supermarket to pick up groceries that they routinely traded for commercials. This time, the manager met me at the checkout counter. He did not look happy.

"Crim, if you want these groceries, you'll have to pay for them," he snapped, "in cash. I did a survey of my customers yesterday. As people came through the checkout, I asked how many times they had heard my commercials. None. Zero. Zip. And only one of them had even heard of your station."

With that sobering ratings revelation, my broadcasting empire tumbled into an inglorious pile of dashed dreams. A week later, I borrowed a flatbed truck from a farmer in our church. At two o'clock in the morning, Nicki and I loaded up furniture and other belongings, slipped out of town without a goodbye and headed to Mother and Dad's house in East Prairie.

We left the transmitter, the console, the used records, the stacks of news clippings, our tarnished reputation, and never looked back. Come to think of it, I don't believe we ever notified the FCC that we had gone off the air. Now, some sixty years later, I wonder if the government thinks we're still broadcasting. Probably not. Nobody in Portageville seemed to know it.

* * *

"I think we should go back to Anderson," I said to Nicki as we sat around my parents' kitchen table. "I'll go back, finish school, and get my degree."

"Sounds reasonable to me," Nicki said.

"But first you'd better figure out who you are and what you want to be. You can't keep hopping back and forth between the ministry and radio."

Mother and Dad nodded in agreement. But then, Mother nearly always agreed with Dad. Married at sixteen and with only an eighth-grade education, she suffered all of her life from an inferiority complex. Although Dad did have the formal education, Mother was much smarter than she knew: keenly observant, a good judge of people, and always learning from life. She was also an imaginative writer, something we discovered from journals after her death. Mother had the additional assets of being a kind, sensitive, and physically attractive woman who had learned to host wonderful parties—attributes that served her well as a pastor's wife. Born Ocie Dell Martin in the tiny hamlet of Steele, Missouri, she could be as strong-willed as the proverbial Missouri mule. But her admiration and love for Dad were unflinching.

In the few months that we'd been married, Nicki had gone from being a pastor's wife to the wife of a failed entrepreneur who clearly lacked both maturity and direction. We discussed the fiasco of our radio station. Was this God's way of reminding me that I was supposed to be a preacher? Did the station go belly up because God wanted me to follow my calling? The reality is, I failed because I was cocky, arrogant, inexperienced, unfocused, and grossly unprepared.

After re-enrolling at Anderson College, I got my old job back at WCBC. But life as a married student was no easier than it had been when I was single, and after a year, I once again was restless. Among the important life lessons I had not yet learned was this one: Wherever you go, there you are. Changing locations, circumstances, or jobs can never calm inner turmoil. When you move to a new environment, the same old doubts, uncertainties, and anxieties move with you. When I heard that the First Church of God in South Bend, Indiana, was looking for a pastor, I applied and was hired. I now had completed two years of college.

Nicki, with her beautiful voice and love of music, sang solos at our services and helped to organize a choir. The congregation was warm and accepting of their new young minister and his wife. I joined the Ministerial Association and the Kiwanis Club. I became a chaplain in the Civil Air Patrol, which gave me access to their two-seat Piper Super Cub. Having a plane available was a real perk, as I had earned my private pilot's license before leaving Anderson and my enthusiasm for flying had grown.

Despite uncertainty about my calling, I mostly enjoyed the job of pastor and worked hard at it. As I had watched my father do during my growing-up years, I visited sick people in hospitals and shut-ins in their homes, officiated at funerals, performed weddings and baptisms, and handled all the other duties and rituals that went with ministry. It seemed I was a natural people person, but it was preaching that I enjoyed most. The pulpit was my stage, the congregation my audience, and it was there, with my mind focused upon the sermon and my delivery of it that I could momentarily push aside the questions that so often haunted me. Strangely, perhaps, preaching became a refuge from those nagging doubts about my faith. Maybe I was preaching to myself, trying to convince myself.

Nicki had agreed on the move to South Bend only after I promised that I would continue my education. I enrolled for theological studies at Bethel Bible College in neighboring Mishawaka. I also signed up for journalism, speech, and broadcast courses at Notre Dame, another clue that my struggle between pastor's study and broadcast studio wasn't over. I didn't consciously think of it that way, but clearly I was preparing myself to go in either career direction.

At Bethel, my curriculum included New Testament studies, Biblical prophecy, and the history of the protestant reformation. The more I delved into these subjects, the more I felt those anxieties that had first troubled me that night on the banks of an Oklahoma lake.

Bethel was a theologically conservative college that interpreted everything in the Bible as literal history, including a six-day creation of the world. Bethel taught that the Bible was divinely inspired, without error, and that every word was historically and scientifically true. The explanations were no more satisfying to me than the ones I'd grown up with. So many of Bethel's assumptions seemed totally out of touch with what is known about the universe; the more I studied the Bible, the less I believed it could all be taken as literal fact. Even if it was God's authentic word, much of it simply had to be metaphor—imagery, figures of speech, allegory. Otherwise, it simply didn't make sense.

Had these professors never heard of Copernicus, Newton, Darwin or Einstein? Were they not bothered by empirical data that clearly cast doubt on many biblical stories? Did they honestly believe that a big fish swallowed a disobedient prophet, vomiting him onto the shore after three days, where God magically caused a tree to grow and give him shade? It was clear that Bethel's mission, as with other Bible schools, was to fortify what already was accepted as truth and never to challenge or question the foundations upon which the assumptions rested.

The more I learned and the more I thought about things, the more difficult it became for me to write honest sermons. Outside the classroom I studied the history of the Bible, how and when it was written and edited, and by whom. I read essays by historians, investigations by archeologists, and opinions of prominent theologians that introduced me to fresh ways of thinking as well as to new areas of inquiry. I was encountering learned scholars who seriously and thoughtfully questioned many foundations of the Christian dogma as I had been taught, and I was seeking the one thing that terrifies many true believers: facts. I wanted objective information, even if it contradicted things my church and my family held to be true.

As the disconnect grew between what I was preaching on Sunday and what I was feeling the rest of the week, I carried on as best I could. When anyone came to my study for counseling—a shaky marriage, a difficult situation at work, a dreaded medical diagnosis—I gave them the same kind of confident message of hope that I delivered from the pulpit on Sundays. Of course, we always ended the session with a confident prayer that God would handle the situation.

I was skillful at saying the right words. After all, I had grown up hearing my dad and my uncle say them. Both my sermons and my counseling must have been believable, because the people seemed to love their young pastor and our small church was growing. The problem was that every day, I was becoming increasingly unconvinced.

Our church believed in miraculous healing, yet I had never seen anyone get well who wouldn't have been expected to recover without prayer. Some who were prayed for remained chronically ill, and some died. It all seemed so random. I spoke often in the pulpit about allowing the Holy Spirit to lead us and to guide our decision making. But whenever I sought such direction in my own life, I seemed to hit a blank wall. I preached that the Bible was the divinely inspired word of God, but the more I proclaimed this, the more I questioned just how true it was. By now I had learned too much about the historical origins of the Bible, its many revisions over time, and the numerous contradictions and absurdities contained within its pages.

Until now, the only career advice I had sought had been from ministers, including Dad and Uncle Alvah. I decided it was time to look for some perspectives from the broadcasting business. In a rather audacious move, I wrote to Paul Harvey, introduced myself as a student who was having trouble deciding between the ministry and newscasting, and said I would like his advice. Paul was at that time America's number one news commentator, with an audience larger than that of Walter Cronkite or Rush Limbaugh. Uncertain that he would even see the letter, I was pleasantly surprised when he wrote back inviting Nicki and me to make the 90 mile drive to Chicago, sit in on his noon broadcast, and then go to lunch with him.

"I hope you don't mind if I invite my number one adviser to join us," Paul laughed as we sat in his office after the noon show.

His wife, Angel, showed up a few minutes later and the two

of them spent an hour and a half over lunch counseling me about my dilemma. I looked around at the fancy restaurant and sure hoped Paul was planning to pay the tab. Paul said he had been raised in the Church of God and knew quite a bit about its doctrines and practices. Whether I was called to the ministry was something he couldn't say, but he did reckon that broadcast news could use good people of integrity—like me.

Oh, yes. He did pick up the check.

* * *

It was a Friday afternoon, several weeks after my meeting with Paul Harvey. I had been at the church, in my study, wrestling with the Sunday sermon and having great difficulty getting anything meaningful down on paper. I walked back to the parsonage next door to the church and went up to our bedroom to rest. I felt an alarming aloneness. Nicki was out, but my sense of isolation was something far beyond her absence. I tried to pray, but the feeling of abandonment only intensified.

Where was God?

The sun was shining through our bedroom window, but a terrible darkness was enveloping me. I dropped to my knees.

"God, if you're there, if you really exist, please say something."

Tears formed in my eyes and my chest tightened.

"Please, God, give me a sign. I have to know. I can't go on like this."

Nothing.

I heard nothing. I felt nothing.

After several minutes on my knees, my arms hugging the bed, I stood up, walked to the window and looked up at the sky, even though I had long ago stopped thinking of God as a being up there somewhere. I hoped that whatever he/she/it was, that God was present with me in that desperate moment.

"God, I really need your help," I pleaded. "I want to be your servant. I want to spread the gospel. Please."

The tears were flowing and my prayer was becoming angry.

I thought of characters in the Bible who had felt abandoned by God—Job, David, Joseph, Abraham, even Jesus—but I had no desire or ability right then to seek comfort in Scripture.

Not since my first crisis of faith in Oklahoma had I experienced such an ominous question mark over everything that I thought I believed, and wanted to believe. Back then I was in my teens, a time when people are supposed to challenge assumptions and search for answers. In adolescence, confusion is part of deal. Now, I was an ordained minister, responsible for the spiritual well-being of a congregation. It was more than my emotions that were at stake; it was my career and my livelihood. My reputation. Also, I knew that somewhere lurking not very far in the back of my mind was the thought: "What will Dad think!"

"Honey, I've made my decision. I have to leave the ministry."

Nicki was well aware of my struggles with faith and shared some of the same questions, so I don't believe she was surprised by my statement during a Sunday afternoon drive in August. We were returning from a youth convention in nearby Mishawaka. It was a few days before our third wedding anniversary.

I knew that many of the things I could not believe disqualified me for ministry in the Church of God. I was ready to launch a quest for truth, unencumbered by the requirement to protect any dogma or belief. I was determined to subject every belief I had ever been taught to the toughest scrutiny, no matter how many sacred cows from my past might be slain in the process. I was trading the comfort of an exclamation point for the vulnerability of a question mark, but I had no choice.

When I announced my resignation the following Sunday morning, I did not reveal to the congregation the doubts I was having about my faith. That would have been hurtful to those who had put their faith in me, and besides, such an exposé didn't seem necessary. I simply announced that I no longer felt a call to the ministry and believed I could best serve as a journalist.

Most members accepted my decision with grace, albeit some disappointment. However, one older lady stood up following my announcement and declared to the entire congregation that I was betraying God. Waving her hands in the air, she shouted,

"Brother Crim, while you were talking, I saw the Devil dancing on your shoulder!"

As she described the vision, her voice rose to nearly a shriek. "If you forsake your calling, Brother Crim, I see your soul *damned to Hell!*"

Her dramatic display made me uncomfortable, but I left South Bend with no anger or bitterness. What I did feel was an enormous sense of relief that my life's vocational compass finally was finding its true north. My faith compass was much less settled, and I was still a long way from having a view of life, God, and reality that I could articulate.

I respected and appreciated the Christian values my parents had demonstrated in our home: love, compassion, grace, forgiveness, and gratitude. I still believed there was an originating and mysterious force behind everything, but beyond that, I had no concept of this force's characteristics—or if it had any. I felt overwhelmed by questions, but I certainly intended to keep following Jesus as best I could while trying to figure it all out. For the time being, however, I would follow him at a distance.

Chapter Six

INTO THE WILD BLUE YONDER

Every new beginning comes from some other beginning's end.

—SENECA

BEFORE LEAVING SOUTH BEND, I had lined up an announcing job at WTVO-TV in Rockford, Illinois. The job didn't pay much, but it did offer free movies and free stock car races, because the man who owned the station also owned the movie theater and the race track. Since neither Nicki nor I had been allowed to attend movies as kids, we had a lot of catching up to do, so the free movies were a real perk.

We began attending Methodist services on Sunday mornings, and I continued to pray and to read the Bible, but more out of habit than conviction. Focusing on the new career gave me a refreshing break from the intellectual war that had raged off and on since I was fifteen, and for a few months, I took a timeout from thinking much about God and faith.

WTVO-TV provided a quick and total immersion into the television business. I hosted an afternoon movie, wrote commercial copy, directed an occasional live show, and selected background music for the newscasts. In today's world of twenty-four-hour cable news, it's difficult to remember that in 1958, most TV stations devoted only about an hour a day to news. Our evening newscast ran fifteen minutes, including weather, sports, and commercials.

We had no reporters. Anchorman Bruce Richardson read scripted copy over photographs, slides, or artwork, interspersed with an occasional short film. It seemed to me that TV was nothing more than radio with pictures, and most nights, the pictures hardly seemed worth the effort.

Color television was still something of a novelty and WTVO still broadcast in black and white. There was no videotape, and we produced all local commercials live in the studio. The local supermarket brought in fresh produce each day, which the director carefully arranged on a black velour background and then dramatically lighted to make it look irresistibly fresh and delicious.

That first television job was a wonderful school for a beginner, but it lasted only four months. Resigning from the church caused me to lose my ministerial draft deferment. One early November afternoon, I had been at the station only a few minutes when Nicki called.

"You have a letter from Selective Service," she said.

From the day I first faced the prospect of military service, I knew the Air Force would be my choice. Already a licensed civilian pilot, flying jets appealed to me a lot more than slogging through fields with a gun as a ground-pounder. At one time I had even entertained the idea of becoming an Air Force chaplain.

"If you haven't opened that letter, then technically, you haven't been drafted," the Air Force recruiter explained. "You can still enlist in the Air Force."

I was sworn in to the Air Force on Veterans Day, November 11, 1958. During basic training, I learned that my less-than-perfect vision disqualified me for flight training. Oh well, hadn't I been advised years ago that certain adolescent activities could make a boy go blind? Because of my civilian background in broad-casting, I qualified for an assignment in public relations, writing news stories and producing radio and television features for the Air Force. My first assignment was to Vandenberg Air Force Base, a newly commissioned missile base in California. We'd been warned that housing prices around Vandenberg would be out of our reach, so we bought a small, used house trailer and an even more used, lemon-yellow Buick Road Master to pull it.

Nicki and I had just passed Flagstaff, Arizona, cruising along listening to the Everly Brothers harmonize "All I Have to Do is Dream," our Beagle, Susie, asleep in the back seat, when suddenly there was a loud bang. The car shuddered and began to swerve, first to the right, then left, then back to the right again. A trailer tire had blown out. Control became increasingly difficult, and in the extended side mirror, I saw the trailer gyrating back and forth, violently. We could feel the trailer pulling our car with it.

As I tried to slow down, there was a loud popping sound behind us. The car seemed to stabilize, but then I watched the full-on horror show through the passenger window. Our trailer hit the shoulder, then began a slow roll down the side of the steep embankment, kicking up dust, and finally coming to rest on its top in what appeared to be a dry riverbed.

I stopped the car. We ran toward our mobile home, now an upside-down wreck. Inside, it was a disaster. Almost nothing had escaped damage. Everything had come loose and the refrigerator door was wide open. My freshly ironed military uniforms lay in a disheveled heap, some splotched with catsup. We pulled as much from the debris as we could salvage—soiled uniforms, canned goods, suitcases, books—and carried it all up the embankment. We filled every available space in the trunk and the back seat of the car. Then we built a wall of boxes between us in the front seat, and when the car could hold no more, we tied things to the roof and under the hood. With our last piece of rope, I tied our yellow mop bucket to the trailer hitch. Anyone watching would have concluded that the real Beverly Hillbillies were about to arrive in California.

What probably saved our lives was the inexplicable release of the safety chains designed to keep the trailer from separating if the hitch failed. Both chains had come loose, allowing the trailer to roll down the ravine without dragging our car with it. Those chains releasing had caused the popping sound.

When they learned what had happened, our parents of course believed that God had answered their prayers for our safety. My own belief about divine intervention was ambivalent at best. I had long been plagued by the obvious question of why some prayers seemed to be answered while others, just as worthy, were not. The church's answers that "only God knows," or "We'll understand it in heaven" were never satisfactory for me. Whether it was God or random good luck that had spared us didn't matter; I still said a prayer of thanks.

We arrived at Vandenberg broke and discouraged. We had not insured the trailer. After paying the motel bill, we had about six dollars between us. Nicki cried herself to sleep our first night in California. But we were determined not to ask our families for more help. We already owed Uncle Alvah a thousand dollars that he had loaned us to buy the trailer.

Broadcasting for Armed Forces Radio Network

By the time we pulled up to the Vandenberg entry gate the next morning, our Buick had totally lost its clutch, probably from pulling the trailer over mountains. The only way I could stop the car to present credentials to the MP was to turn off the key. Then, in order to proceed, I had to start the car in gear and watch the bewildered MP in my side mirror as we lurched and galloped onto the base.

I reported for duty and recounted our sad saga to my new commanding officer, Major Laridon. My story must have been convincing because his response was to reach into his pocket and hand me $50.00.

"You know I'm not supposed to do this," the major said, "and I expect you to pay me back as soon as you can."

That loan allowed us to rent a converted garage apartment in nearby Santa Maria, where we shared a small bathroom with the owners, both of whom were schoolteachers. Our bathroom, between the garage and the kitchen, had a swinging partial door that offered a minimum of privacy. The first time I was seated on the commode, I looked down to see the couple's two-year-old son on his hands and knees looking up at me from under the door. From then on I took a small suitcase with me, strategically placing it in front of the opening.

Nicki got a job as secretary to the Base Exchange officer and I found part-time announcing work at the local radio station. Within a month, I had paid back the major, and within a year, we had paid off our debt to uncle Alvah, rented a decent apartment, and bought a new subcompact car—a British-made Ford Anglia.

During our two years in California, an information officer at Strategic Air Command headquarters, Lieutenant John Halbert, had noticed my work and decided I should join the headquarters operation at Offutt Air Force base near Omaha.

Once reassigned there, I continued to produce radio and television features and, among other duties, assisted in the production of the Rock Hudson movie *A Gathering of Eagles*. One of my most memorable jobs was when they dispatched me to the public address microphone to read a welcoming citation when President Kennedy visited the base.

Despite many lingering questions about God, I had not given up on faith, although I still didn't know exactly what I believed. We stayed loosely connected to the church. I led a youth group at the local Methodist church, Nicki sang in the choir, and on the base, I served as a volunteer chaplain's assistant.

In late 1960, toward the end of our first year in Omaha, we learned that Nicki was pregnant. We had been married for six years and were both joyful at the prospect of a baby. Nicki was in her fourth month when we decided to visit her parents in Ohio. We couldn't afford plane tickets, so we made the trip by train.

The long and bumpy journey turned out to be too much for Nicki, and by the time we arrived in Hamilton, she was hemorrhaging. Doctors were unable to save the baby. We never learned whether it was a boy or a girl. We both were so overcome with grief, maybe we didn't want to know. We were later blessed with two very wonderful children, but today, more often than I care to, I find myself wondering about our lost baby.

My enlistment was up before the U.S. got deeply involved in Vietnam, so I never saw combat, but I did experience firsthand the most harrowing event of the Cold War: the Cuban missile crisis.

In October 1962, the world was on the brink of nuclear conflict as the United States and Soviet Union faced off over Moscow's decision to place missiles in Cuba. As Russian ships carrying the missiles confronted an American blockade, Strategic Air Command was placed on DEFCON-2. The only higher state of readiness is DEFCON-1, signaling that nuclear war is imminent. Today, a friend of mine who was serving overseas at a B-47 base remembers that pilots were strapped into their seats with jet engines running, ready if given the order to carry their nuclear payloads to the U.S.S.R.

During the tense final hours of the crisis, scores of us serving at Strategic Air Command headquarters were hustled down elevators and deep into the underground. There, under forty-five feet of concrete and steel, we were sealed off and presumably protected from a nuclear blast.

I took no comfort in this since Nicki was at her job in the Base Exchange office, protected only by a thin roof of corrugated steel. I had no desire to survive if a nuclear bomb was going to annihilate SAC headquarters, killing my wife and all of our friends who were totally vulnerable on the ground above us.

While the generals and colonels huddled in front of consoles under huge screens, ready to launch B-52 bombers and intercontinental missiles if ordered to do so, the rest of us watched and waited in front of TV monitors to find out if the apocalyptic movie *On The Beach* was about to become a documentary.

Hours seemed like days, but Soviet Premier Nikita Khrushchev eventually blinked, backing down to President Kennedy's demand to remove the missiles. The Soviet ships turned back. The world was saved.

Even though I hadn't qualified for Air Force flight training, using my civilian license, I managed to log nearly 200 hours of flight time in aero club planes. I was dispatched to Air Force bases across the nation to interview missile launch officers, military legends such as General Jimmy Doolittle, and many show business celebrities when they performed at Air Force bases.

By December, 1962, I had given my country four years of service. The Air Force had given me much in return: a college degree; experience in writing, reporting, and broadcasting; some badly needed maturity; and at long last, a sharp focus on where I wanted to go and what was required to get there. At the age of

27, I was now ready to pursue broadcast journalism in earnest.

The next step was to earn a master's degree.

Northwestern University's Medill School of Journalism was considered to be one of the best J-schools in the country, but gaining admittance there with my checkered academic background was a long shot. Defying the odds was not a new concept to me and the positive reinforcement of my childhood must have given me the confidence to try. I hoped that my real-world experience would count for something.

The application required an essay explaining why I wanted to pursue a journalism career. I remember my composition being heavy on platitudes and a bit sanctimonious. Journalism, I declared, was *my calling*, and I proceeded to lay out my reasons in almost missionary terms. Pompous or not, something must have resonated, because Medill accepted me and offered me a fellowship with full tuition and a small cash stipend.

Interviewing KC-135 pilot for SAC radio service

Nicki soon got a job at the Evanston hospital, and before long, I started bringing in some money, too. WLS, the ABC radio station in Chicago, hired me as a part-time news writer. Juggling classes, schoolwork, the fellowship, and the radio job was exhausting, but during four years in the Air Force, I had learned how to squeeze the most out of every hour.

Interviewing Jayne Mansfield during the USO show

When the station posted an opening for a news announcer, I auditioned and got the job.

That move from part-time writer to full-time newscaster quadrupled my salary and certainly got me noticed at Medill. WLS was the number-one rated Top Forty station in the Midwest, and for Chicago-era Baby Boomers, the names Dick Biondi, Art Roberts, and Clark Weber still trigger memories of sock hops, first romances, and doing homework while listening to the radio. The first airplay of a Beatles record in the U.S. was on the Dick Biondi show, so to broadcast the news on such popular programs made me something of a minor celebrity on campus.

It's been said that the reason the Wright Brothers succeeded when others failed is because there were two of them. That certainly applied to my success in graduate school. Nicki played a critical role in getting me through the long, grueling days—helping me with research, editing and typing my thesis, all while holding down her own full-time job at the hospital.

During my final week at Northwestern, Phil and Cele Eisgrau invited us to their swank waterfront apartment for a farewell dinner. I had become friends with their son, Mike, who was a classmate at Medill.

"You know they'll be serving wine," Nicki said as we pulled into their parking garage off Lake Shore Drive.

"Yes, I'm sure they will," I said.

Neither Nicki nor I drank, although our abstinence at this point was out of habit, not conviction. We both believed there was nothing wrong with consuming alcohol in moderation. Even the Bible we'd grown up with records that Jesus's first miracle was turning water into wine at a wedding party in Cana. Not only that, the Scripture describes it as the *best* wine of the entire evening. We were pretty certain it wasn't Welch's grape juice.

"Have you decided what you'll do when they offer wine?" Nicki persisted.

"What will I do? I think I'll ask for the red," I replied.

We both laughed.

Chapter Seven

THE BIG BREAK

Life isn't about the big break; it's about one significant life transforming step at a time.

—TIM STOREY

"HI, MORT. This is Jerry Graham. I'm program manager at WNEW."

I knew that WNEW was the number one New York radio station for news. It had spawned a long list of broadcast journalists who went on to become national network TV correspondents, including Reid Collins, Marlene Sanders, and Ike Pappas.

"I hear you're about to graduate from Medill. Are you interested in New York?"

Interested? I was ecstatic at the prospect.

To do well at WNEW almost guaranteed a chance to go

national. Nicki was as excited about moving to New York as I was about working at WNEW. We found a row house in Forest Hills, Queens, a quick subway ride from Manhattan. The quaint brick home, built in 1928, was cozy with a wood-burning fireplace and a diminutive backyard opening onto a

common grassy courtyard. To us, it was a mansion. But even more importantly, I was about to become part of the nation's media elite.

Life in New York did not get off to an easy start. As a newsroom rookie, I was reminded from the first day that I was now in the big time. More than once during the early weeks I wondered if I had gotten in

Delivering the news in New York

over my head. The newsroom competition was fierce as each of us was encouraged to outdo the previous newscast with more clever lines and compelling copy.

My toughest competitor was an ambitious and talented young newscaster named Alan Walden. Alan and I alternated hourly newscasts, and my relentless goal was to come up with a lead line more impressive than what Alan had written for the previous show.

My best lead line came just three weeks into the job. It was so blatantly sexist that if I used it today, I would be suspended or fired, but this was the 1960s, the real-life *Mad Men* era, before Betty Friedan, Gloria Steinem, and women's liberation. The opening story was about showgirls at the Copacabana nightclub going on strike. Their biggest issue: they wanted expanded restrooms. Too many women, too few stalls.

At the time there was a commercial running on our air for Contadina canned tomatoes, and it included a musical jingle touting the product's richness: "Who put eight great tomatoes in that itty bitty can?"

New Yorkers were familiar with the jingle, so playing off the commercial I opened my newscast with these words:

"Who put all those great tomatoes in that itty bitty can? That's what the Copa girls are asking tonight…"

It was tabloid journalism, but when I returned from the studio, the entire newsroom broke into applause. Even Alan Walden was clapping. I had passed the test and proven that I could write New York-style with the best of them.

At WNEW I encountered my first serious conflict between conscience and career. Cigarette advertising had not yet been banned from television and radio; cigarette smoking was endorsed by such notables as actor-politician Ronald Reagan, football great Frank Gifford, and even some doctors. Winston cigarettes sponsored one of my newscasts, and although I wasn't required to read their commercial, I was expected to introduce the newscast with the words:

"Brought to you by Winston. Get the fine tobacco taste of a Winston."

I cringed at the idea. Years of indoctrination about the sin of smoking had left a deep emotional imprint, despite the fact that I had smoked briefly during my months in Blytheville. I also worried that reading a tobacco endorsement would hurt the people who believed in me, most of all my family.

I sought the advice of our former pastor in Chicago, Denzel Lovely. We had attended his church during my time at Northwestern, and I respected Dr. Lovely's wisdom.

"Mort, throughout your life and career you will face challenges of conscience, and there may be times when you have to choose between loyalty to the job or to your values.

I can't tell you if this is one of those times," he said. "Life doesn't always present us with neat, black-or-white choices. Sometimes it's necessary to wade through a little mud in order to reach a worthy goal. Only you can assess what your goal is, and how dirty you consider this mud." He then reminded me of German theologian Dietrich Bonhoeffer, who had struggled with the choice of assassinating Hitler or following his strong moral code against murder. The comparison between taking down the heinous Hitler and plugging cigarettes seemed like a stretch, but I got the point. I decided to read the Winston intro, but I never felt good doing it.

A few weeks after I began working at WNEW, the station hired my friend Steve Bell, who also had graduated from Medill and was working as a TV anchor at WOW-TV in Omaha. Like Nicki and me, Steve and his wife, Joyce, had grown up in conservative churches where movies, dances, drinking, and card playing were prohibited. Joyce's father had been a Quaker minister and Steve's dad a Sunday school superintendent. The four of us quickly bonded. Steve and I called ourselves the brothers we'd never had.

Besides its strong reputation for news, WNEW was a powerhouse in the music industry. It was not unusual to see Frank Sinatra, Barbra Streisand, or Leslie Gore walk into the studio for an interview with our number one on-air star, William

B. Williams. It was Willie B who coined Sinatra's unofficial title, Chairman of the Board. Willie B.'s show, *Make Believe Ballroom*, was to recording artists what *The Tonight Show* became for comedians. If Williams got behind a record, he could quickly shoot it to number one and make the artist an overnight sensation.

Within two months of arriving at WNEW, I was assigned to deliver a half-hour newscast at 11 p.m., which included a commentary by David Schoenbrun. He had been a CBS correspondent in France during World War II and was one of the famed Murrow Boys (the second generation of that illustrious group). Legendary broadcast journalist Edward R. Murrow had recruited him to practice the same sort of thought-provoking, incisive, and high-standard coverage for which Murrow became famous. Schoenbrun was finishing out his storied career at WNEW, and to be working side-by-side with a Murrow colleague was heady stuff for a preacher's kid from West Frankfort.

Sometimes a New York story would become national news. That happened on the evening of November 9, 1965, right at rush hour. It was cold, and with so many people cranking up the heat, turning on lights, and cooking dinner, the energy drain in the heavily populated Northeast pushed the electrical system past the maximum. One by one, power grids throughout the region began to fail, and within minutes, WNEW and all of New York were totally in the dark.

Just as fast, however, our radio station was back on the air with emergency generators, and our news team swung into action for one of the biggest stories we would cover that year. All over the city, it was pure chaos: massive traffic jams as the stop lights went out, people trapped on stalled elevators and left stranded in various ways. For the elderly, the dependent, and people in hospitals, it was downright dangerous.

While the blackout was a major inconvenience for everyone, for me it was both personal and alarming. Nicki was expecting, and could deliver at any moment. She was home alone in Queens, in the dark, without even a functioning subway to transport her if she needed to go to the hospital. The blackout also had disabled telephone service in that pre-cellphone era, so I couldn't call her. Reporters were radioing in that nothing was moving in Manhattan, and the Queens Borough Bridge was a virtual parking lot. Driving home to her was not an option.

The blackout covered eighty thousand square miles and affected thirty million people. Our news team did a commendable job of relaying the story to those listening on portable, battery operated radios or in cars. We emphasized the human side of the story, interviewing pedestrians, trapped drivers, police officers, EMS crews—anyone we could find who would help our listeners understand the crisis in personal terms. Steve Bell turned in some remarkable reporting that helped us win several major awards for our coverage.

In New York, it ended by mid-morning the following day and I finally was able to get home to Nicki. She was fine. One day later, Steve and I rushed her to Mount Sinai Hospital as fast as my Thunderbird could negotiate the New York City traffic. We needn't have hurried. Albert Morton Crim, Jr., didn't arrive until early the next morning, his first but not last experience with procrastination.

Sometimes it's the feeling we experience during a dramatic event that we remember as much as the event itself, and my recollection of my emotions the day Albert was born is vivid.

Seeing for the first time this little miracle Nicki and I had created filled me with an inexplicable sense of divine presence. We had hoped for, planned for, and dreamed about this new person who would be coming into our lives, and now that he had arrived, I was filled with gratitude beyond words.

Thank you, God, I found myself spontaneously whispering as I stepped out the door of Mount Sinai Hospital and into the Manhattan dawn. A pink-orange sky backlit the city's gray skyscrapers as the sun began its daily show beyond the East River. It was all so amazing. Life was *awesome*. I felt fresh, newly alive, and invigorated as I contemplated the wonderful days that surely lay ahead for us. My news career seemed poised for a limitless trajectory, and now we had been blessed with a healthy boy to share that future and to create one of his own.

Who could know what this remarkable little baby would become? What he would achieve? It was exciting and breathtaking, and my sense of God in that moment required no explanation. It was beyond description. Perhaps I was discovering that all true encounters with God are too profound to be described by mere words.

In early August, 1965, WNEW sent me to Cape Canaveral to cover the launch of Gemini Five, an eight-day earth orbital mission flown by astronauts Gordon Cooper and Pete Conrad. I was to co-anchor coverage of the flight with Alan Walden. I took great pleasure in a *New York Times* ad which declared, "Crim and Walden Cover Conrad and Cooper." It did not escape my notice that I'd been given top billing over Walden, my chief competitor in the newsroom, despite Alan's longer tenure at the station. When I pointed this out to Nicki, she quickly observed that my name was probably first only because Crim and Walden made for a better alliteration with Conrad and Cooper. Nicki had a wonderful way of keeping me from ever getting too full of myself.

The Cape Canaveral assignment opened an important door to my next stop: the ABC Radio Network. Tom O'Brien, vice president of news for ABC Radio, had been a correspondent and still enjoyed being at the scene of the action. He had a big, booming radio voice and an Irishman's massive frame to match. Whenever there was a space shot, the ABC news team could count on the boss being with them at the Cape.

I ran into Tom at a NASA briefing and he recognized me as soon as I introduced myself.

"I've been listening to you on WNEW. When you think you're ready for the network, give me a call."

I had worked at WNEW for one year when ABC Radio hired me to anchor ten newscasts each week, and to report from the field. Joining the network was a stunning moment for me. I would be sharing the national airwaves with radio titans I had long admired: Paul Harvey, Alex Drier, Bob Considine, and Edward P. Morgan. That little radio station in Arkansas seemed a lifetime away.

I was thirty years old, life was good, and still today, I remember my six years in New York as among the happiest and most professionally satisfying of my career. Partly it was the exhilaration of working in New York, the heart of the industry, but also it was the nature of the news itself. The 1960s were the decade in which a U.S. spy plane was shot down over Russia, the Cuban missile crisis came close to triggering nuclear war, the war in Vietnam divided the nation, race riots broke out in major cities, and college campuses erupted with building occupations and protest demonstrations over social issues. President Kennedy, his brother Robert, and Martin Luther King, Jr., were assassinated, and a bullet permanently paralyzed Alabama's segregationist governor, George Wallace, when someone tried to kill him.

John Glenn became the first American in space, and Neil Armstrong the first man on the moon. It was the era of Woodstock and miniskirts, Malcolm X and Medicare, and Hare Krishnas and the Beatles. Everything was changing fast, and to be a national newsman in New York was to have a front-row seat to the greatest show on earth. Whether on assignment filing a report or sitting at the desk preparing my next newscast, I was engaged in writing the first drafts of history. Some days I couldn't believe they were actually paying me to do it.

Covering space shots for ABC

On the longer, featured programs, the newscaster would be introduced by an announcer. One Saturday morning, minutes before I was to deliver *News around the World,* a man walked into the studio and sat down at a microphone across the table from me. I was busy reviewing copy and barely looked up.

"Good morning, Mort. I'm your announcer."

It was a familiar voice. He was a bit on the rotund side, thinning hair, appeared to be in his seventies, and wore glasses and a broad smile. His face was not immediately familiar, but I knew that voice. He extended his hand.

"I'm Milton Cross," he said.

Of course. For more than four decades, his had been the renowned voice of the Metropolitan Opera. My father loved classical music and Milton Cross had been a regular radio visitor in our home on Saturday afternoons. Now this legendary announcer was finishing out his career by introducing news programs and reading commercials. This celebrated voice, Milton Cross, was about to introduce *me*.

The red light above the control room window flashed on.

"This is News Around the World," he intoned into his microphone.

"Now, here with today's report, Mort Crim."

The names Francesco Cavalli or Monteverdi never rolled off that golden tongue with more earnestness or finesse than did the words *Mort Crim* that Saturday morning. One of my most treasured keepsakes, along with that memory, is the two-volume set of *Complete Stories of the Great Operas* by Milton Cross. It is inscribed: "To Mort Crim, great newscaster and a fine person."

My desk at ABC was in a large office, which I shared with Ted Koppel, Charles Osgood, Jim Harriott, and media psychologist Dr. Joyce Brothers. Steve Bell left WNEW and joined us a short time later. Koppel, Osgood, and Bell would all go on to have significant careers in national television, but in 1965, we were all young radio network neophytes.

Our newsroom was a smorgasbord of nationalities, races, religious beliefs and personalities. Having grown up in a predominantly white, protestant, midwestern environment, being suddenly thrust into the middle of such rich variety was eye-opening.

Except for my uncle Al Safir and Medill classmate Mike Eisgrau, I had not personally known many Jewish people. My concept of Catholics was shaped in large part by Protestant prejudice. At ABC, I was working side by side with Raj, a practicing Hindu from India; with Avi, a conservative Jew who observed a kosher diet; with Robin, a devout Catholic who attended mass at least once a week and wouldn't eat meat on Fridays; and Fred, a professed atheist who seemed more Christian in his attitude than many Christians. Before New York, I had never known any atheists—at least none who admitted it.

It was becoming clear to me that the belief system we start with in life may have little to do with truth. It will have everything to do with what we're taught. What our parents believe. What our group thinks. What our culture endorses.

Raj was a Hindu because his parents, his family, his friends, were Hindu. All around him there was support for his Hindu beliefs. Avi didn't start out life with a clean religious or philosophical slate; he was Jewish because his family was Jewish. That's the faith he grew up believing to be the right one.

It also seemed obvious to me that few true believers in any religion recognize (or will admit) the degree to which their culture determines their beliefs. Such an admission would be acknowledgement that their beliefs might be wrong, and this would be a serious threat to their faith.

Yet, recognizing the biases that are built into us from birth is the starting point for any rational, objective search for truth. If we are blind to the forces and influences that formed our beliefs, our search will be conducted within a bubble of unawareness. Real fact-finding will be impossible.

On that dark night of doubt along the banks of an Oklahoma

lake, seeds of recognition about a larger world had germinated in my mind. Here in the heterogeneous melting pot of New York, they were coming into full flower.

Even as my spiritual understanding was increasing, Nicki and I were less and less involved with church. We did attend Sunday services occasionally at Manhattan's renowned Marble Collegiate Church. We donated to the church and participated in communion, but that was about the extent of it. Whenever I was invited to speak in churches, on Christian college campuses, or at religious conventions, I frequently accepted but I avoided talking about theology. I spoke in more general terms about Christian principles, morality, and applying Jesus' teachings to the modern world. I couldn't speak about specific beliefs since my own were too ill-defined.

I had a deep longing to find God, but questions, doubts, and skepticism had created an intellectual wall that I couldn't seem to break through. Sometimes I envied my family for the apparent ease with which they believed. Nicki and I often discussed my spiritual struggle, and while she harbored some doubts of her own, her faith never seemed as tentative as mine.

So far, I had developed more ideas about what God is not than what God is. Andy Williams had recently released a song, "He's Got The Whole World In His Hands," but it seemed to me that God had put the whole world in our hands. I hadn't yet resolved the inconsistencies I saw between the idea of divine intervention in human affairs and the apparent randomness of good and bad things happening, but it was clear to me that God is no magic genie that answers our wishes if we simply pray hard enough or often enough.

Trying to approach my inquiry like a good journalist, I

was reading everything I could find that seemed to address my questions—from J. B. Phillips' *Your God Is Too Small* to Bishop James Pike's *A Passionate Pilgrim*. Leslie Weatherhead's *The Christian Agnostic* and Harvey Cox's *The Secular City* were particularly helpful.

I studied the works of renowned theologians and mystics, including Paul Tillich, Karl Barth, Meister Eckhart, and Dietrich Bonheoffer. I read biographies of Albert Schweitzer, C.S. Lewis, Gandhi, Martin Luther King, Jr., and Mother Teresa. I researched the history of the New Testament writers and the findings of archeologists. I began to see that there were many ways of looking at the Bible and interpreting it; I had grown up believing there was only one.

Chapter Eight

GOODBYE NEW YORK

Go out on a limb. That's where the fruit is.

—JIMMY CARTER

TOM O'BRIEN was committed to radio.

He never wanted to rely on the television correspondents to cover really big stories. He believed radio would get whatever time those reporters had left over after their TV assignments, and he was right. Also, a TV correspondent was inclined to simply write a report and read it into the microphone. Tom wanted more than that; he wanted background sounds, color, action, and interviews. He believed that only correspondents working exclusively for radio would put the listener into the middle of the story.

This is why I was dispatched to the Kennedy Space Center, along with Merrill "Red" Mueller, to report on manned space flight. Frank Reynolds and Jules Bergman did an excellent job of handling the TV side of things, but Red and I would guarantee that radio listeners got the coverage they deserved.

On July 16, 1969, I was an eyewitness to the most historic event of my lifetime: the launch of the first humans who would set foot on the moon. My description of that launch is recorded in a commemorative vinyl album published by ABC: "Now you can hear those thunderous engines as the sound moves over our way."

I felt my voice quiver in synch with the vibrating ground. I gripped the microphone more tightly, moving it closer to my lips, hoping to be heard above the deafening roar from more than seven million pounds of rocket thrust. We reporters were three miles from the launch pad, far enough away to be safe, but close enough to feel the Saturn's power, and to smell the kerosene-saturated smoke that covered the launch pad and was now wafting our way.

I was privileged and lucky to be among this corps of space correspondents watching history in the making.

"That's the largest, the biggest, the loudest sustained noise that man has ever created."

I was now yelling into the microphone, unable to hear my own words, but hoping the audience could. The ground trembled. For a few moments, the television newsmen were silent. Walter Cronkite, David Brinkley, and Chet Huntley, sitting in their anchor booths just to the right of where I was standing, didn't need to say anything. The picture their audience was watching said it all.

Kennedy Space Center with Merrill "Red" Mueller (c) and ABC Vice President Tom O'Brien

Today it seems everybody has access to television, even in the world's most remote villages, but that was not true in 1969. Millions around the world—in automobiles, factories, farm fields, and offices—were experiencing this remarkable moment by radio. Those tuned to ABC were depending upon me to create the picture with my words.

"The rocket has cleared the tower. The powerful Saturn taking three young men and an ageless dream on their way to the moon.

A white rocket the size of a skyscraper, fighting its way free of gravity, and it looks like a beautiful, perfect launch. Apollo Eleven, still clearly visible, and by this time it should be more than a mile high."

For Nicki and me, the journey from small-town announcer to national news correspondent had itself been something of a rocket ride. My background as a civilian pilot along with my experience covering Air Force missile launches helped earn me the regular assignment to the Space Center. The Apollo program was just gearing up, and Red Mueller and I reported on every moon flight through Apollo 12—six in all.

Writing about current events was more satisfying to me than writing sermons had ever been. As a reporter, I could verify facts, interview sources, and be reasonably certain that what I was saying was true. Of course, I had a lot to learn in the coming years about the relationship of facts to faith. In time I would discover that you don't always discover truth by simply adding up facts—that some truth comes to us through intuition, imagination, experience, and encounter. But in those early and heady New York days, that's how I felt.

As much as I enjoyed newsroom work, it was reporting from the field that really got the journalistic juices flowing. Being at the scene of the action and describing events as they occur is the red meat every serious reporter craves, and covering the Space Program was as good as it gets.

For one week prior to an Apollo launch, ABC would move our news operation into a suite of rooms at the Cocoa Beach Holiday Inn, turning it into a remote studio. There I would prepare and deliver my daily newscasts, then attend NASA briefings, conduct interviews, and hang out with the astronauts. Most of them stayed at that same Holiday Inn.

One afternoon while taking a dip in the motel pool, I looked around and saw that I was swimming with Alan Shepherd, the first American in space; Frank Borman, commander of the first spacecraft to fly around the moon; and Wally Shirra, the astronaut who provided CBS viewers with launch details while sitting next to Walter Cronkite. Recently I found a photograph of our two-year-old son, Al, next to Shepherd beside the swimming pool. Al was too young to know that someday he would treasure that historic photo with the space hero.

Albert Junior with Alan Shepherd

The days leading up to a launch brought all the network heavyweights to Cocoa Beach, and you never knew whom you would run into. On May 18, 1969, about a half hour before the launch of Apollo 10, I was just leaving the restroom when I heard banging on a stall door and someone with a familiar broadcaster's voice muttering words not appropriate for TV. Working from the outside, I was able to get the jammed door unstuck and out walked Walter Cronkite, obviously in a hurry to make it back to his booth before the commercials ended.

Swimming with Apollo astronauts Wally Schirra (seated) and Frank Borman

The Sixties was a great time to be a reporter and the challenging assignments just kept coming. In 1966, I was sent as part of the White House contingent to cover President Lyndon Johnson's seven-nation tour through Asia and the Pacific. The nineteen-day trip was to include visits to all of the nations whose governments supported the U.S. in the Vietnam War: New Zealand, Australia, Thailand, Malaysia, South Korea, the Philippines, and finally a presidential visit to Vietnam. Heads of state from the allied countries were to meet with Johnson in Manila for a summit conference on the highly controversial war. Frank Reynolds, the ABC White House correspondent, was covering it for television.

There was a Presidential motorcade at each stop. Correspondents and columnists rode in air-conditioned buses near the back of the line while photographers and camera operators were positioned aboard a flatbed truck at the front. Producer Mark Richards and I chose to ride on the truck where our microphone could pick up all the sound and action as background for my reports. In those years, ABC television news was still an also-ran behind CBS and NBC, but when it came to radio, our network led the pack, thanks in large part to Tom O'Brien's insistence that we send our own correspondents to cover the big stories.

On the second day of the trip, Ray Scherer ran up to the truck, a tape recorder hanging from a strap over his shoulder. He was NBC's White House correspondent and was covering this trip for both television and radio.

"Joining us, Ray?" I asked.

"Thanks to you guys," he replied, not seeming too happy about it.

"My desk wants to know why I'm not getting the natural sounds they're hearing on ABC."

Ray and his tape recorder were on the truck with us for the rest of the trip.

Opposition to Johnson's war policies was building, both at home and abroad. In Melbourne, Australia, chanting anti-war protestors tossed cans of red and green paint onto the president's limousine as the motorcade moved down the street. Sirens blared, tires screeched, protestors chanted, and pandemonium broke out. It was a noisy story made for radio. I recorded my report with the uproar in the background, jumped off the slow-moving flatbed truck, and looked for a telephone.

The only way to get recorded material to the states quickly in those pre-satellite, pre-cellphone days was to feed it over a landline telephone. We radio correspondents carried a wire designed to electronically transmit sound directly into the telephone's circuitry. We did this by unscrewing the mouthpiece of the phone and attaching two alligator clips to the mouthpiece terminals.

As I jumped from the truck, I spotted a police station. Identifying myself as part of the President's entourage, I asked if I could make a collect call back to the states. The dispatcher pointed to a black telephone that looked like something from the 1940s, and probably was. Try as I might, I could not get the mouthpiece to unscrew. It seemed my only choice was to read my report into the phone, but without the background noise it would sound dull—exactly the kind of colorless report a TV correspondent might send, and the kind Tom never wanted to hear. However, one thing a field correspondent learns is to improvise: I pulled out a handkerchief, twisted it into the shape of a donut and curled it around the mouthpiece, creating a crude sound chamber. Then I pressed the recorder's tiny speaker against it and fed ten minutes of material back to New York. As poor as the sound quality was, back at ABC, Tom was delighted. I never knew if Ray Scherer got his recordings to NBC radio, but the next day he was back on the truck.

The focal point of the trip was Manila and the Vietnam summit conference. On our ride from the airport into the city, we passed massive billboards welcoming President Johnson—a virtual wall of signs all along our route.

"I never realized LBJ was so popular in the Philippines," I said to Frank Reynolds in the seat beside me. Frank, who had been to Manila before, laughed.

"Those billboards aren't about Johnson. They're there to hide the depressing poverty on the other side. If it weren't for those signs, we'd be looking at row after row of tin-roofed shanties, and worse. Marcos doesn't want the visiting Presidents to see them." He was speaking, of course, about the Philippines' corrupt president, Ferdinand Marcos.

Interviewing Philippine President Marcos at the Manila Summit Conference

If we had been shielded from Manila's uglier side, our first night in town exposed us to the opulence and splendor enjoyed by Marcos and his former beauty queen wife, Imelda. Known for their extravagance, they threw a big party for the press at the

Malacañang Palace, the president's official residence and workplace.

After an elaborate smorgasbord of Filipino delicacies—served from long rows of tables under torch-festooned tents in the presidential courtyard—it was time to dance. The palace had arranged for a live orchestra, and each of the male correspondents was invited to dance briefly with Imelda. Never having been allowed to attend dances when I was growing up, I was not good at it, and tried hard not to step on her shoes. Little did we know at the time how many hundreds of pairs she owned.

There were enough reporters and camera crews on the trip to fill two chartered 707 jetliners, so we sometimes had to share hotel rooms. In Manila, at the Filipinas Hotel, I was paired with ABC's diplomatic correspondent, John Scali, who later would be named U.S. ambassador to the United Nations. The summit had ended and I had turned in for the night. At about two o'clock, there was a single rap on our door. Sitting up in bed, I saw a folded slip of white paper sticking out from under it. Scali had not yet returned from wherever he'd gone for the night (partying on the road by traveling correspondents could fill another book) so I turned on a light and opened the folded note. It was on White House stationary and addressed to me. The message was brief:

"Mort, be at the U.S. Embassy at 6 a.m. Bring whatever equipment you need with you."

It was signed by Bill Moyers, the President's press secretary. I had been with Moyers at dinner earlier in the evening, so something must have come up rather quickly to prompt this late-night memo. Mark and I were scheduled to accompany Lady Bird Johnson the next morning to Corregidor, where she was to honor American troops who had fought the Japanese on that crucial island in World War II. A White House directive took precedence over those plans, however, so a few minutes before six o'clock, I arrived at the embassy, an easy walk from the hotel. A Marine guard posted at the entrance checked my press credentials, then motioned me in. A few correspondents were already there drinking coffee and mingling with administration officials, including Secretary of State Dean Rusk and Special Assistant for National Security Affairs Walt Rostow. Within a few minutes, Bill Moyers was calling everyone together for a briefing.

"The President has decided to make a secret visit to Vietnam," Moyers began.

Some of us smiled at the use of the word 'secret'; the possibility of such a trip had been rumored among the Press Corps for days, and several hours earlier *The New York Times* had reported on the upcoming trip. White House leaks are nothing new.

"You are the reporters who've been selected to provide pool coverage," Moyers continued. "Each of you will be responsible for providing material to the other news people."

I was the only radio reporter in the assembled group of about twenty journalists and cameramen.

"This mission is not without risk, and if any of you elect not to go, you'll stay here in the embassy until the President returns."

I glanced again at the Marine with the gun guarding the door.

"You will have no communication outside this room until the President is safely back," Moyers concluded.

The press plane took off first, with Air Force One and the President only a few minutes behind us. The White House staff wanted reporters in place so they could film the President stepping onto the Cam Ranh air base and being greeted by General William Westmoreland, commander of U.S. forces in Vietnam.

About a half hour away from Cam Ranh Bay, our pilot announced:

"Ladies and gentlemen, as you know, Air Force One is coming in right behind us. This is an extra security measure decided on by the White House. They figured if the Vietcong got wind of the President's visit and tried to shoot him down, they'd get us first. You and I, Ladies and Gentlemen, are the decoy." Maybe Donald Trump wasn't the first president to consider us enemies of the people.

"You think he's joking?" I said to CBS correspondent Marya McLaughlin, the designated pool reporter for TV.

We both laughed.

As we descended the airplane's steps, I heard some of the waiting GIs laughing. A couple of them pointed at me and one let out a wolf whistle. I realized these guys in full combat gear were amused by my clothing. With Corregidor still on my mind, I had put on black cotton slacks and a Barong Tagalog, a fancy, embroidered Philippine shirt that I had purchased two days earlier. Perfect attire for strolling around a memorial with Lady Bird, but sorely lacking the gravitas of a war correspondent.

As I stood there among the troops, dressed like some vacation dude in a Chevy Chase movie, I was grateful to be a radio correspondent who would be heard but not seen.

* * *

On March 29, 1967, about two years after I joined ABC, the American Federation of Television and Radio Artists called a

With LBJ at Cam Ranh Bay, Vietnam

strike. Nearly everyone who appeared on national television or radio, and most who worked for stations in major markets belonged to AFTRA. Our union was a strange mixture of talent: news anchors, reporters, announcers, singers, dancers, clowns, jugglers—anyone and everyone who faced a TV camera or spoke into a microphone.

Most network journalists, from news stars like Walter Cronkite and David Brinkley to correspondents like Steve Bell and me, had personal services contracts. AFTRA's role was to protect those thousands of other performers who were not advanced enough in their careers to have agents, or who worked in chorus lines or had bit parts in soap operas. These people depended upon AFTRA's minimum wages, called 'scale,' to make a living.

Walking the line with fellow correspondent, Al Edel

Walking a picket line was a new experience for most of us and produced a comical moment one morning as we paced back and forth in front of ABC headquarters on Sixth Avenue. Our line included a very young Peter Jennings, and a not-so-young Howard Cosell, the acerbic and legendary sportscaster. Howard was decked out in a long, cashmere overcoat and felt hat, his neck draped with an expensive-looking, ivory-colored silk scarf. The sandwich-board sign he was wearing, *ABC UNFAIR TO AFTRA*, looked comically out of place on a prosperous TV star. But Howard marched that picket line as though he didn't know how he'd pay for his next meal.

A city bus stopped in the middle of traffic about six feet from the curb. The driver opened the door, stepped off the bus, waved a fist in Cosell's direction and yelled:

"Howard, you son-of-a-bitch, you've got a lot of nerve pick-eting out here in your thousand-dollar suit. What if you had to do what I do for a living? You ought to be ashamed of yourself."

Before Howard could respond, the irate driver was back in his seat, pulling away with a busload of smiling passengers. It was the first time I had ever seen Howard speechless.

A few of the best-known television names refused to honor the picket lines. NBC's Chet Huntley went to work, com-plaining that news people had no business being tied to a union dominated by announcers, entertainers, and singers. But his on-air partner, David Brinkley, refused to cross the picket line, and the breach this caused between the famous pair ultimately hurt their ratings. Walter Cronkite's news show pulled ahead of the first-place *Huntley-Brinkley Report* after the strike ended, and stayed there.

Even though Huntley was the biggest name to cross the picket line, many of those who honored the strike shared his unhappiness; among them was Walter Cronkite. Like Huntley, Cronkite believed that news people should not have their careers linked to the entertainment folks. Named in a 1976 *U.S. News and World Report* opinion poll "the most trusted man in America," Cronkite believed that broadcast journalists should form their own, separate union. He believed that what news people did was a public service. Sure we shared the same airwaves, but our role was distinctly different, and in his view there was something unseemly about tying journalism careers to those of actors, singers, and dancers. (This was a few decades before the line between news and entertainment had become so blurred that it was hard to tell the difference.)

Over at NBC, *Today Show* host Hugh Downs was similarly troubled. Hugh had an office across the street from NBC, and he invited a handful of us over to talk about the situation. It was generally agreed that we didn't like being coupled with the entertainers, but there was no consensus on what to do about it.

Meanwhile, Cronkite was forming his own ad hoc committee. Having met me a few times at Cape Canaveral (not to mention that I had rescued him from a jammed restroom stall), he asked me to join his committee to represent network radio journalists. We had several meetings before we all decided there were just too many obstacles to forming a new union. Research showed it would be a bigger deal than Walter had thought, and most importantly, without all those variety show and soap opera actors, a news union wouldn't have much clout with management. (After the strike ended, I was invited to join AFTRA's national board. Mike Wallace was on the board representing television news people; adding me gave radio a voice in setting union policy.)

On April 10, with the network strike in its thirteenth day, ABC's White House correspondent Frank Reynolds and I sat in a waiting area at JFK Airport. Our flight to Uruguay was due to depart in less than an hour, and neither of us knew for sure whether we would be on it.

President Johnson had called a meeting of Latin American leaders to a summit at the resort town of Punta del Este. Frank was being sent to cover for television and I was going for radio. Neither of us had crossed the picket line, so now we were in a quandary. Rumors were rampant that the strike was about to end; however, if it was still on when we arrived at the summit meeting, what should we do? We could report on the summit and be scabs to our colleagues, or refuse to report and then be personally responsible for all of our trip expenses. Not a good choice.

We sat in the terminal weighing the decision. Do we stay or do we go? We watched the television monitor, eager for the latest word. About twenty minutes before boarding time, a bulletin appeared on the screen and a voice announced, "The television and radio strike is over. After nearly two weeks, AFTRA and the networks have reached agreement..."

We didn't wait to hear more. Grabbing our briefcases, we raced to the airplane. We were back in the broadcast business, right along with the announcers, actors, jugglers, and singers.

Not every country can provide its leader with an Air Force One, so our airliner made a stop in Santo Domingo to pick up the President of the Dominican Republic, Joaquin Balaguer. He and his entourage took over the entire first-class section of the plane. About a half hour into the flight, tape recorder hanging from my shoulder, I went forward and requested an interview, which was granted. As a television correspondent, Frank couldn't do that. While we radio guys always carried our tape recorder with us, Frank's cameraman and camera were on another flight.

Unfortunately, so was my luggage.

We had been advised by the White House to bring a tuxedo for the formal state dinner. At the Montevideo airport, I watched in dismay as the last piece of luggage was unloaded. All I had now was what I was wearing: an old, light-green, seersucker suit and a short-sleeved sport shirt.

Almost immediately there was an event to cover, followed by a dinner. I not only showed up that evening in my heavily wrinkled seersucker suit, but covered every single event of the three-day conference in the same clothing. Once again, I was grateful to be a radio reporter who was only heard and not seen.

At the White House party with President Johnson and daughter, Lynda

In June 1967, two months after the Punta del Este summit, all hell began breaking out in cities across America. It was the start of the infamous urban riots, and one of the most destructive was occurring in Newark, New Jersey, just across the river from Manhattan. The looting, shooting, and devastation went on for six days, leaving more than two dozen dead and hundreds hurt. On the second day, I was dispatched to cover it. As always, Nick would be looking for the sound and feel of the story, not just reports spoken into a microphone. With interviews, descriptions, and natural background sounds, I tried to convey the mood and create word-pictures of the smashed windows, overturned cars, empty cans, sticks, and bricks pitched out onto the street, along with the broken remains of Molotov cocktails that rioters had tossed at police. Of course, there was also the human side of the story: people killed and injured, displaced, businesses ruined.

National Guard troops had been called in to back up local law enforcement, and within minutes after I arrived, a new confrontation erupted. At one point, I took shelter under a car as rioters and guardsmen exchanged shots and bricks. I could hear the zing of bullets sailing over the car, and I could see the reflection of new fires dancing on shattered glass that littered the sidewalks.

With mayhem all around me and police sirens providing the background, I described into my tape recorder what I was seeing and hearing. Later, I recorded interviews with a couple who lived in the area. It was a tragic and depressing scene, but I was getting the ROSRS—radio on scene reports—that would make the situation real to ABC radio listeners.

Covering the riots helped prepare me for an assignment that I didn't know was coming. Warner Press, the Church of God publisher, asked me to write a book about the relationship of faith to the real problems of the world. Their editors believed that my prior experience as a minister, combined with my current role as a national journalist, should give me a unique perspective on the subject. But since my own beliefs had evolved significantly from those held by most in the church, I was reluctant. Given all my doubts, I wasn't sure I could write what the publisher was asking for with honesty and integrity. On the other hand, if I stuck with Jesus' teachings and how they should be applied to racism, bigotry, injustice, poverty, and war, perhaps it was doable. I might be able to write such a book without reference to anyone's orthodoxy.

I completed the book, *Like It Is!*, in a year, explaining in the preface how I had left the pastorate but not going into detail about my ongoing questions of faith. It was a positive book pointing to a future where the church would tackle the same issues that, in my view, were most important to Jesus: caring for the poor and marginalized in society, loving others as we love ourselves, welcoming the stranger, accepting those who are different, and taking on the structures of power. I did not explore my own ambivalence about who Jesus was, his precise relationship to God, or dozens of other theological issues that for me remained unresolved.

Our pastor at Marble Collegiate Church, Dr. Norman Vincent Peale, had written the best-selling *Power of Positive Thinking*. He agreed to write a forward for my book. I hoped Warner Press and the public would think as highly of my work as Peale did:

"Mort Crim's book literally shook me up. It challenged me personally and really made me face up to myself, to my attitudes and my participation in the great social movements of our time. *Like It Is!* has the genius of motivating the reader to start asking questions of himself, real and searching questions…This book by a radio and television newsman is the best work on the relation of Christianity to the problems of our time that I have read."

Of course, I was deeply gratified by Dr. Peale's words, and even more heartened when Warner Press not only published the book, but simultaneously released a British edition. The book sold well and eventually enjoyed a second printing in the U.S.

The big take-away for me was this: I can live my faith, make a positive difference in the world, promote a vital, life-changing, society-changing Christianity without having all my questions answered. My doubts were real, but they didn't have to define my developing faith.

* * *

The year was 1969. I had been at ABC Radio nearly five years when commentator Edward P. Morgan left ABC to join PBS and I was named to replace him. Morgan had been a radio

superstar, the liberal version of right-leaning Paul Harvey. Moving into his time slot was both exciting and humbling.

Within a year, I was given an even better time period: 8 a.m.—morning drive time—when radio has its largest audience. *News Around the World* had been a staple of ABC Radio's lineup for years, and only Paul Harvey at 8:30 had as large an audience as this fifteen-minute premier newscast.

Named to succeed ABC's legendary commentator, Edward P. Morgan

Paul's show originated in Chicago, but when he was in New York, he broadcast from our studios. On several occasions after we were both off the air, Paul had invited me to join him for breakfast in a diner down the street. He always expressed interest in my family and my career; having counseled me when I was in South Bend, I think he took some personal pride in my success at the network.

I had been delivering *News around the World* for about a month when Paul arrived in our newsroom to prepare his morning newscast. At about three minutes before time for my newscast, I was in the studio, head down, studying my copy. Over the intercom I heard a familiar voice.

"Good morning, Mort."

It was Paul, leaning against the wall behind the sound engineer, arms folded, and looking into my studio through the glass.

"I just wanted to come in and see how a *pro* does it," he said with a grin.

After our first meeting when I was a confused young pastor, Paul had become something of a mentor, critiquing my work and offering advice throughout my Air Force and college years. Now, the number one news commentator in America had just acknowledged me as a peer.

Even though I had just started the 8 a.m. newscast, I was nearing the end of my five-year contract with ABC. It was the Spring of 1969, and I realized that my radio career had gone about as far as it could go. I was thirty-four and if I wanted to expand into television news, I needed to take action.

There had been very few TV opportunities for me at ABC; I had been sent to cover stories for the network's nightly news program when television needed an extra correspondent, and twice I had substituted as anchor on WABC-TV's local morning newscast, but none of this had led to any regular TV assignment. I needed some guidance.

Well, America's number one radio newscaster had helped guide me into that profession. Maybe it was time to contact the nation's number one television anchorman, Walter Cronkite. I called and he invited me to his CBS office.

"Would you consider leaving New York to work for a local station?" he asked.

I hadn't really thought about that.

"That could be a good way to gain some on-camera experience and also do some important work. Local stations need good news people."

It was significant to me that the Dean of national newscasters had respect for local news and thought that it mattered.

"I have a good friend who owns our CBS affiliate in Louisville, Kentucky," Cronkite continued. "His name is Barry Bingham. His father was America's ambassador to England under FDR. He owns the Louisville *Courier-Journal and Times,* as well as the TV station. I think his son, Barry Junior, is running the operation these days. I'd be happy to put in a call for you." Sure, a call from Walter Cronkite couldn't hurt.

Cronkite followed through and a week later, the news director at WHAS-TV, Bob Morse, called me. Yes, they were looking for a new evening anchor and Cronkite had told them that I was a solid journalist.

The Louisville *Courier-Journal* had such a good reputation that it was cited in Northwestern's journalism classes as one of the nation's best newspapers, in the same league as *The New York Times, The Wall Street Journal, The Washington Post* and *The Christian Science Monitor.* Cronkite had told me that the Binghams wanted this kind of standing for their television station.

Nicki and I spent a lot of time weighing the Louisville offer, and I discussed it with Steve Bell during our morning commutes into Manhattan. Two years earlier, we had both moved our families from Queens to Tenafly, New Jersey, thinking suburbia would be an easier place to raise our children.

"You know, there's something else about going to Louisville," I suggested to Steve one morning on our way into the city. "I've occasionally toyed with the idea of a political career, and building name recognition at a local anchor desk wouldn't be a bad way to start." Even during my foray into the ministry I had been fascinated by the idea of running for office. Maybe it was my politician grandfather's influence, but the idea of service to others had been ingrained in me since childhood. Years of covering elected officials had increased my fascination with the political process; I loved reporting, but sometimes I had a nagging suspicion that we journalists were the play-by-play announcers in life, whereas politicians were actually on the field and engaged in the game.

If I could make a solid impact on Louisville, perhaps I could become a viable candidate for office. I was born less than a hundred miles from Louisville and felt a cultural kinship to people in this part of middle America. Another potential plus, should I decide to enter politics, was the Bingham family; they had a long history as leaders in the Democratic Party, and their newspaper was a strong voice for liberal and progressive causes. If I gave enough speeches, got heavily involved in community events, and built a solid name, was it too farfetched to think that an anchor job in Louisville might lead to political opportunity? Wouldn't that be a natural transition and simply increase my ability to bring about positive change? At least that's what I believed the best politicians try to do when they're acting at their best.

Over the years I had made a slow transition from Republican to Democrat, and my political conversion paralleled the spiritual changes occurring in my life. I'm certain that my switch in loyalties was puzzling to my parents, because I had grown up in a black-and-white world: Republicans were independent, industrious, and clear-headed, whereas Democrats were closet socialists, big spenders, and fuzzy thinkers. Although I voted for Richard Nixon in 1960 (the first year I was old enough to cast a ballot), I watched the party of Lincoln become a haven for racists and bigots such as Strom Thurmond. I recognized that many Republicans, including my parents, were committed to racial equality, but passage of the Civil Rights Act under President Johnson had many so-called Dixiecrats fleeing the Democratic Party and joining the Republicans.

Eight years later, Nixon took advantage of the angst over civil rights and developed his Southern Strategy. He used code words, clearly understood by Southerners, in a thinly-veiled appeal to racists whose anger had simmered to the boiling point since the Civil Rights Act became law. Nixon's Strategy of pitting 'us against them' was ultimately successful, and may have been the prototype for Donald Trump's ascendance to the Oval Office, with his overt support from white supremacists, neo-Nazis, and an assortment of other bigots.

As the GOP drifted further away from principles of fairness and equality, I had to re-examine my own political allegiances. By the early seventies, it was clear that the Democratic Party's platform and policies aligned more closely with the core of my own beliefs. It seemed to me then, and does even more starkly now, that looking out for the white, wealthy, and privileged was becoming more important to many Republican leaders than caring for the hopeless, the helpless, and the marginalized. For all the questions I still had about God, I had never given up on Jesus and his clear mandate to care for the least fortunate among us.

Steve was not surprised by my political interest and this

wasn't the first time we had discussed it. But politics aside, he did wonder if leaving New York was the best move for my broadcasting career. Nicki shared his reservation about walking away from the network. I had not mentioned to her my thoughts about politics. She had endured all the angst associated with my move from the ministry to journalism. It didn't seem fair to even suggest that there might be yet another career change lurking somewhere down the line.

I accepted the Louisville offer one July afternoon in 1969. The next day, Tom O'Brien called me into his office.

"Mort, ABC's got a television job for you. How would you like to go to Vietnam?"

Chapter Nine

MY NEW KENTUCKY HOME

Hit the reset button . . . Today is a new day. Fresh start, begins now.

—GERMANY KENT

HAD ABC'S OFFER to become a war correspondent come twenty-four hours earlier, my career, and my life, might have followed a completely different track. But by the time Tom O'Brien informed me of the opening in the Saigon bureau, I had already signed a contract with WHAS-TV. The wheels were in motion for my transition to local TV, and the publicity department was in high gear. Walter Cronkite, whose network program followed the local newscast on WHAS, had recorded several promotional spots for my television debut with me seated beside him at his CBS anchor desk.

Many of my colleagues were skeptical about my leaving the big city for the hinterlands; for some of them, Kentucky might as well have been Kathmandu. I found that when someone has worked in New York for a while, they start believing that civilization ends at the Hudson River.

Nicki and I were not concerned about culture shock. We loved New York with its vibrancy, energy, and seemingly infinite number of restaurants, shows, and people. Rarely was there a dull moment, and covering the news there—well, it doesn't get any better. But there had been life before New York and we knew there would be plenty of personal fulfillment in Louisville. Yes, cashing in nearly two decades of radio experience for a shot at television was a gamble, and there was no guarantee that I could make it back to New York, but it was a risk I was willing to take. Nicki wasn't so sure. It had been such a long, arduous trek to a top spot in network radio, did it make sense to turn my back on national exposure for a local job in Louisville? Nicki still did not know that in the back of my mind, the dormant political bug had started to stir. She couldn't guess that I viewed the move to Louisville not only as an entrée to television, but possibly politics as well. I never shared these thoughts with her, and that was a major mistake. But I had put her through so much grief trying to figure out a career path during our early years of marriage that I was reluctant to introduce such a crazy notion. After all, these political thoughts were nothing more than fantasies. Weren't they?

Louisville is a crossroads city, combining the energy and drive of the North with the hospitality and charm of the South. It didn't take us long to become comfortable in this pleasant, mid-sized city, home to mint juleps, the Kentucky Derby, and carpeted with the state's famed bluegrass (even though in reality bluegrass is a deep green).

Louisville wasn't New York, but the old River City's heart throbbed with the vitality of exciting sports, night life, culture, the arts, and a growing number of restaurants for every taste. Lee Corso had just arrived to coach University of Louisville football, and the respected Louisville Orchestra had recently hired Jorge Mester from Mexico as its conductor. The world-renowned Actors Theatre was under the artistic direction of Jon Jory, son of veteran actor Victor Jory.

We found a two-story, colonial style home about fifteen-minutes' drive from WHAS. It came with a tennis court and a treehouse, which immediately caught the eye of four-year-old Albert. Bowman Field wasn't far from our home, a perfect venue for pursuing my interest in flying.

Although our roots in the Church of God ran deep, we were no longer comfortable with the church's literal interpretation of Scripture and its restrictive lifestyle expectations, so we opted for Second Presbyterian.

At WHAS-TV the new job fit me like a tailor-made suit. Radio friends in New York had worried about my transition from microphone to camera, but I hadn't. I had delivered hundreds of sermons and speeches, was very comfortable at the podium, and thought that looking into a camera and reading the news should come quite naturally—and it did.

My first newscast was on a Monday at 6 p.m., following one of those videotaped promos from Walter Cronkite, which we played at the end of his CBS newscast.

"Now stay tuned for Mort Crim, who'll have the latest local news here on channel eleven," Walter said.

As she sat in our den watching that first show, Nicki may have been more nervous than I was and she was no doubt relieved when I didn't embarrass both of us. She was on the phone as soon as I returned to the newsroom.

"Good job, honey! You looked like you'd been doing it all your life."

Perhaps, in a way, I had been.

Even though I was enjoying television work, there were times when I had my own doubts about the wisdom of having left New York. Occasionally, while sitting in the anchor chair and introducing a report on some highway pile-up or a school board vote, I would have flashbacks of covering stories of national or international importance. I would recall traveling with the President; describing space launches; interviewing astronauts, senators, and Broadway stars; and having the United Nations as part of my beat. Compared to stories I had covered at the network, some of the events that made news in Louisville did seem rather trivial. It took me awhile to appreciate how a city council decision or a property tax referendum could have more direct impact upon the viewers' lives than a dozen bills passed in Washington.

As the weeks went by, both Nicki and I became more at ease with the decision to leave ABC, and we were adjusting to the new celebrity lifestyle that was part of being on TV every night. The first time someone recognized me in a restaurant, I remembered a conversation with David Brinkley during a plane ride to New York following a space launch. When we checked in at the ticket counter, it seemed everyone was staring at the famous newscaster.

"What's the toughest thing about being such a celebrity?" I asked Brinkley, seated next to me on the flight home.

"Socks," he deadpanned, with the dry understatement for which he was famous on the *Huntley-Brinkley Report.*

"Socks?" I asked.

"Yeah, I like to buy my socks in a discount store. And every time I get to the checkout counter, I can see people looking at me and whispering. I figure they're all thinking, 'What the hell is David Brinkley doing buying his socks in a discount store?'"

Although I was starting to get a taste of celebrity, it would be a few more years before I fully understood how totally and completely television exposure strips away any semblance of privacy. Brinkley had been at the game long enough to know.

My co-anchor at WHAS was affable, wavy-haired Ken Rowland, whose folksiness and horn-rimmed glasses were more reminiscent of a favorite uncle than of a television anchorman.

A few weeks after I arrived at the station, Ken invited me to attend a meeting of a women's group where he was giving a speech. He talked mostly about national and international affairs and the audience appeared to hang on every word. I had read most of what Ken said in the current issue of *U.S. News and World Report,* but it didn't matter to the ladies whether Ken's material was original. He was the familiar face they watched each evening and trusted. When Ken finished giving his analysis of the world situation, the small room burst into applause and the women exchanged big smiles of approval. Then they gave him a standing ovation.

It was a lesson in the power people cede to their TV anchormen, and I remembered a quip by one of my broadcast professors at Medill:

"If you don't know how to pronounce a word, just say it with authority."

The professor was joking, but clearly there is a certain aura of authority that comes with simply showing up on television every night. Maybe the idea of moving from TV anchor to politician wasn't that crazy after all.

Launching a TV career in Louisville

Two years into the job, I still had not confided in Nicki about my interest in politics. But, as months passed, the idea grew. Delivering the news twice a day was giving me something every politician craves: name recognition. Since arriving in Louisville, I had been giving speeches to Kiwanis and Rotary Clubs, Jaycees, business conferences, church organizations, and an assortment of women's groups. I accepted every invitation. The positive responses after these appearances increased my curiosity. How many of these people might vote for me if I *should* decide to run for office?

Despite these private thoughts, I had no particular plan to run for anything. Even with my increasingly high profile in the community, there would be many obstacles. Because I had not been born in Kentucky an opponent could easily brand me as a carpetbagger. Nevertheless, I continued to ponder the possibilities.

Life at home was good. Nicki was enjoying our return to the Midwest, and since I didn't report to the newsroom until mid-afternoon, I could usually spend several hours with her and Al before heading for the TV station. Pushing aside occasional daydreams about running for office, I focused on my work: conducting interviews, researching stories, and preparing and delivering daily newscasts. I wrote much of my own copy, and occasionally went out with a camera crew to cover the news, just as I had as a network correspondent.

As much as I enjoyed television, I had not lost my love of radio. TV was a team sport, with the anchorman serving as quarterback to a crew of reporters, writers, editors, and videographers. Radio was more like tennis: one person with a typewriter (today, a computer) solely responsible for both content and delivery. I enjoyed the independence and freedom of that, as well as the challenge of painting pictures with words. So I created a short daily feature, *One Moment Please,* and offered it for sale to other radio stations. WHAS-TV's General Manager, Ed Shadburne, liked the idea and signed the station on as a partner, investing in advertising and providing me with an office and secretary for the project.

One Moment Please gave me a national platform to talk about things that mattered to me. These ninety-second motivational stories were about relationships, success, perseverance, overcoming failure, surmounting obstacles, tolerance, generosity, and helping others. Most of the news I had to report was about human failure, conflict, brokenness, and tragedy—the worst in human nature. My radio commentaries emphasized the best.

Perhaps I was finding in *One Moment Please* a way to continue ministry without ecclesiastical constraints or religious trappings. *One Moment Please* essays drew upon my Christian heritage, found their foundation in the teachings of Jesus that I'd learned as a child, and gave a literal voice to my values. And while I hoped *One Moment Please* would be financially successful, it wasn't money that had motivated me to create it. I wanted to provide the audience with inspiration in their daily struggles, hope when their world felt chaotic and scary, and courage to take on their challenges. In a way, I wanted to provide a counterbalance to the depressing news we journalists presented every day.

As the series developed, I increasingly sensed the largeness of a God too big to be contained by labels, description, dogma, or religion. The best parts of my heritage—the authentic elements of Christian teachings—were driving and directing my work. I didn't recognize it then, but I believe the creation of *One Moment Please* was the beginning of a fuller understanding of the God I had been trying to find since that teenage crisis of faith in Oklahoma. As a young person, I had thought that the discovery might come through some convincingly dramatic moment: a sudden, mind-blowing insight. Instead, I was quietly encountering the mysterious life force we call God in the simple, day-to-day act of doing something for the purpose of helping others, and investing in a cause bigger than myself. I was learning what Karen Armstrong would later articulate in her book, *The Case for God*, that true religion is a practice, not a theory or a set of propositions. Finding God is not like finding a lost book. It's more like finding happiness; you don't find it by looking for it directly. Happiness is what happens when we do the things that produce it. For me, this was becoming the way to discover God.

The feature quickly found an audience. Within a few weeks,

we had signed more than a dozen radio stations. Later renamed *Second Thoughts*, the series eventually was heard on more than thirteen-hundred radio stations as well as the Armed Forces Radio Network. Clearly, there was an audience hunger for positive, inspiring stories. Writing five fresh episodes each week plus running the business side of syndication and anchoring the newscasts kept me busier than I had been in New York. I loved the hectic schedule. I was doing what I wanted to do and relishing every minute of it, and I was meeting some really fascinating people— none more colorful than Colonel Harland Sanders.

Sanders had adopted the title *Colonel* after the governor gave him one of those Kentucky Colonel certificates that his staff hands out by the hundreds. Sanders made the designation so synonymous with his name that he was usually referred to simply as *The Colonel*. He had earned a small fortune as founder of Kentucky Fried Chicken. He should have made a large fortune but wasn't sophisticated enough to realize what he had. A group of investors, headed by John Y. Brown, Jr., paid the Colonel two million dollars for a company that was actually worth many times that. Eventually the new owners turned it into a multi-billion-dollar international enterprise. Fifteen years later, Brown became governor of Kentucky.

I first met the Colonel when we served together on a state advisory board. *Like It Is!* had just been published, and I presented him with an autographed copy. It was the beginning of a friendship that lasted until his death at the age of ninety.

Once, when my parents were visiting us, the Colonel invited our family to join him and his wife, Claudia, for dinner. He knew Dad was a minister, and halfway through our meal the Colonel said, "Reverend Crim, did Mort tell you that I got religion?"

Serving on an advisory board with Colonel Sanders

Frankly, I wasn't aware that the crusty old Sanders had anything to do with church.

"That's good," Dad smiled, amused, I'm sure, by the Colonel's phrase "got religion."

"Yep, I've given up drinkin' and chewin' tabacky."

Dad smiled again and nodded.

"And," the Colonel continued, "I'm tryin' real hard to give up cussin', but goddammit, Reverend Crim, that's a hard one!"

"Colonel, you just keep working on it," Dad said, trying hard to suppress a chuckle.

Sanders and his wife, Claudia, lived in a spacious antebellum-style home in Shelbyville, just east of Louisville. Nicki and I visited them on several occasions and after the Colonel died, we continued to exchange Christmas cards with Claudia until her death. Claudia told me that the Colonel loved *Like It Is!*, and took my book with him whenever he traveled.

* * *

On July 26, 1971, Apollo Fifteen was launched from Cape Canaveral.

Normally, a moon shot would have had me glued to the television set. But on this day, there was only one launch I could think about: the impending birth of our daughter.

My aunt Vera was on furlough from her medical missionary duties in Kenya. She had delivered hundreds of African babies in far more primitive surroundings, and Baptist Hospital permitted her to assist in Carey's birth.

"Everything's fine," Aunt Vera had announced, as she emerged from the delivery room.

The moment I saw Carey, lying behind the nursery's glass window, swaddled in a pink blanket that seemed coordinated to her glowing little face, I was overcome with the same powerful emotions that I felt after her brother's birth six years earlier.

"Now, go home and get some rest," Aunt Vera instructed.

Less than an hour after arriving home, the phone rang.

"Get back to the hospital right away," Aunt Vera said. There was urgency in her voice.

"Carey has a blood disorder and we're taking her to Children's Hospital."

I rushed to the maternity ward. Aunt Vera had our newborn cradled in her arms and was practically running toward the door, a staff nurse close behind her.

"They have an ambulance ready to take us to Children's. I'll see you there."

There was no time for details, but I already knew: Nicki's blood was Rh negative and mine, Rh positive. If this mismatch creates a problem, usually it will be during the second or third pregnancy; Nicki's miscarriage while I was in the Air Force meant that this pregnancy was the third.

By the time I got to Children's Hospital, Carey was already in an incubator under a bilirubin light designed to counter jaundice. Her skin, which had been a rosy pink when I first saw her, was now a sickly yellow. My heart sank.

"They plan to transfuse her," Aunt Vera explained. "They'll replace all of her blood. They hope that procedure, along with medication and the bilirubin light, will pull her through."

I knew we were in for a few hours, or even days, of uncertainty. I instinctively began to pray. It's what my parents had always done in a crisis, and it's what I had done as a minister. But what words should I use now?

In my search to understand God, I had become increasingly skeptical that prayer had the power to change physical outcomes, even though I had heard my parents and grandparents talk of my own healing when I was four years old. They always considered my survival a divine miracle. According to the story, I was near death with a worsening case of whooping cough. Then, a preacher they all called Old Brother Palk anointed me with oil and prayed for me. He was widely reputed throughout southern Illinois to have the gift of healing. Almost instantly I began to improve, according to the story. My parents were convinced that prayer and divine intervention had saved my life.

At this point in my struggle to find truth, I believed that there is a mysterious power secreted within the cosmos. I felt, as Albert Einstein once observed, that "something deeply hidden has to be behind things." But my years of study and serious thinking about the issue, along with my observations as a journalist, had convinced me that this mysterious force was not the

God I had learned about in Sunday school. I saw no evidence of a divinity that grants personal wishes when we pray. For me, the story of that God was a fairy tale.

In nature I saw hints of plan and design. In human heroism and sacrificial love, I sometimes sensed an unseen power or presence that defied mere logic. But I saw no convincing proof of a divine being that rewards good and punishes bad. The random tragedies, horrors and undeserved suffering that I had witnessed as a reporter were evidence to me that God does not intervene, directly or miraculously, in the affairs of humans.

Even before I began a serious search to understand the nature of God, I had difficulty reconciling the conflicting things I'd been taught. How could an all-powerful, all-merciful, all-loving and just God be so inconsistent, capricious, and unreliable when it came to distributing His mercies? I had seen too many babies with grotesque birth defects, innocents slaughtered in war, lives and hopes wiped out by floods and other disasters to believe that God was some kind of cosmic director, orchestrating the human drama.

I had heard ministers try to explain these contradictions, but the reasoning always seemed convoluted. A divinity that randomly blessed some people and cursed others wouldn't be a creator I could respect, and certainly wouldn't be the essence of love described in the New Testament.

Nicki was thirty-seven and we presumed that Carey would be our last child. During the nine months of pregnancy, we had fallen more in love each day with this little baby-to-be. My desperation over the possibility of losing her drove me to pray, even though I couldn't bring myself to ask God for a miracle. I prayed that both Nicki and our new little daughter would be surrounded by the love I felt for them. If God is love, as my parents believed, then I wanted that love to envelope Nicki. I asked for serenity and strength. I prayed for the courage to face whatever lay ahead. I asked that I might be able to trust this *something*, this mysterious force I called God, no matter the outcome. I prayed that my own anxiety might be replaced with the sort of calm the Bible calls 'peace that passes understanding.'

I was at the hospital every day until I headed for work in the afternoon. On the third day, Aunt Vera called me. Her voice was upbeat.

"Carey is going to be fine," she happily reported. "The transfusions worked."

Whatever reservations I had about miracles and divine intervention in human affairs, my next prayer came quite effortlessly: "Thank you, God."

* * *

We had been in Louisville for nearly three years. I was nearing the end of my contract with WHAS, although the station clearly was eager to renew it. Al was seven and in first grade; Carey was eleven months old and talking non-stop. Our newscast ratings were up, the syndicated radio series was adding new stations every week, and I was getting more speaking invitations than I could handle. Nicki liked being closer to her family in Ohio. We were feeling settled. The stars all seemed to be perfectly aligned.

I was preparing for the 6 p.m. newscast on a Thursday afternoon when the phone rang.

"This is David Salzman at KYW-TV in Philadelphia," said the voice on the other end.

"How long does your contract at WHAS have to run?"

"Actually, I'm nearing the end of my agreement," I said.

I was less than three years into my first job as a TV anchorman in the nation's thirty-ninth largest television market. Philadelphia was the fourth. I was honest with Salzman.

"I don't have any desire to leave Louisville, but I suppose we could talk." He probably thought I was trying to strengthen my hand for negotiating a better deal, but it really was the way I felt.

"Fine. We can fly down Monday and meet for dinner between your early and late newscasts."

The conversation had lasted less than a minute, but it left my head spinning. If we did move to Philadelphia, it would be the end of any political ambitions. It had taken nearly three years for me to be fully accepted as a Kentuckian and as part of Louisville's social fabric and civic life. And I still hadn't shared my aspirations with Nicki; not since our first year of marriage when I had mentioned perhaps running for Governor of Illinois, our home state, had I brought up the subject. I'm certain she never took that remark seriously. Would she even remember the conversation? In those days I was having enough difficulty deciding between the pulpit and the microphone. Nicki had probably dismissed that comment as part of my confused struggle to find a focus.

Now I needed to tell her about my feelings. If I was serious about running for office, we should stay in Louisville—this was the place where a political career could be feasible. But first I had to tell her about the phone call from KYW.

Her reaction to the Philadelphia idea was generally affirming. Nicki had never believed that we would stay in Louisville. She fully expected that someday we would return to New York, where I would work for one of the television networks, so when

I told her that politics might be enough to keep me in Kentucky, it came as a shock.

"I knew a long time ago you had mentioned something about maybe wanting to be a Governor or something, but I figured that was a passing fad," she responded.

I couldn't blame her for thinking that.

"I don't even know that I'm serious now," I said. "But it is something I've thought a lot about and I do think here in Louisville, over time, it would be doable."

"What would you run for?" There was skepticism in her tone.

"Well, it wouldn't be for dog catcher," I responded, trying to lighten the mood. "Maybe Congress, but that would be a long shot. We live in a pretty Republican district."

"I think it's crazy," Nicki said firmly.

"You've worked twenty years to become a broadcast journalist. Now you've got a good start in television, things are going well. I can't think of anything riskier than walking away to start a new career in politics."

She was absolutely right. *Crazy* was exactly the word that kept coming into my mind whenever I'd thought seriously about it.

"I wouldn't like it," Nicki said. There was an edginess in her voice.

"If you think you have no privacy now, it would be ten times worse in politics. They'd be looking at every little detail of our lives, our parents, our kids, and our finances. I think it would be terrible."

She seemed much more emphatic than when she had questioned my decision to leave New York and ABC. We both had some drunks in our families, and a second cousin of mine had done jail time, but the skeletons in our closets were few and I thought certainly manageable. Then Nicki shocked me with these words: "If you ever decide to run for office, I'll go stay with Mom and Dad until the campaign is over. I don't want anything to do with politics."

The forcefulness and finality of her response was startling. We had always discussed and sometimes argued over decisions, but in the end, we inevitably had reached agreement. Now this political option clearly was not to be discussed. Argument over. Nicki had just delivered a resounding *No*. And while it wasn't a word she used, I'm sure I distinctly heard in her tone, *Hell no*.

On Monday, I left the studio after the six o'clock news to meet the KYW-TV management at a downtown steakhouse. As I approached the table, all three men stood and one of them reached out his hand.

"I'm David Salzman. I spoke with you on the phone. This is John Rohrbech, our General Manager, and our News Director, Mike Von Ende."

We all shook hands and sat down.

I was flattered that the station's three top executives thought hiring me was important enough to bring all of them to Louisville.

It was Salzman who did most of the talking. There was the usual small talk during the meal, and then he opened the real conversation.

"Of course, you know what we're here to talk about."

I nodded.

"Our senior anchorman, Vince Leonard, does an excellent job. He's been with the station a long time, but we're not sure how many more years he has left so we're preparing for the future."

I thought Vince must be in his sixties; later I learned that he was forty-six. Such was the youth-culture mentality that dominated much of the TV business at that time: the preferred demographic, the audience age group every TV station coveted, was eighteen to forty-nine. It was commonly believed that kids under eighteen didn't have a lot of money to spend, and folks over fifty didn't spend as much as those in their middle years.

"We'd like to pair you with Vince, and we're prepared to make a very generous offer."

We talked for a few more minutes about details, the size of the newsroom, the number of reporters, what specific shows I'd be anchoring, how many stories a week I would be expected to cover, and finally, how much money they were offering.

"How much are you making now?" Salzman asked.

I was always taught that in any negotiation, the party that throws out the first number loses. But I knew it wouldn't be too difficult for them to find the answer, so I told him.

"We'll double it and pay all your moving expenses," Salzman said without hesitation. "This would be a great career move for you."

I told them that I would think about it, discuss it with Nicki, and get back to them.

As I prepared the eleven o'clock news, it was difficult to keep my mind on my stories. I got home shortly before midnight, and then sat down at the kitchen table with Nicki and reconstructed the KYW conversation. We drank coffee and talked until about 1:30 a.m. With a baby daughter certain to wake up early and a seven-year-old son to get off to school, we had to get some sleep. But even after going to bed, we kept talking. We were facing a big decision.

It took us about two weeks to make up our minds. We agreed that this move would be good for the family, good for my TV career, and would put us closer to New York, assuming that my ultimate goal was still network news.

I knew that leaving Louisville would mean an end to any political ambitions I might still harbor, but those were just daydreams anyway. Nobody was asking me to run for anything. Besides, without Nicki's support, there was no reason to think further about it.

WHAS made a perfunctory attempt to keep me, offering a salary increase and some additional perks, but I think they recognized that this was a career opportunity I couldn't refuse. I negotiated a deal with WHAS to retain my syndicated radio series, *One Moment Please*, permitting me to take it to Philadelphia.

One week before we were to leave, with my KYW-TV contract signed and the moving van scheduled, I delivered my final speech in Louisville. It was a commencement address at DeSales High School. As I took my seat, the man next to me leaned over and whispered into my ear. If the audience was still applauding, I can't say. His words were all that I could hear.

"Mort, I'm an official in the local Democratic Party. I've been authorized to ask if you would consider running for Congress."

Chapter Ten

CITY OF BROTHERLY LOVE

I immediately regret this decision.

—RON BURGUNDY

ON MY VERY FIRST DAY in Philadelphia, I was having doubts about the decision to leave Louisville. I hoped the demands of my new job would keep me from thinking too much about the blown political opportunity, at least for a time.

"So they brought you in on a Saturday," I said to the tall, distinguished anchorman standing at the sink, dabbing a small sponge to his cheeks.

"Yes, a bit of a bummer," he said, glancing briefly in my direction.

The station had decided to videotape some promotional

spots on the news set with Vince Leonard introducing me to the Philadelphia audience. Vince had been the primary news anchor at KYW-TV for fourteen years, coming to Philadelphia from Indianapolis when he was thirty-three. I had been in town for three days. As I stationed myself two sinks away and pulled out my own makeup kit, Vince loosened a little.

"Where do you plan to live?" he asked, his tone less wary.

"Not sure. Nicki and I are looking at some homes on the Main Line. Possibly Devon."

"We're in Malvern," Vince said, "not far from Devon. Nice area. You'd like the Main Line."

Vince did not seem unfriendly, but he was definitely reserved. If he wasn't welcoming me with enthusiasm, there was a reason: Vince had to wonder if the station had brought me in to replace him. After years at the top, KYW's news ratings had started to slip a bit and I was being added to Vince's six o'clock show as a co-anchor, something he had never had. But he was gracious to me and graciousness, I would learn, was a part of Vince's nature.

Besides co-anchoring with Vince, I was assigned to anchor my own newly created show, *Newswatch 5:30*, and to co-host *The Noon News*, KYW's top-rated midday program, hosted by the city's Grand Dame of television, Marciarose Shestack.

"Whatever you do, don't call her Marcia," News Director Mike Von Ende cautioned me as I arrived in the newsroom the following Monday morning.

"She's Marciarose. It's all one name."

Our first show together went quite well. I felt comfortable anchoring with her, and she invited me to join her for lunch.

"We need to get acquainted, and there's no better place than the Head House Tavern," she said.

Marciarose knew all the top restaurants in Philadelphia, and I would eventually learn that the maître d's all knew her. In addition to being a highly respected television personality, she was well-connected socially and married to one of the city's most prominent attorneys.

"Jerry and I will be happy to introduce you around," Marciarose said as we left the restaurant and headed back to the newsroom.

Marciarose, my noon co-anchor at KYW-TV

KYW occupied a new building just a block away from Independence Hall, where the Revolutionary Congress had hammered out our Declaration of Independence. The Liberty Bell was now housed there, and eventually I would become its voice; for several years Walter Cronkite's voice was what tourists heard when they touched the audio button, but the National Park Service decided the script needed updating and asked me to record a new one. (No, it wasn't CBS News, but replacing Cronkite as the Liberty Bell's voice was still a boost to the ego.) Betsy Ross's house was an easy walk from our studios, and the streets around our station were constantly filled with tourists. The very air seemed rich with American history.

After three years in Louisville, Philadelphia definitely felt like the big time. We found a tri-level house on a wooded lot in suburban Devon, about ten minutes away from Vince and Frankie Leonard's. It had a swimming pool and looked like an idyllic place for a family. Our new home was close to Valley Forge National Park and the hills, streams, valleys, tall trees, and centuries-old inns that surrounded it made our neighborhood seem like an extension of those historic grounds.

On what was still my first day, I was learning my routine. After lunch, the team for the station's primary newscasts at 6 p.m. and 11 p.m. began to arrive. At 5:15 p.m., I headed for the Newswatch set. Normally, arriving in the studio five minutes before air time is sufficient, but *Newswatch 5:30* was a brand new program and this would be my first time to solo-anchor at KYW. As it turned out, the extra minutes came in handy because a stage manager stopped me at the studio door.

"Where you going with that?" he demanded.

I was holding my script in one hand and a letter mounted to a piece of foam board in the other.

"Is that a prop?" he asked, pointing to the foam board.

"It's a letter that I'll be referring to in the newscast," I responded.

"Are you showing it on camera?"

"Yes, that's why it's mounted on the board."

"Then it's a prop. You can't take it into the studio. Stage manager has to do that. Union rules," he added, as he took the 'prop' from my hand.

He then pointed to a small wooden table near the studio door.

"That's where you put props," he explained. "We have to carry them in for you."

It was not the last time that I would hear the term *union rules,* and I quickly learned how much the prospect of a union grievance affected both work and relationships in the world of major-market television.

About eighteen minutes into the show, I introduced Big Al Meltzer with his sports report. We bantered for a few seconds, he welcomed me to KYW, then delivered the latest on the Eagles and the Phillies, spicing the news with his own comments and pointed suggestions for the coaches.

Weatherman Bill Kuster also said how glad he was to have me aboard, gave a brief forecast, and announced that he would be doing his six o'clock forecast from Kuster's Garden. At 5:58 p.m., I signed off and had two minutes during commercials to move over to the six o'clock set and take my place beside Vince.

By 6:30, I had made it through my first noon show, my first solo appearance as a KYW anchorman, and my first co-anchored show with Vince. I wondered how the City of Brotherly Love was feeling about the new guy in town.

In the 1970s and 80s, before twenty-four hour cable news, the local anchorman occupied a unique place in the community. He was a major celebrity, talked about, written about, publicly admired, and publicly criticized in much the same way as a professional athlete. New York had a cross-section of celebrities from the worlds of politics, sports, and Broadway. Hollywood had its movie stars. But for cities like Philadelphia, it was the talking heads that appeared on television every night that grabbed the limelight.

One of the most exciting things about the news business is that you never know what is going to happen next. Working next door to the studios where Mike Douglas taped his syndicated afternoon talk show gave our newsroom access to the biggest names of the day. Sooner or later, everyone who was anyone—from Frank Sinatra to the Rolling Stones, Truman Capote to Moe Howard of *The Three Stooges* fame—appeared in Mike's interview chair, and often we could get them over to our side of the building for a newscast appearance. But not all of Mike's guests were well-known stars, or even human stars— and one made his way into our newsroom uninvited. It was a Thursday afternoon in early September, and as I started to enter the newsroom, two reporters and a producer came rushing out.

"Don't go in there!" one of them yelled. "It's a war zone!"

Whatever was happening, the battle was still raging; shrill shrieking mixed with banging, clanging, whacking, thumping, and pounding. From the open doorway I could see desks littered with debris, broken typewriters on the floor, and papers scattered everywhere.

I cautiously stepped into the newsroom where two Philadelphia police officers pointed at the ceiling. The commotion seemed to originate there. Several of the ceiling tiles had been broken out along with the light fixtures attached to them. Dust, staplers, clipboards, typewriters, and tangled wires covered the floor.

"What's going on?" I asked the police.

"We're trying to get Marvin."

I knew we had a couple of staffers with short tempers but couldn't imagine one of them going berserk. Besides, neither of them was named Marvin.

"He got loose from his handler and ran down here from the Douglas studio."

It turned out that Marvin was a trained chimpanzee who had been performing on Mike's show. Something frightened him and once he broke loose, so did all hell. According to our staff, the chimp picked up heavy typewriters like they were plastic toys and tossed them across the room. He overturned a couple of desks and flung news scripts and wire copy everywhere before leaping up into the ceiling, where he continued to wreak havoc and yell at the top of his simian lungs. With the help of the police, the chimp's trainer finally was able to calm Marvin and coax him down. Meanwhile, we had some serious cleaning up to do before showtime.

It was one of those rare times when those of us who cover the news became the news; Associated Press distributed a photograph of me on the floor assessing the damage to my office, and it appeared in newspapers across the country. Of course, our competitors across town couldn't resist wisecracks about it.

"If a monkey got loose in the Eye-Witless newsroom, how would you know?"

Usually, the weapons newsrooms used against each other were not monkey business at all, but things such as special reports that we prepared for sweeps (ratings periods) and an endless flow of promotional spots advertising why each news team was better, faster, smarter, and more personable than the other. KYW's special series often were journalistic jewels that made us proud, but sometimes they were so silly we wanted to hide. One highly advertised series during the May ratings period had the titillating title, *Why Your Bra is Killing You.*

Another time we heavily promoted a series about dirty hotel beds, and another on why you couldn't trust food in even the best restaurants. The idea was to arouse so much fear, anger, or curiosity in viewers that they would be compelled to watch. Sensational as it was, our hype seems tame when compared to the way nearly every story today is breathlessly bannered as *Breaking News.* Maybe those promotional campaigns were an omen of the idiocy to come.

Promoting the news at KYW was big business and the station invested huge amounts of money in it. Professional movie crews were brought in to produce some of our thirty and sixty-second spots, and often the entire team was sent on location to film them. We were treated like movie stars at these shoots, complete with personalized directors' chairs.

Some of the best scenes were shot at Philadelphia's famed Italian Market. Our anchor team strolled the market in casual clothing, joked with proprietors and with each other, and generally tried to convey the idea that this group of good friends was strongly connected to the city.

If the special series were designed to make viewers watch us, the goal of these promotional spots was to make them like us. To that end, we were encouraged to accept invitations to speak and to emcee events when asked. I did a lot of both, and signed on with the city's top speakers' bureau.

Being a local anchorman, it was never a problem getting the best table at a fine restaurant or being seated even when there were no tables available. Police stops for traveling a few miles over the speed limit rarely resulted in a ticket, and on one occasion, a state trooper said he would let me go with a warning if I'd give him an autograph for his wife. Of course, there was a downside, including the nearly total loss of privacy. Every move in public could be subject to scrutiny, and occasionally a critique by some newspaper or magazine columnist. If a columnist didn't like you, the criticism could be scorching.

The celebrity aspect was harder on my family than on me. Rarely did we sit down in a restaurant without me being recognized, and occasionally someone would approach our table. Usually, it was a quick, "I watch you every night," or a request for an autograph. I can't count the number of paper napkins that have my signature on them. Occasionally, there would be a serious intrusion by someone who wanted to talk, sometimes endlessly. Nicki didn't enjoy this but she knew such interruptions went with the territory.

I once shared an elevator with two women on my way up to see my accountant. One of them ventured,

"Hey, you sure do look like Mort Crim."

"Interesting," I said. "You're not the first person to tell me that."

The elevator door opened and I went off to keep my appointment, leaving them wondering, "Is he or isn't he?"

Sometimes you just have to have some fun with the celebrity thing.

I had been at KYW for two months when General Manager Alan Bell called Vince and me into his office.

"We're bringing in a new reporter from Houston to work with you guys," Alan said.

"She's very good, and we feel lucky to be getting her. I'm putting her on *Newswatch 5:30* with you, Mort, and eventually we'll be working her into the six o'clock and eleven o'clock.

"Her name is Jessica Savitch. She's young, but she's a helluva reporter. She looks great and has the potential to be an excellent anchor."

I doubt that Alan had ever said of me or Vince that we "look great," but hiring women for their sex appeal has a long tradition in television—a practice Fox News has perfected to a fine art.

"I thought *Newswatch* was doing just fine," I responded, no doubt sounding as defensive as I felt.

Newswatch 5:30 had been created specifically for me. At least that's what I'd been told, and ratings were starting to build. I couldn't see any reason why Alan would want to add a co-anchor and certainly not this early in the game.

"The show is doing well, and you're doing fine," Alan assured me. "But we think that adding a female to the show will broaden its appeal to women."

I'm certain Alan also expected Jessica to improve the show's appeal to men. He had seen her on videotape and she was drop-dead gorgeous.

"You said she's young," I questioned. "How young?"

"Mid-twenties, I think."

"I'm not sure this is a good idea," I said. "How much experience can she have at that age?"

There was an implied sense of superiority in my comment, as well as an obvious desire to protect my turf.

"Wait 'til you meet her," Alan assured us. "I think you'll be impressed."

I was not eager to share solo billing any more than Ron

Burgundy was, and as we left Alan's office, I experienced more than a little guilt. I began to feel the weight of sins I'd been taught about while growing up in the church: envy, jealousy, vanity, and pride. And what about the good old golden rule? I wasn't treating Jessica the way I would want to be treated, and she wasn't even here yet. Reluctance to share the spotlight might have been a normal anchorman reaction, but what I was feeling was not consistent with my values and I knew it.

Many newsrooms in the early seventies were still something of good old boys' clubs, but my resistance to Jessica was more out of conceit and self-importance than male chauvinism. After all, I already was paired with a woman on the noon show, and in the newsroom, I worked every day with women reporters and writers. Nicki and I discussed the situation and she listened patiently as I expressed my frustrations. Then, as she always did, she provided some wise, down-to-earth counsel and perspective.

"You can fight the decision or you can make the best of it. Is this something you really feel is worth going to the mat over?"

By the time Jessica arrived in our newsroom, I had made my peace with the idea of having her beside me on the *set*.

"Call me Jess," she said, arriving for her first day of work and dropping a tan leather satchel on my desk. It was something between a briefcase and a purse.

Alan had shown us her video, but in person, she seemed much smaller, although just as pretty. She's definitely got the looks, I thought, but can she write? How will she do in the field? Can she ask tough questions? Is she ready for the fourth-largest TV market in the country?

"You'll have a busy few days getting settled in," I said. "But once you feel comfortable enough, I'd like to take you out to dinner and fill you in on the routine here."

"Great. I could use a good briefing from somebody already on the job," she said.

I wondered if she understood how much I had resented the idea of having a co-anchor.

Jess jumped right into the job and covered a story that afternoon, and it was clear immediately that she knew how to report the news. Her writing was crisp, thorough, and accurate. Her delivery was not bad, although she did have an ever-so-slight speech impediment, which she would soon correct with the help of Lilyan Wilder, a well-known communications coach in New York.

In the days to come, Jessica also proved herself to be a hard worker, showing up earlier than her schedule demanded. She also stayed later than required if she thought her story could be improved by some rewriting or additional editing before the eleven o'clock news. Clearly Jessica was determined to make it on the basis of talent and hard work.

On her third day on the job, she came into my office. "Mort, is that dinner invitation still good?"

"Of course," I responded.

"How about right after the six o'clock?"

The restaurant was an easy walk from the station. After we'd ordered wine and studied the menus, I cut to the chase.

"Jess, you may be aware that I have been less than enthusiastic about your joining me on the anchor desk."

She seemed a bit startled by my candor.

"I do want you to know that it's not about you. Yes, I have had some concerns about your experience, but to be perfectly honest, it's mostly that I haven't felt that I needed a co-anchor.

Our ratings have been building and I think we've been doing quite well the way things are."

Jessica stared at me, probably trying to determine whether I was sincere.

"Please understand, I'm not trying to take anything away from you," she said. "But this is a great opportunity for me."

"Yes, it certainly is," I said.

I had selected a remote table near the rear of the restaurant to avoid any newspaper reporters who might be within earshot. My arrival at KYW had generated a lot of newspaper and magazine coverage, and I knew the pending addition of a co-anchor to my show would be grist for the gossip columnists if word should leak out.

I leaned into the table.

"While I've not been anxious to share the anchor desk with you, I want you to know that I will never do anything to make your life difficult. To the contrary, I'll do everything I can to help you succeed."

Jessica looked at me, obviously a bit skeptical.

Then, after a brief pause, she reached her hand across the table. We shook on the deal, dinner was served, and we never again spoke about my reluctance to have a partner on *Newswatch*.

In the years that followed, the truce we declared over drinks that night deepened into a special friendship. When Jessica finally did arrive at the *Newswatch* anchor desk about two months later, neither of us could have guessed the mutual attraction we would feel, or the strong bond that would develop both on and off the set.

The team of *Mort and Jessica* premiered in July 1974 amid a flurry of well-planned publicity and anticipation generated by our promotion department. From both media and audience response, it seemed we were an immediate hit. Despite my early misgivings, Jessica's television performance was pure magic; when she looked into that lens with her captivating blue-green eyes, her gaze was magnetic. I quickly realized what an asset she was to the news team and to the station. Within a few weeks, the phrase *Mort and Jessica* was spoken around town as though it were a single word. While Jess would alternately share anchor duties with Vince and me on the six and eleven o'clock shows, it was *Newswatch 5:30* that made the two of us a team in the public's mind.

Now, when I emceed a banquet or made a speech, someone would invariably yell, "Where's Jessica?" as though it was unnatural for one of us to be there without the other. Jess encountered the same kind of response at her public appearances. Viewers sensed that we had on-air chemistry. What they could not know was just how much that same chemistry was at work off the air. Over the months, anchoring the news side by side every night on *Newswatch*, a very strong and dangerous personal connection had begun to grow.

At home things were going smoothly enough, but Nicki and I seemed to be talking less to each other. Like all couples, we had our disagreements, but we were never given to serious arguments. Now the silent stretches between conversations grew longer. Nicki had been my childhood sweetheart and the only girl I'd ever loved. She was, and always had been, the light of my life. I believed that she and I were the very definition of soulmates. Statistically, marriages that begin as early as ours have a poor prognosis, but

Vince, Jess, and Mort. The press dubbed us "The Dream Team."

we had always believed we would beat the odds. Divorce was something that never entered my vocabulary or thoughts, partly because of a strong religious upbringing and my personal belief in the sanctity of our wedding vows. A kind of moral arrogance caused me to presume nothing could ever threaten our marriage.

The attraction Jessica and I felt for each other was physical, to be sure, but also deeper. Our feelings seemed to connect at the intellectual and emotional level, based partly upon our mutual enthusiasm for the television news game. We held the same views about the role of journalism in a free society, and our passion for the craft was strong. We agreed on the kinds of stories we should be covering, sometimes putting us at odds with management. There is a unique sort of bond that often develops between people who work fervently together for a common cause, and we were partners in a mission.

As a journalist twelve years her senior, I became her mentor, and without recognizing it, my growing feelings for Jess were making me perilously vulnerable. Our jobs required that we spend a lot of time together, but we found ourselves looking for excuses to see each other outside of work.

At the same time, my resentment toward Nicki was festering. Privately, I was unfairly blaming her for my failure to pursue politics. I was convincing myself that her resistance was the only reason I had given up the idea and left Louisville. Had she not been so strongly opposed, we would still be in Louisville and I might be running for office. At least, that is the lie I told myself.

It didn't take Vince long to recognize that I was not out to take his job. I had been at KYW only a few months when he asked if I'd like to become a partner in the airplane. Vince was co-owner of a Cessna Centurion that was kept at Wings Field, a small historic airport in suburban Blue Bell where the Aircraft Owners and Pilots Association had been formed just four years after I was born. Vince and I had talked often about our love of flying and to be invited into ownership of the Cessna was a sure sign that he trusted me.

The plane was a popular topic of conversation around the station, too.

"Hey, why don't we fly your plane down to Louisville for the Kentucky Derby," Big Al suggested one evening as he, Vince, and I were having dinner between shows.

Al had not piloted an airplane in years, but he had been a cadet in the closing months of World War II and had never lost his love of flying.

"I'll kick in for the gas. Bet we could be there in a little over four hours.

Friendship with Vince bonded around an airplane

"Crim, you lived there. I'm sure you could get us tickets."

The Run for the Roses was less than a week away, and this year was the Derby's one hundredth anniversary. Tickets were always at a premium for the world's most famous horse racing event, and would be especially difficult to find this year. Hotel rooms would have been booked for months.

"Don't you know anyone you can call?" Al asked.

"I could call Colonel Sanders, but I don't think even he will have enough clout to find a hotel room now."

The idea of attending the Derby's centennial was appealing. During the three years I'd lived in Louisville, I had never attended the Derby. I was always anchoring from the studio while our reporters and sports anchor covered the activities at Churchill Downs.

With little hope of success, I called my old friend.

"Colonel, this is Mort."

"Great to hear from you," Sanders responded with a twangy voice as familiar as his trademark white suit and black string tie.

"How are things in Philadelphia?"

"Just fine, Colonel. A couple of colleagues and I were talking about coming to the Derby next week, and I figured if anyone had connections for a hotel room, it would be you."

"Don't be ridiculous," the Colonel said. "You boys will stay at our house. I wouldn't think of putting you up in a hotel."

Even though the Colonel and I had become friends, I never expected that kind of invitation.

"Are you serious?" I asked. "We can't impose on you and Claudia like that."

"No imposition. Just tell me when you're coming and where to pick you up."

"We're going to the Derby," I reported back to Vince and Al, "and we're staying at Colonel Sanders' house." I think Al and Vince were impressed.

On Friday, May 3, the day before the Derby, the three of us climbed into our airplane, lifted off from Wings Field and headed southwest to Louisville.

We landed at Bowman Field, the airport where I had earned my commercial pilot's rating, and before we got the engine shut down, a long, white limousine was pulling up to our plane. The uniformed driver got out, opened the rear door, and out stepped the Colonel in his trademark outfit.

"Glad to have you boys here," the Colonel said as we headed for his house in nearby Shelbyville.

"Claudia's looking forward to seeing you again," he said, glancing my way.

The Sanders home had several upstairs guest rooms, all of them opening off a hall that ran the circumference of the open living room. Claudia met us at the door and ushered each of us into our individual quarters.

"You boys just relax and do whatever you want between now and tomorrow," she said.

"We'll leave for Churchill Downs about eleven o'clock."

The next day, the same white limousine that had picked us up at the airport took us to Churchill Downs, where the Colonel escorted us to his private box.

The Kentucky Derby is much more than a horse race. It's an all-day festival where women put on their finest hats, men dress in summer jackets, and everyone sits around sipping mint juleps and soaking in the pageantry and splendor. As people passing our box caught a glimpse of the Colonel, unmistakable with his familiar white mustache and goatee, they waved or stopped to say hello. Some asked for an autograph or picture with him. He was an authentic down-home celebrity. I was also asked to pose for a few pictures with fans who remembered me from my Louisville days.

At around one o'clock, the Colonel asked,

"You boys hungry?"

We said we were, and the Colonel took off across the grass to find some food. Yes, it was chicken.

That evening, he and Claudia invited us to dine at the Colonel's Lady, which was across the way from their home. The Colonel's Lady was a restaurant that Sanders owned and named in honor of Claudia. Tonight, the man who had created the world's most famous fried chicken recipe ordered steak.

"I like chicken," the Colonel said, noticing our amusement

at his selection. "But you can get tired of it. Sometimes I just like a good piece of beef."

By the time we got to bed it was late, and the three of us would have enjoyed sleeping in. That was not to be.

"Rise and shine, boys," the Colonel called up to us early the next morning. "I've got breakfast on."

The seductive aroma of frying bacon blended with a whiff of baking biscuits and brewing coffee made it much easier for us to hit the deck, even though it was only 6 a.m.

"Got a special breakfast for you boys," the Colonel said, pouring some homemade batter onto a sizzling griddle.

"Ever had wheat germ pancakes? They're my own recipe.

Colonel Sanders makes our breakfast

And I've whipped up some red-eye gravy for the biscuits." What the Colonel set in front of us wasn't just a meal. It was a feast.

After breakfast, the Colonel joined us in his limousine for

our ride to Bowman Field. After seeing us off, he headed to the commercial airport to catch a plane for Madrid.

We marveled at the man's stamina. At 85, he was jaunting off to Spain to film commercials for Kentucky Fried Chicken's European operation. I wondered if somewhere, hidden away with his famous formula for fried chicken, he had some secret herbs and spices for staying young.

Vince and I had always enjoyed flying together, but that enjoyment was about to end. When Alan Bell learned that three of his prime anchor talents had made a flight together in a light plane, he put a clause in Vince's next contract prohibiting us from ever flying together again. Vince and I would later laugh about this, noting that far more Philadelphians died on the Schuylkill expressway than in plane crashes, yet his contract did not prevent us from carpooling.

Chapter Eleven

A LONG, DARK TUNNEL

Never blame another person for your personal choices—you are still the one who must live out the consequences ...

—CAROLINE MYSS

ON ELECTION NIGHT, just two months after we arrived in Philadelphia, I had watched the national returns on TV and paid close attention to the Kentucky congressional race. Gene Snyder, the congressman I might have challenged, won re-election, but in a real squeaker with a margin of just forty-three hundred votes. Most of those had been in Louisville, where I was best known. I had to wonder whether I might have pulled enough of those votes to beat him. I began to feel a melancholy that I couldn't shake.

As regrets about leaving Louisville grew, both my feelings for Jess and my resentment of Nicki intensified. I was increasingly depressed. Nicki sensed it. She would ask me what was wrong. I was never able to answer. Failure to talk it out was a huge mistake. Throughout our marriage, we had been able to discuss most issues freely, my despondency over politics being the one exception. Now the communication channel seemed to be slowly closing.

Little by little, my depression was beginning to cloud all the positive things happening in our lives. Al was adjusting well to second grade, Carey was growing up, Nicki and I both liked our home, and we were making friends outside the TV station. Materially, we appeared to have it all: a nice house with a pool, luxury cars, and enough money to enjoy the good life. We dined at the finest restaurants, attended the best shows, vacationed in exotic places, and were showered with all the perks that came with being a well-known television personality. In the Anchorman movies, Ron Burgundy made a parody of the line "I'm kind of a big deal," but the truth is, being a major-market anchorman in the seventies really was a big deal! We certainly had come a long way from southern Illinois.

At the TV station, the job couldn't have been going better. Ratings were up. The audience and most of the newspaper and magazine columnists seemed to adore our entire news team. We liked each other and viewers could tell that our friendships extended beyond the studio. Columnists often referred to Vince, Al, Bill, Jess, and me as the *Dream Team*. We called ourselves *Camelot*.

Jess and I looked for opportunities to see each other between newscasts, especially on those nights that I didn't go home for dinner. Because it was so natural to see us paired on TV, whenever we were together at a restaurant, it never raised an eyebrow. I don't think anyone, even our colleagues, knew just how close we had become.

For a long time neither of us spoke to the other about our feelings, though I'm sure we both were beginning to recognize them. One night after the early newscast, Jess and I drove to the airport, got into my plane, and flew to Atlantic City for dinner. Well, that was the plan, but we hadn't thought through the timeline, so it ended up being just a beautiful night flight. Once we got to Atlantic City, there was no time for dinner and we barely made it back to the studio in time for the late newscast. I'm not sure why we did such a foolish thing. Maybe we enjoyed the thrill of knowing there was some risk in it.

A cryptic Christmas gift from Jessica

A few times I drove Jess to New York for her voice lessons with Lilyan Wilder. Accompanying her to these sessions gave us additional time together, and a chance to share lunches out of town. It was an easy drive from Philly to Manhattan, and we were always back in the newsroom by midafter-noon. For a while, we joked about our deepening friendship.

"Jess, we could never have an affair," I said to her one after-noon. "We have such high public profiles in this town, it would be about as subtle as the McDonald arches."

We laughed.

The following Christmas, Jess handed me a small package. "Merry Christmas," she said.

I opened the box. In it was a twenty-four-karat gold key fob in the shape of McDonald's famous arches.

Even though we had long sensed what was happening, the moment when we acknowledged it was traumatic. It was on a Friday night. I had offered to drive Jess to the train station after our eleven o'clock news for her weekend trip to Baltimore to visit her boyfriend, Ron Kershaw, with whom she had a rocky, on-again-off-again relationship. Ron had met Jessica in Houston and moved east with her. We made the drive in silence but the atmosphere in the car was emotionally charged. It felt like we both wanted to say something, but couldn't.

"Jess, I think you and I have a problem," I blurted out as we stopped in front of the train station and I opened her door.

"Yes, Mort, I know we do," Jess responded, putting her arms around me.

Without another word, she kissed me, then walked into the train station and did not look back.

I drove home in a state of disbelief. Without stating it in so many words, we had acknowledged our feelings, and it now felt like I was on a dangerously out of control, run-away train. My first thought was of Nicki and our two children. Whatever conflicted feelings I was dealing with, I did not want to hurt Nicki. Whatever the solution, I could not jeopardize our marriage and family. By the time I arrived home, I was an emotional wreck.

Nevertheless, a week later, our long-simmering emotional relationship became a full-fledged affair. Jess had invited me to her apartment for some "Chinese carry-in" between newscasts. There's no doubt we both knew we were setting ourselves up for something more than dinner. That evening not only released months of pent up emotion, but also unleashed a torrent of guilt and regret unlike anything I had ever felt.

A romantic involvement with Jess was wrong. It violated everything I believed about commitment and marriage. Besides, I still loved Nicki very deeply. My dark cloud of depression began to grow blacker every day. I was sinking into a tunnel with no glimmer at the end of it. I wasn't sure there was an end. I tried to pray, but was anyone listening? At times it felt like walls were closing in on me; there were moments when it was hard to breathe. I was in love with two people, or believed I was, and could see no way out of the dilemma. I became increasingly frightened of my own feelings. Of course I should have opened up to Nicki, but in my confused mental state, I was convinced that I would have to untangle all of these emotions and solve this problem by myself.

Nicki began expressing more and more concern for my dark moods, and our children must have sensed that things were not good with their dad. I was starting to be affected physically. One day, shortly after taking off in our airplane, I began to feel faint and had trouble catching my breath. Nicki had flown to Ohio on a commercial plane to visit her parents, and the plan was for me to fly there for the weekend and to bring her back.

As I climbed out of the traffic pattern at Wings Field, I felt like I might pass out. I started breathing so fast and so hard that I wondered if I could get the plane back to the airport. I managed to land, found another pilot I could hire, and we resumed the trip with me in the co-pilot seat. It was the first in a series of such attacks.

I was becoming an emotional wreck, but life had to go on. There were holidays to observe, family vacations to take, children to rear, stories to cover, and a challenging job at the anchor desk. The days may have been mostly joyless but I managed to trudge through them, taking care of my responsibilities at home and in the newsroom as best I could.

In the fall of 1973, Nicki and I flew to England for a much-needed vacation. We spent several days in London, then rented a car and toured the British countryside down through Bath and on to Land's End. On Sunday, October 7, we were driving back to London and stopped in Salisbury to attend church services at the historic Salisbury Cathedral. When it came time for prayer, the priest said, "Let us say a special prayer for those caught up in the Middle East war."

War? What war? It was the first time I'd received a news bulletin in church.

This was years before cellphones, so we left the church, found the nearest pay phone, and I called the KYW newsroom.

"Yeah, Mort, we didn't know how to reach you. Are you ready to head for Tel Aviv?"

Vacation was over.

"I can get a flight home from London, and you go on and cover the war," Nicki said. She had been married to a journalist long enough to know that when the story breaks, the reporter goes.

"Don't worry about me," she added.

The truth is, I worried about Nicki a lot. About the way my feelings for Jessica had the potential to really hurt her. About our future. About our children.

In those years, major-market TV stations often sent their anchors out of town, and even out of the country, to cover major events that had a local angle. Putting the anchorman in the middle of a significant national or international story was a photo-op no news director wanted to miss. It made sense that KYW would want to have a presence in this conflict; Philadelphia's Jewish population was the fifth largest in the nation, and there were a substantial number of Arab-Americans in our coverage area. Most of them had roots in Syria or Lebanon, and Syria and Egypt had joined forces to launch this war against Israel. On a story like this, KYW also could get more bang for the buck by distributing my reports to all the Westinghouse-owned television stations.

"You leave Heathrow at 8 p.m. tonight, and you'll be staying at the Tel Aviv Sheraton," the assignment editor said. "We have a driver set up for you and we're hiring a local film crew in Israel."

Flying into Lod International Airport (the name was changed to Ben Gurion two months later, in honor of the former Prime Minster) was a surreal experience. Israel clearly was on a war footing. The entire city of Tel Aviv was under a blackout. Lights inside the airplane were turned off before we began our final approach, and the pilot landed on a dark runway.

Our taxi driver used only his parking lights on the way into the city, and there were few cars on the road. The hotel was virtually dark, as were all the buildings around it. At the check-in desk, the clerk handed me a flashlight and told me to keep the shades drawn in my room.

At 7:30 the next morning, an Israeli army major met me in the lobby. He'd been assigned to be both driver and guide. After a quick breakfast, we picked up our freelance Israeli crew—a photographer and a sound engineer—and headed north to cover the conflict.

The war had been launched with a coordinated attack; Egyptian forces pushing their way into the Sinai Peninsula to the

South, and Syrian tanks moving into the Golan Heights in the North. Within hours, Israeli forces had mobilized and quickly halted the Egyptian advance. Now the real action was with Syria, which had made threatening gains into Israeli-held territory.

If my arrival into a city under wartime curfew had felt strange, the drive to the front lines was bizarre. How many wars, I wondered, can be covered after breakfast as a day trip? The plan was for me to return each evening to the hotel, sleep in a comfortable bed, take a shower, have some coffee and breakfast, and then commute again to the battlefield.

Our route to the Golan Heights took us through the ancient city of Nazareth. With my study of the Scriptures and my background in theology, I was disappointed that we had no time to stop and visit sites that I had read and heard about all of my life.

Somewhere outside of Tiberius, we stopped at a roadside coffee shop. As we were paying for our drinks, we heard jets. Running out the door with coffees in hand, we looked up and saw a Soviet-built Syrian MIG in a dogfight with an Israeli Phantom. They were duking it out right over the road where we were standing. The noise from the jet engines was so loud we couldn't determine if shots were being fired, but before we finished our coffees, the Syrian MIG turned tail and headed back toward the border.

Watching air combat take place during a coffee break added to the weirdness of an already strange conflict, where journalists and even some troops commuted daily to the front lines. Our destination was an Israeli encampment near Mount Hermon. Syria had regained control of Israel's sector of the strategic mountain on the first day of the war, and Israeli forces were poised to take it back.

It was a grim ride from the coffee shop to the encampment.

Wreckage of burned-out Syrian tanks and the bloated bodies of Syrian soldiers lay alongside the road. The first three days had seen one of history's bloodiest tank wars; hundreds of tanks destroyed, thousands of soldiers dead, and thousands more wounded. Half a dozen Phantom fighter jets like the one we had seen in the sky had been shot down.

Burned-out Syrian tank near the front lines in Golan Heights

In the no-holds-barred tank battle for the Golan Heights, the Israelis had prevailed, despite being heavily outnumbered: fifty thousand Syrian infantry versus six thousand Israelis; twelve hundred Syrian tanks against Israel's one hundred and seventy. But Israeli commanders had out-thought and out-maneuvered the Syrians, and Israeli troops had out-fought them.

By the time I arrived to cover the conflict, the momentum clearly had shifted to the Israeli side. My weeklong coverage consisted of describing the carnage, interviewing Israeli troops and commanders, and comparing notes with my colleagues from other media after our evening briefings back at the hotel. I witnessed a couple of brief skirmishes between the two sides, and frequently heard the exchange of artillery fire, but the main battles were over, and most of the casualties had occurred during the eighteen hours of continuous combat prior to my arrival.

Although we had missed much of the action, we were keenly aware that this was a war zone, we were on the front lines, and danger was never far away. On my third evening at the hotel, I learned that a journalist for the BBC had been killed hours earlier by an incoming Syrian rocket. It happened less than a mile from where I'd been reporting. At ABC Radio, I'd had ample opportunity to be a working reporter. As a television anchorman, I didn't have as much time to be on the scene of events, so I welcomed assignments like the Arab-Israeli War. In addition to sending back daily satellite reports, we gathered enough film footage to support an hour-long documentary, which we assembled after I returned to Philadelphia.

Even though there's always some risk when reporting from a war zone, I frankly had felt in more danger while covering the Newark riots. Still, the sounds of battle and the sight of dead soldiers were reminders of my own mortality. Would I live long enough to find the truth about God? Would I have to wait for my own death to find out for sure if there's anything beyond this life?

Being in Israel, always referred to by my parents as the Holy Land, revived some of the big questions about life that had dogged me. This was where Jesus lived, where he taught, where he died. This land gave birth to the Bible, its history as well as its myths. Someday, I thought, I'll come back and visit the places I've heard about since childhood. I wondered if I might have found more answers by then.

Between the vacation and the war assignment, I had been

away from the anchor desk, and Jessica, for three weeks. I also wondered if my feelings for her had changed at all.

*   *   *

We had signed off after the eleven o'clock news. Vince, Al, Bill, and I said goodnight in the parking garage between the TV station and Independence Hall. I had been home only thirty minutes when I began having symptoms of a heart attack; profuse sweating, numbness, rapid breathing, and a sense of impending doom.

"Call Vince," I told Nicki.

Vince lived only a few minutes away.

Nicki first called EMS, and then called Vince. He arrived a few minutes ahead of the ambulance, and with Nicki in his car, followed the ambulance to the hospital.

After the usual protocols for a suspected heart attack—EKG, bloodwork, X-rays—the emergency room doctor informed us that I had not suffered a heart attack. He suspected hyperventilation. I told him about the episode in the airplane.

He explained how I could control hyperventilation, and within a short time I was back to flying my plane again. I was also feeling an increased need to share my emotional state and my dilemma with someone. I knew I needed help, but who? Where? For months I had bottled it all up, and some days I felt as though I would explode if I didn't find someone to talk to about it. Finally, I flew to New York to meet with my longtime attorney and friend, the man who had negotiated all of my contracts, Donald Hamburg.

"Don, I think I've fallen in love with Jess," I said, struggling to hold back tears. I was shaking. "I don't know how it happened. It's awful. I'm an emotional basket case."

Don knew Nicki almost as well as he knew me, and he also knew Jess. At my recommendation, she had hired him as her agent. Don reminded me that he was a lawyer, not a psychiatrist, but he did offer some advice as my friend.

"Don't let an affair wreck your marriage, Mort. You say you still love Nicki. Find someone who can help and do it right away."

Flying back to Philadelphia alone in my plane, I knew that it was past time to seek professional counsel, but what if a newspaper columnist found out that I was seeing a psychiatrist? Despite my ongoing faith struggles, Nicki and I still attended church most Sundays, so I made an appointment with our pastor, Dr. David Watermulder. I didn't mention my relationship with Jessica but told him that I was in an emotional crisis and desperately needed help. Dr. Watermulder recommended a psychiatrist, Dr. Joseph Hughes.

"He's an older man," Reverend Watermulder said. "He's nearing retirement but he's had lots of experience counseling men your age."

Men my age? Did our pastor think I might be undergoing the proverbial midlife crisis? Amid all the anger, regret and despondency, I had not thought of that possibility.

I immediately liked Dr. Hughes, felt comfortable with him, and for three months the two of us sat at his desk over lunch, usually a sandwich, and talked about feelings. About life. About my regrets over not having pursued a political career. About my relationship with Jess, my love for Nicki as well as the anger I felt toward her, and my desire to save our marriage.

At my first visit, he prescribed a mild tranquilizer and a

mood elevator, which he said were designed to get me through the crisis phase. The first few sessions left me wondering if I was making any progress, but after a few weeks, I began to feel slightly better about myself and about life in general.

"You grew up in an environment where guilt was a very strong emotion," Dr. Hughes explained during one of our sessions. "Your church advocated *holy* living, and you expected perfection of yourself. The truth is, humans are neither holy nor perfect. We're all just imperfect humans."

He was right, I had expected perfection of myself. Our church taught that it was possible to live a completely holy life; that, empowered by the holy spirit, we could live without sin. To confront the fact that I was broken, flawed, and capable of violating my own moral code was humbling. It was also an important and necessary revelation.

"You also married so young," he went on, "that you never had much of a chance to know yourself very well before committing to another person."

That also was true. Now at the age of thirty-eight, I had been married half of my life. It was Dr. Hughes's opinion that I was a prime candidate for a midlife crisis.

"It's important for you to realize that feelings are neither right nor wrong. They're just feelings. We can't control how we feel, we can only control how we act."

For someone who grew up in a church where the mere thought of adultery was as much a sin as the act itself, I found Dr. Hughes's words reassuring. Perhaps I would never be capable of controlling my feelings for Jess, but he was telling me that I had the power to decide whether to continue acting on them. He also helped me to recognize that my anger at Nicki was really anger with myself.

"I suspect that you had some reluctance to give up a solid broadcasting career and enter the uncertain world of politics. But it was easier to blame Nicki for the decision than to confront your own lack of courage."

As much as it hurt, I knew this insight was right on target.

"As for Jessica, you may always have strong feelings for her, but you don't have to let those feelings destroy your relationship with Nicki."

I'm confident that Dr. Hughes helped save my marriage and quite possibly my life. I'm not sure how much longer I could have withstood the emotional battering, nor how many more of my dark moods Nicki could have handled.

"You've got to end the affair," he said firmly.

"Then concentrate on the parts of your work that you really enjoy."

"What should I tell Nicki?" I asked him.

"Don't tell her any more than she wants to know. Be honest with her if she asks, but it's possible she would rather not know any details of your relationship with Jessica. Work on rebuilding your relationship. Focus on your children."

Because Jess and I had to continue as co-anchors and colleagues, it was crucial that we learn how to maintain a friendship without stepping over the line. We knew it would be difficult, but we also knew it was the right thing to do. It was the *only* thing to do.

During my involvement with Jess, I had been unable to involve God. My belief that God does not directly intervene into our lives and my own deep sense of shame and guilt prevented me from seeking the kind of help that would have come so naturally to my parents. As I came to a deeper understanding about God as the eternal essence that resides within each of us, I began to realize that trust in that power—the very essence of love—can be an enormous source of strength, courage, and hope in life's most perilous moments. Instead of crying out to a God out there, I had only needed to seek the living presence that's as close to us as the air we breathe. At the time, I lacked such an insight.

Later, I believe I did encounter God in a profound way, and it came through Nicki's response to my behavior. I felt unworthy. Ashamed. In the face of my guilt, she showed compassion and understanding. At our wedding, Nicki and I had pledged *for better or for worse,* and now I had put her through incredible pain. Her response was to honor that vow in the most tangible way.

Until the end of her life, Nicki never asked about Jessica, and she seemed uninterested in details of that relationship. Nicki showed me in very personal terms what it means to love someone who doesn't deserve it; to forgive someone who doesn't merit it; to offer understanding to someone who doesn't even understand himself.

Of all the beliefs I grew up with, one that remains true for me is this: God is love. Nothing, not the deepest ocean, the highest mountain, or the darkest deeds can ever separate us from that love. The God I had searched for in books, in reason, in vigorous debate, and in church, I was discovering in Nicki's compassion, understanding, grace, and forgiveness.

Chapter Twelve

TURNING THE PAGE

Nothing in the universe can stop you from letting go and starting over.
—GUY FINLEY

IN EARLY 1977, it was a foregone conclusion that Jessica would be leaving KYW for a network job. Both ABC and NBC were interested in her, and she'd had some discussions with news executives at CBS. The entire TV news industry recognized that Jessica was a hot property. It was clear that her biggest decision would be which offer to take.

While I also had network ambitions, my situation was a bit more complicated. Since bringing my syndicated commentaries, *One Moment Please*, from Louisville to Philadelphia, the radio series had grown considerably. We also had placed it on more than seventy television stations. If I went to one of the networks, they almost certainly would require me to stop the syndication and to sell my production company.

I was starting to get inquiries from both NBC and ABC, and the prospects at NBC looked quite promising. I received a telephone call from Joe Bartelme, news director at WNBC-TV in New York. He followed it up with a hand-written note suggesting a local anchor position on WNBC-TV plus some national exposure delivering several of the network's news minutes during prime time. He suggested that subbing on *The Today Show* also might be part of the deal. In one conversation, he was so specific that Nicki and I thought it was pretty much a done deal. We spent a Sunday afternoon driving through suburban New Jersey sizing up potential properties.

At about the same time, ABC News called and said they had a network opening: anchoring one of their two weekend newscasts and working as a Capitol Hill correspondent during the week. The position would require living in Washington and commuting to New York for the weekend show. Tom Jarriel, ABC's White House correspondent, was currently anchoring the weekend programs but he was moving to the magazine show, *20/20*.

I met with David Burke, ABC's Executive Vice President for News, who explained the job in detail and said it was mine if I wanted it. I was curious about the logistics.

"If I spend weekends in New York and cover the Senate during the week, what are my days off?" I asked.

"Well, frankly, when the Senate's in session, you really wouldn't have any. And when a key Senator goes off on a junket, you'd be expected to go along and cover the trip."

Al was twelve and Carey was six. This simply wasn't a time in their lives when I could take a job that demanded working seven days a week. After what Nicki and I had just come through, it was definitely time for me to put family first.

"It sounds like an incredible opportunity," I told Burke.

Then, with some reluctance, I said,

"Maybe someday, but not right now."

I recognized the risk in saying no. In the television business, the same opportunity rarely knocks twice.

The NBC job did not materialize. Bartelme, who had tried to hire me a few years earlier when he was news director at WCCO-TV in Minneapolis, was moved to another position at NBC. The job he and I had discussed ultimately went to Chuck Scarborough, an anchorman from Boston.

With both NBC and ABC no longer in play and with my contract at KYW nearing the end, I began to explore other options. While KYW would eagerly have renewed my contract, I really didn't want to stay in Philadelphia, given the trauma Nicki and I had been through. Ralph Mann, a highly respected talent agent who had co-founded International Creative Management, had been watching my progress since Louisville. ICM was considered one of the two best talent agencies in the country, along with William Morris, and Ralph personally managed an impressive stable of news people including Jane Pauley, Charles Osgood, Peter Jennings, and Floyd Kalber. His telephone call couldn't have come at a better time.

"I'd like to represent you," Ralph said.

I told him about losing out at NBC and explained why I had declined ABC's offer.

"I'll check around and see what's out there," he assured me.

I have to admit it was a bit unsettling to be ending the job in Philadelphia without knowing where I was going next. During those uncertain days, I recalled a statement by the late Basket Mosse, one of my broadcast professors at Medill:

"The only security you'll ever have in this business is what you carry right up here," he would say, pointing to his head.

Now it was time to draw upon that reserve of inner confidence.

Before my last day of work at KYW, I had signed a contract with WBBM-TV, the station owned by CBS in the nation's third largest market: Chicago.

As we drove out of Philadelphia on a calm, summer day, Nicki and I could not have imagined the headwinds we were about to face in the Windy City.

Chapter Thirteen

MY KIND OF TOWN?

Don't spend your life looking back, thinking what you should have done.
—NISHAN PANWAR

"IS THE NEXT CRONKITE HERE?" That was the headline above my picture on the front page of the *Chicago Daily News* entertainment section.

Bill Kurtis would not be pleased. He already was annoyed by a Frank Swertlow column in the *Sun-Times*, suggesting that my presence beside him on the anchor desk made Kurtis 'look like a Boy Scout.'

But if Bill would be upset, Donna would be furious. Donna LaPietra was Bill's ten o'clock news producer and his lover. Their affair was an open secret in the newsroom, where Bill and

Donna literally ran the operation. Jay Feldman had the title of News Director, but everyone knew that Bill and Donna were the newsroom's real bosses.

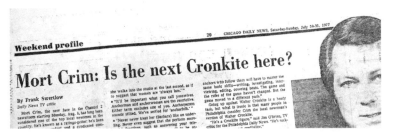

Chicago Daily News headline

From the moment I arrived they perceived me as a threat, and Donna began orchestrating a not-so-subtle campaign to make sure I would not succeed. Maybe if I'd known the full story behind my hiring, I would have understood their resentment. On the other hand, if I had known the full story, I probably wouldn't have taken the job.

I had been told by CBS management that Bill Kurtis was expected to leave WBBM-TV soon and go to New York to be the host of the CBS Morning News. The Chicago station was bringing me in to take over his job when that happened. The problem was, they never told Bill. From his perspective, I had been hired to put the squeeze on him if he negotiated a new contract. Where the truth lies we may never know, but it was crystal clear: Bill and Donna did not want me in *their* newsroom.

The idea of Bill becoming a network anchor was plausible. Not only had he earned respect as a first-rate journalist, but his former mentor, Robert Wussler, had moved up to CBS headquarters in New York and was president of the network.

Until Bill left WBBM, I was expected to co-anchor with him at 6 p.m., substitute for him when he was off, and co-host the station's *Noon Show* with longtime TV personality Lee Phillip. This exposure, plus reporting and documentary assignments, would make me a familiar face to the audience before I—presumably—moved into Bill's chair.

That may have been management's plan, but fate had a different idea. Just days before I was to start work at WBBM, Wussler left as president of CBS amid rumors that he had been fired. With his departure, it seemed likely that Bill would not get the CBS morning job. Whether he would remain at Channel Two seemed uncertain; rumors were rampant that WMAQ-TV, the NBC station in Chicago, was hot to hire him. For the second time in less than a year, an executive shuffle in New York had cast a shadow over my future.

While Bill and Donna had loyal supporters among the staff, others resented the pair's authoritarian style. A few also disliked the way they perceived that I was being treated, and I became a sort of rallying point for the dissatisfied. Newsroom tensions were palpable. It was anything but a fun place to work.

Bill was not overtly hostile to me and we were civil to each other while working at the anchor desk, but we never went out of our way to otherwise engage in conversation. Donna's demeanor was downright cold if not antagonistic. Dividing anchor reading assignments was a conundrum for the producer. He knew that Bill's contract required that he have at least 51 percent of the on-camera time during any newscast. The producer believed, incorrectly, that my contract had the same stipulation. Even wise King Solomon would have had trouble figuring out how to give each of us more than half the show. So, each time Bill confronted him to complain about not getting enough airtime (and that was almost daily), the producer felt trapped in a no-win situation.

I found my greatest professional satisfaction as cohost of the noon show with Lee Phillip and the weekend public affairs program, *Two on Two*, with Walter Jacobsen. Both Lee and Walter were pleasant to work with, and Lee was especially welcoming and supportive. Whenever major figures in politics, entertainment, business, or sports came to Chicago to appear on the *Noon Show*, I usually interviewed them.

I had been on the new job for only a few months when Scott Craig, one of Chicago's most highly respected documentary producers, asked me if I'd like to be the anchor-reporter on one of his projects. It was an investigative look at insurance redlining in Chicago, examining the way insurance companies charged poor people outrageous premiums based upon where they lived. We won an Emmy for our program, which contained some of my finest writing and reporting.

Home, a refuge from the newsroom chaos

I also was given several special reporting assignments by the station, some of which took me out of town. Getting away from the newsroom tension was always a relief, and on a few assignments I was able to rent an airplane and fly myself and the crew. This added an element of fun. But for Donna, whatever I did was never good enough—and her criticisms, voiced mostly behind my back, could be scathing.

If the TV station was a cauldron of turmoil, thankfully things were better at home. Nicki and I were growing closer. The move out of Philadelphia and into new surroundings was proving to be healthy for our relationship. Chicago is a great city and we loved our new home in Evanston, only a few blocks from the Northwestern campus.

Al, however, did not share our enthusiasm for the move. At age twelve, he found it gut-wrenching to be pulled away from lifelong friends, and breaking into a new school was difficult.

"I hate you for doing this, Dad," he had tearfully told me not long after we arrived.

His words cut deeply. They took me back to my own adolescence and the pain I had felt when Dad's move to a new church meant a new town, new school, and new friends. I had attended seven different schools in five towns before completing high school. At least Dad had a good reason: he believed he was following the Holy Spirit. I was merely following my personal ambitions.

It took most of the year for Al to make the adjustment to Roycemore, the private school where we enrolled him. He developed a few friendships in the neighborhood and seemed to be enjoying hockey, a sport he discovered during our time in Philadelphia. My son still chuckles about a picture he took in the Flyers locker room, not realizing until the prints came back that he had captured one of the star players in the background doing a full Monty.

One upside of the move for Al was front-row concert tickets

for some of his favorite bands, including KISS, Aerosmith, Jefferson Starship, and Ted Nugent. All of these acts were represented by ICM and my agent, Ralph Mann. Ralph always provided us with backstage passes so that Al could meet his music idols in person.

Because of Al's age, I accompanied him to the concerts, sitting through hours of music that was foreign to my own tastes. Even worse, the tickets inevitably were down front, close to humongous speakers so unbelievably loud they made jet engines sound like electric razors. I endured the noise by wearing earplugs. Al used to tell his friends that his dad actually slept through an Aerosmith concert. It was true.

Carey was just starting first grade when we left Philadelphia, so it seemed that her adjustment to Chicago was much easier. The fact that she seemed to have been born both adaptable and congenial certainly didn't hurt.

* * *

On December 4, 1977, I received some news that made all the newsroom upheaval seem trivial.

"Your mother just called and she wants you to phone her right away," Nicki said as I walked through the door.

"She sounded upset."

I dropped my brief case and immediately called my parents in Houston.

"The doctors say it's malignant," mother said. She was crying.

"They plan to remove part of his lung tomorrow. We won't know until then just how bad it is."

I hung up the phone in shock and disbelief.

How could my father, who had never smoked, never worked

around asbestos, never done *anything* that might account for this, have lung cancer? Dad was only sixty-three. He had gone into the hospital for prostate surgery but a routine X-ray showed something suspicious and a needle biopsy confirmed the worst.

We flew to Texas to be with them during the surgery at the M.D. Anderson Cancer Center. The surgeon didn't pull any punches.

"We believe we got the primary tumor," he told us, "but given its size and location, we can't be optimistic about the long term. In all likelihood, the cancer has metastasized. We will be doing additional tests."

I followed the surgeon into the hall, leaving Mother quietly weeping in the waiting room. Before I could ask anything further, the doctor put his arm on my shoulder.

"I know you love your dad and will try to do everything you can to keep him with you. Let me tell you, as someone who lost his own father to this disease, don't become so obsessed with saving him that you lose the valuable time that's left.

I made that mistake with my own dad," the surgeon confessed.

"Enjoy every minute you have with him."

On the flight back to Chicago, I tried hard to accept the words dad had said before we left.

"It's okay, Mort. I'm in God's hands."

I wanted to trust. To believe. To know that everything would be okay, but what did that really mean, *in God's hands?*

I knew dad wasn't suggesting that God would miraculously heal him. Although he had much more faith than I did that such miracles are possible, I knew his theology well enough to understand that was not what he was saying.

It's in God's hands for Dad meant that he was enveloped by a love so powerful, so deep, so complete, that nothing could separate him from it, not even death. Maybe he would get well, maybe he wouldn't, but for him being *in God's hands* meant he would win either way.

Three weeks later, in the early winter of 1978, I received a phone call at my office. It was Nicki.

"Honey, I don't want you to be alarmed, but the doctor wants to biopsy that lump in my breast."

I knew about the lump. Nicki had discovered it a couple of weeks earlier but we had not been concerned. Two previous biopsies in years past had been benign. Surely this was just one more harmless manifestation of her fibrocystic disease.

"I'm sure it's nothing to worry about," she assured me.

Three days later she went into Evanston Hospital for the biopsy, but when they brought her back to her room, she had undergone a double mastectomy.

"We don't know if the cancer is contained," her doctor told me.

"We've sent her lymph nodes to the lab. If they come back clean, she has a better than 90 percent chance of beating this."

A few days later her doctor called with the results. I held Nicki as she listened. I felt her body tense up and saw tears well up in her beautiful, sad blue eyes.

"Three of the nodes had cancer," she said as she hung up the phone.

I pulled her close. The odds had been explained to us, so there was no glossing over the seriousness of the situation.

"They want to do three months of chemotherapy to kill any cancer cells that might have escaped from the original tumor," she said, her voice quivering. She knew as well as I that her chances of surviving more than five years were just a little more than fifty-fifty.

"Honey, you don't know how terrible I feel hitting you with something like this when you're already dealing with your dad's illness," she said, as though getting cancer had been her fault. It was typical of Nicki to be thinking more about me and our kids than about herself. I suddenly felt a paralyzing fear and a fresh recognition of just how deeply I loved this incredible woman. The prospect of losing her was terrifying.

"Babe, we'll get through this. We've survived a lot, and we are going to beat this," I said, not daring to believe otherwise. Then, as though trying to reassure myself, I repeated what Dad had said.

"It's okay, we're in God's hands."

Dad's words had come from a deep place of confidence and trust. Mine came from frightful anxiety and desperate hope. Whether from faith or from fear, I knew the words were true. Nothing I could do would change the outcome. Dad and Nicki were, indeed, in God's hands, and for better or worse so was I.

Both Dad and Nicki eventually made uneventful recoveries, but Dad was living on borrowed time. Nicki had a slightly better than even chance of beating her cancer, but Dad's prospects for survival were dire: eighteen months to two years, the doctors predicted.

Nicki's chemo was difficult. In 1978, oncologists did not know as much about controlling nausea as they do now, and she spent far too many hours hovering over the toilet. Even when she wasn't vomiting, there were many days that she felt just plain lousy. She lost all of her hair but never her sense of humor, and she did find some classy wigs.

"This looks so much better than my old hair, don't you think?" she quipped one day while looking into the mirror.

We shielded Al and Carey as much as we could. There was no reason to discuss with them statistics and survival rates. Besides, we couldn't *know* how long Nicki might live. Anything the doctors could tell us was a guess. We told each other that a cure might be found soon, or at least new treatments that could increase her longevity.

Occasionally we attended the Presbyterian Church in Evanston, but I had been too preoccupied with the challenges at work to worry much about the meaning of life and the nature of God. Even though faith and religion had not been uppermost in my mind since we arrived in Chicago, I did pray for Nicki and for Dad. My old faith had been dying since our final days in South Bend, and a new one was still being born. But I had reached some conclusions: God is bigger than all of our descriptions. God is not a king, a ruler, a father, or even a *he*. All such descriptions are merely metaphors; personifying God by literalizing them, it seemed to me, reduced God to the same status as the gods of Greek and Roman myth. The Bible says God is love, and if love is the ultimate creative force, then that made sense to me. But how does one pray to a non-being? That I hadn't yet figured out, but prayer felt like a natural response, so I asked God to grant peace, courage, and wisdom to Dad, to Nicki, to Mother, and to all of us.

As my personal world was falling apart, life in the newsroom was not getting any easier. Bill still hadn't made up his mind whether to stay or move across town to NBC, and the columnists were conjecturing almost daily about what he might do. They also speculated about my future, or lack of one, at WBBM. I continued to host the noon show with Lee, and to co-anchor early news with Bill. Occasionally, Donna would assign me a special report or an interview, but the most important ones always went to Bill.

I had been at WBBM for ten months when Nicki completed her chemotherapy. Her hair and her energy both returned. Dad had undergone radiation treatments and was now once again teaching and serving as dean of students at Gulf Coast Bible College in Houston, a position he had held for several years. A semblance of normalcy returned to our home, but in the newsroom, storm clouds were gathering.

Bill is staying.

The news broke into the newspapers and ricocheted through the station. It ended months of tension over Bill's future, but added new uncertainty about mine.

In the short time I had been there, News Director Jay Feldman had been replaced by an older, seasoned journalist, Dick Graf. I had been in my office for only a few minutes when Dick walked in. I presumed he wanted to discuss the implications that Bill's decision had for my career.

"Mort, we need to take a walk down to Dave's office," he said without his customary smile.

Dave Nelson was the new General Manager brought in to replace Neil Derrough when Derrough was moved to New York to manage WCBS-TV. As Dick escorted me down the long hall, I said, "Okay, Dick. I know this is about the Kurtis deal. Can you give me a heads up? What's this going to mean for me?"

"You're about to be fired," Dick said without breaking stride.

I was shocked by Dick's directness and by the suddenness of the decision.

"This makes no sense," I said.

"There's plenty for me to do around here, even with Bill staying. What about the *Noon Show*? *Two on Two?* The special reports? And somebody's still got to sub for Bill and Walter."

Dick stopped, looked directly at me, and said, "You didn't hear this from me, but Bill made it part of his deal. If he stays, you have to go."

So, there it was.

It was a short meeting. Dave thanked me for the work I'd done, said he understood it had been a difficult year for me, and in what could have been a line from *The Godfather,* insisted that my firing was nothing personal, just business. Of course, he never mentioned the part about Bill's ultimatum. I'm not sure why Dick chose to tell me about it, but perhaps he felt I was being undermined by CBS and he owed it to me to explain why.

"I'll get with Ralph and we'll work out a buyout of your contract," Dave concluded.

It was only the second time in my life that I had been fired. However, getting canned at WHBU in Anderson, Indiana, had been my own fault.

But that's not the end of the story. Years later, Bill Kurtis was tapped to narrate Will Ferrell's *Anchorman* movies, which Ferrell said Jessica and I had inspired. One of the great ironies of my career was meeting up with Bill in New York at the premiere of *Anchorman 2: The Legend Continues.* Who would have dreamed during our uneasy time together at WBBM that a news anchor parody would bring us together again in real life, thirty-six years later?

Returning to my office, my first call was to Nicki and the second to Ralph. I had been back at my desk for less than an hour when Neil Derrough called. As part of the CBS hierarchy, he knew what was happening and wondered if I'd be interested in coming to New York to co-anchor a newscast on WCBS. I wasn't sure whether he was actually making an offer or simply trying to assuage his conscience for having gotten me into the WBBM debacle. I thanked him and said there were some other options I'd like to consider. He didn't push for an answer.

In the next couple of weeks, I received inquiries from KNXT-TV, the CBS station in Los Angeles, and an offer from WCAU-TV, another CBS-owned station that happened to be my old competitor in Philadelphia. Even KYW called and asked if I wanted to come home. But going back to Philadelphia with all the painful memories wasn't something I was ready to consider. Besides, it would have felt like a step backwards.

The KNXT management flew Nicki and me to L.A. for an interview and a look around the newsroom. My immediate impression was that Los Angeles TV stations were too show-business oriented. They didn't seem to practice serious journalism. Besides, having spent most of our lives in the East and Midwest, neither of us was enamored by the idea of moving to the West Coast. Despite my Air Force years at Vandenberg, California felt like a foreign country.

Then ABC called. Would I be interested in coming to Washington as a network correspondent? There was no immediate anchor position available, but this could be an entrée to bigger things. Network opportunity had, indeed, knocked twice.

But family concerns had tempered my national ambitions. Dad's cancer, and now Nicki's, had changed my priorities. The ABC offer presented the same challenge to family life that a similar opportunity had posed a year earlier. As I thought about

ANCHORED

what was facing two people I so dearly loved, working for the network was no longer that important. My time at WBBM was almost up and I was in the process of cleaning out my office when the phone rang. It was Joel Chaseman, president of Post-Newsweek Stations, the chain of television stations owned by the Washington Post Company. Before the Post had hired Chaseman away from Westinghouse, he had played a direct role in my selection for the anchor job in Philadelphia. When I began syndicating a television version of *One Moment Please*, Joel was my first customer and purchased the series for all five of the Post-Newsweek TV stations.

"Someday you're going to work for me again," Joel had joked as we put the syndication deal together over the phone. Well, maybe he hadn't been joking.

"Joel, nice to hear from you."

He wasted no time on small talk.

"Before you commit yourself to anything, I want you to consider working for us," he said.

"You probably know that we've just acquired the NBC station in Detroit and we're planning to rebuild the news operation there from the ground up. We'd like you to be our lead anchor."

"Detroit?" I said, probably with some astonishment in my voice.

"I know what you're thinking. And I know you must be considering other possibilities. But you really do need to look at this. I think it could be a great opportunity for you."

"I don't know, Joel. It's very flattering, and I certainly have high regard for you and for the Washington Post people. But Detroit?"

Joel knew as well as I that the Motor City was suffering hard

182

times. The nation was slipping into recession and the saying was, "When America catches cold, Detroit catches pneumonia." The city, which once ran as smoothly as a new Chrysler, relied almost totally on the auto industry for jobs, and the Big Three carmakers were getting beat up pretty badly by foreign imports, especially those from Japan.

The 1968 riots had decimated much of the city. White flight to the suburbs had critically eroded Detroit's tax base, and its reputation for crime and political corruption was legendary. Detroit often was referred to as "Murder Capital, USA." Someone had even manufactured a coffee mug that read, "I'm so bad I vacation in Detroit."

"Yes, it's a tough town," Joel countered, "but we intend to create a first-class news operation, and I'm hoping you'll be a part of it. I'd like for you and Nicki to fly to Washington and meet with the guys who'll be running the operation. At least don't say no until you understand our plan."

That seemed fair, and what did we have to lose?

"Okay," I said. "We can do that."

Nicki had never been to Detroit.

"Maybe we should go over and look at the place before we spend their money on airline tickets," she suggested. We found a sitter for the kids, drove to Detroit, and spent the afternoon driving around the city.

We passed the TV station, but didn't go in. The address was 622 West Lafayette Boulevard. *622?* The number jumped out at me. Nearly two years earlier, a New Jersey psychic named Joan Durham had predicted at a party that the number 622 would figure prominently in my future income. I've never had much confidence in psychics, and our church was strongly opposed

183

to any kind of fortune tellers (work of the devil), but this coincidence did strike me as strange.

After surveying the downtown, we toured residential areas that we had been told might be good places to live, among them the Grosse Pointes, Birmingham, and Bloomfield Hills. These suburbs, home to Detroit's auto titans, had everything Detroit was thought not to have: lush manicured lawns, stately homes, and wide clean streets. Maybe living here wouldn't be so bad.

Three days later, we stepped off a plane at Washington National Airport. Post-Newsweek had arranged for a limousine to take us to the Madison Hotel. As the bellhop opened the door of the Dolly Madison suite, the sight of fresh orchids greeted us from an exquisite vase on the table. Next to the flowers, we found a chilled bottle of champagne. A note from Joel welcomed us to Washington.

"Well, Post-Newsweek sure does know how to make a good first impression," I laughed, and Nicki agreed. "But remember, the job is in Detroit, not Washington," she said, reminding me of the obvious.

We'd just finished unpacking our suitcases when the phone rang.

"Mort, this is Jim Lynagh."

Lynagh had managed Post-Newsweek's Washington station, WTOP-TV, and now was heading up the Detroit operation.

"Hi, Jim. Eager to meet you," I said.

"Once you're settled in, let me know. I want to bring over Jim Snyder. Jim is going with me to Detroit to manage our news operation until we have it established."

Snyder's role was evidence of how serious they were about creating a first-class news operation. Jim was Vice President of

News for all the Post-Newsweek stations. He enjoyed a national reputation, and previously had worked as a producer for Walter Cronkite. That they were sending him to Detroit to launch a local news department told me Detroit definitely was going to be a priority.

"We should be ready in an hour or so," I said. "Why don't we say three o'clock?" At a minute after three, there was a knock on the door.

"Wow, you guys did it up right," I said, with a sweep of my hand toward the suite's luxurious lounge.

"Glad you like it." Jim Lynagh smiled, introduced himself and Jim Snyder, and we all sat down to talk about Detroit.

They didn't ask about my ill-fated year in Chicago. By now, just about everyone in the industry knew what had happened.

"We're taking over a station that's in last place," Lynagh began. "The news operation needs a lot of work and the ratings are awful. We're pretty much number four in a three-station market. There are nights when our early news gets beat out by reruns of *Little Rascals*." I thought he was joking. I would later find out he wasn't.

"There are some good people there," Snyder said. "But basically we plan to rebuild from the ground up and adhere to Post-Newsweek's philosophy of serious journalism."

My ears perked up and I'm sure Nicki's did, too.

"We've already changed the call letters to WDIV," Lynagh continued.

He explained that the "D" was for Detroit and the "IV" were the Roman Numerals for "four," the station's channel number.

"Channel Four has been WWJ since the station started,"

Lynagh explained, "and we think changing the call letters is an important way of telling the community that this is a new station and a new day."

"We will be doing a lot of political coverage and some important investigative journalism," Snyder said. "We're already hiring very experienced and savvy reporters, and we're bringing John Baker in from our Washington station as Executive Producer to run the day-to-day.

We sure would like it if you'd join us. It's going to be an exciting next few years. And it could be fun."

We talked for about an hour. Nicki and I both had questions about Detroit, about the city's dismal reputation, and about raising children there. I was not overly concerned about how such a move might affect me professionally. Detroit ranked in the nation's top-ten television markets, and still enjoyed a worldwide reputation as the automobile capital and the birthplace of the famous Motown sound. But the 1968 riots had left scars, both physical and psychological, and I wondered if Nicki and I really wanted to live there.

Both Lynagh and Snyder stood to leave, but at the door Snyder lingered.

"Mort, how old are you?" he asked.

"Just turned forty-three," I said.

"Well, professionally, you probably have about another twenty-five years or so ahead of you," Jim said. He paused.

"I know you're considering some places that are a lot more glamorous than Detroit." He paused again, then shook my hand and stepped into the hall. Just before I closed the door, he turned to me and said, "Seems to me there could be a lot worse ways to spend the second half of your career than helping an old, beat-up city find its way back."

The limousine, the fancy suite of rooms, and the flowers had been nice touches. But it was Jim's final statement that penetrated right to the heart of who I was, or at least who I wanted to be: helping an old, beat-up city find its way back.

While Jim could not have known the impact of those words, Nicki knew.

The hotel room door clicked shut. For a few moments, neither of us spoke.

Then Nicki broke the silence.

"We're going to Detroit, aren't we?"

Detroit bound, with Jim Snyder and Jim Lynagh

Chapter Fourteen

WEIGHING ANCHOR

A new challenge keeps the brain kicking and the heart ticking
—E.A. BUCCHIANERI

"I MAKE MORE FUCKING MONEY than Mort Crim."

Bill Bonds was literally jumping up and down on top of the table he'd commandeered as his stage. He was pointing his finger and shaking it at me.

"I make more goddam money than any anchorman in this town," he shouted.

Members of Bill's Channel Seven news team snickered, and tried to keep his moving feet from knocking over their beers.

They had seen versions of this act before: a drunk-out-of-his-mind Bill Bonds was nothing new to his friends, or to most of Detroit. Bill's suit coat was draped over the chair he'd just vacated, and his tie hung loose below his open collar.

Our weatherman, Sonny Eliot, raised a mock toast, egging him on.

"You tell 'em, Billy."

Sonny turned to see how I was taking all this drama. It was only my second week in Detroit, and my first night at the Lindell A.C., the sports and media bar where Lions, Tigers, and Redwings regularly mixed it up with newspaper scribes and so-called media celebs like Bill and me.

"This guy's a piece of work," my co-anchor, David Wittman, laughed.

We all knew what had lit Bill's fuse. That morning, the *Detroit Free Press* had reported that I had signed a five-year, million-dollar-deal with WDIV, a figure that would have made me the highest-paid news anchor in Detroit. Bill's ego couldn't let the story stand unchallenged.

It wasn't the last time I would witness an out-of-control Bill Bonds. Billy, as his friends called him, once went on his own newscast (no doubt after an extended dinner hour) and challenged Mayor Coleman Young to a fistfight. The mayor was in his late sixties and of course it never happened, but if the flamboyant anchorman and colorful Mayor had agreed to fisticuffs, the event could have sold out Cobo Hall.

Bill was king when I arrived in Detroit, and he was sure he would chew me up and spit me out as he had every other chal-lenger to his ratings dominance. His well-publicized fondness for the bottle, as well as his short temper and prolific profanities, all seemed to endear him to hardscrabble Detroiters; he was one of them, and never hesitated to mix personal commentary with his news reports. This was before the arrival of cable news channels, where the line between news and opinion has been virtually obliterated. No one ever accused Billy of being fair and balanced; but to his legion of fans, it didn't matter.

Even the cocktails he regularly enjoyed between the early and late news didn't seem to dull his quick wit and ability to unleash zingers—often at the expense of his own co-anchor, or reporters in the field.

Bill figured I had about as much chance of dethroning him as a white guy had of becoming Detroit's mayor. Many before me had tried, but Bill and his co-anchor, Diana Lewis, seemed to have a hammerlock on first place in both the early and late time periods. He had been the town's dominant anchor for nearly a decade.

Sonny, who had been on Detroit TV even longer than Bill, was well aware of the challenge ahead of us.

"You've got your work cut out," he said.

"The guy's bigger than life." *Monthly Detroit* magazine described him this way:

"A sermonizing, convincing anchorman, who says as much with his expressions as with his voice. His intensity and furrowed brow tell us he is deeply troubled by the daily round of horrors and miseries he is forced to report."

Bill eventually climbed down off the table and walked over to me. Red-eyed, he stuck out his hand and said, "Welcome to Detroit." A light mist of perspiration glistened on the TV makeup he had not bothered to remove after work. Both of us had come directly from delivering our eleven o'clock newscasts.

"That's our competition," Sonny said with a mischievous grin, as Bill staggered back to his Channel Seven friends and lit up a cigarette.

Bill Bonds first came to prominence while covering the 1967 Detroit riots. He had brief stints in both Los Angeles and New York, but the coastal types didn't seem to buy his act, and both times he ended up back in Motown. He also had played himself in a couple of movies, including *Escape from the Planet of the Apes.*

I studied him for a minute or so. Yes, this was going to be an interesting contest of both style and substance, because the contrast between us was striking. Bill was loud, arrogant, hard-drinking, profane, funny, and at times totally outrageous. Post-Newsweek had hired me, in part, because they believed I was none of those. I was thirty before I had so much as a glass of wine, and even now, I was at most a light social drinker. As for profanity, that was something virtually foreign to me. Audiences saw me as the Pat Boone of newscasters, and my squeaky-clean public image was the complete opposite of Bill's.

I have a strong sense of humor, but it tends toward the dry and subtle side. Compared to Bill's raucous style, I was considered by some critics to be stiff, and maybe too restrained. Columnist Bob Talbert enjoyed tagging me with the handle, Mort *Grim*. But that was okay. Post-Newsweek and WDIV had no intention of trying to out-Billy Channel Seven, and neither did I.

My bosses counted on the main anchor at their flagship Detroit station to be a solid journalist who could deliver the news straight, objectively, and with authority. They calculated that since my steady, low-key style had helped move Philadelphia's KYW-TV into first place, maybe such a consistent and dependable approach would be enough to dethrone Bill Bonds and the Channel Seven gang. And although the battle between Bonds and me would become fierce, I was determined that it would never become personal. When my picture appeared on the cover of a local *TV Guide*, Bill sent me a copy, which he had autographed across my face with the inscription, "Here's wishing you relatively good luck."

Years later, the two of us would appear in a Red Cross ad campaign called *Good Buddies*, urging people to give blood, including a photograph of Bill and me, laughing and embracing.

From day one, there was much private and public debate over WDIV-TV's chances of ever winning the news wars. *Monthly Detroit* magazine introduced me to the city with a front-page headline over my photograph that asked:

BECOME BUDDIES FOR LIFE.

IT'S EASIER TO GIVE BLOOD TOGETHER.

TV competitors, but comrades for charity

"Can the Company That Brought You Watergate Whip Bill Bonds?"

That company, of course, was the Washington Post, new owner of WDIV, and my employer.

But would no-nonsense, hard-hitting journalism work in a blue-collar town seemingly addicted to Bonds's loose-cannon commentary and on-air antics? One reason people tuned in to Channel Seven was because they never knew when Billy would implode, and they didn't want to miss it. In bars around town, bets were placed on just when Bonds' infamous toupée would fly off during one of his notorious rants.

Driving home from the Lindell that evening, I wondered what influences and forces had produced this flamboyant character. There was much I didn't know about Bill Bonds, but I was certain of this much: competing with him would never be dull.

* * *

"Crim, did you have any idea what you were getting into?"

Jim Snyder watched as I unpacked boxes and set up my desk a few feet away from his.

"Not the best arrangement for either one of us," Jim said, peering over the top of his glasses.

"But I promise not to listen in on your phone calls, and please ignore mine."

Jim, known for his ethics but not his sense of humor, smiled slightly. He wasn't one to talk about his faith, but I soon learned that Jim was a devout Catholic who took the tenets of his religion seriously. His strong commitment to practice *real* journalism and his no-nonsense approach to making a positive difference in the community marked him as a man on a mission. So was I.

Space was at a premium in the old, cramped building that housed the TV station, so Jim had suggested that we share an office until new facilities could be built for both of us in a partitioned-off section of the newsroom. That newsroom, which was claustrophobically small, housed our entire operation: desks for reporters, producers, and assignment editors, as well as teletype machines, police radios, camera gear, boxes of copy paper, blank video tapes, stacks of notebooks, and anything and everything else needed to run a big-city newsroom.

Crowded into a slightly larger studio just off the newsroom was the news set. I thought it was rather plain and uninspiring but figured Snyder would soon get around to sprucing it up. After working in spacious, electronically sophisticated studios at WBBM-TV in Chicago and KYW-TV in Philadelphia, these relatively antiquated Detroit facilities might indeed have had me wondering what I'd gotten myself into. But this was a new and exciting assignment, and I was happy to accept the temporary office arrangement.

The outmoded building was the least of our challenges; the station's image in town was the big one. Not only were we putting new faces in front of the camera, but changes were just as dramatic behind the scenes. We hired new producers, reporters, assignment editors, and writers, bringing some in from other Post-Newsweek stations. But it seemed that for every new hire, somebody was fired. It was a scary and anxious time for everybody who had worked for the Detroit News Company, and you could feel the uncertainty as longtime employees worried if they would be next.

In the executive suites, more than thirty years of good-old-boy culture was under siege, and several executives were shocked when Jim Lynagh, the incoming general manager, ordered them to shut down their private bars. Within a few months, most of the leftover managers had been replaced.

For those of us coming in, it was exhilarating. But having recently experienced in Chicago the trauma of being let go, I really felt bad for those on their way out.

A clear sign of Post-Newsweek's commitment to WDIV was the decision to put Jim Snyder in charge of the news department. His national reputation as a leader in broadcast journalism would be severely tested in Detroit. But Jim assured us we would have all the resources needed to win our tough race with Channel Seven.

* * *

"How's it going?" Nicki asked, as I walked in from the garage, suit coat slung over the arm that held my briefcase.

It was Friday night, the end of my first week at the station.

"Well, it's hard to tell after only a week," I said, dropping my briefcase onto a couch in the den and walking ahead of Nicki into the kitchen.

"As soon as I clean up a little, I'd love a glass of wine."

It was a little after midnight. I was exhausted and had driven straight home to Grosse Pointe without taking time to remove my TV makeup.

Nicki opened a fresh bottle of Merlot and had two glasses setting beside it on the coffee table when I returned to the den.

"The newscasts went well," I said, settling into my favorite chair.

"But it's hard when you don't know anybody, and frankly, we've got so many new people that most of them don't know each other. Plus, we're all adjusting to new routines."

Nicki laughed. "At least nobody hates you," she said, in an obvious reference to the impossible situation I'd just left in Chicago.

I laughed too.

"Well, not yet. Wait 'til they get to know me."

We both laughed.

Nicki and I loved our new home on Alger Place, a comfortable, traditional, two-story brick house just a block from Lake St. Clair. On a nice night, with the windows open, we could hear sea gulls, frogs, and other sounds of nature. It was only a twenty-five-minute drive to downtown Detroit, but Grosse Pointe, home to Detroit's automotive pioneers and legends, felt like it was a thousand miles from the city.

Both of the children had been asleep for hours. Not being there for the children's bedtimes was one of the real disadvantages of working late-night television. But I planned to be home for dinner between the early and late shows and hoped to devote lots of time to the kids on weekends. Al was now thirteen, and Carey was seven. They were growing up fast.

"Things have got to be better than in Chicago," Nicki offered, smiling at the thought.

"I know. It will just take time," I said.

"But I don't have a single doubt about our decision to come here."

"Neither do I," Nicki said.

She had just finished chemo before we moved to Detroit, and we were starting to feel more hopeful about her future.

* * *

Jim Snyder and General Manager Jim Lynagh both understood the importance of inserting me fully into the lifeblood of the community. They raced me through a whirlwind of 'get acquainted' tours, making sure that I met face to face with every major mover and shaker in Detroit, including Mayor Coleman Young, Henry Ford II, and Chrysler boss Lee Iacocca.

It was also important that I get out on the street with camera crews, report stories, conduct interviews, and establish my credentials as a newsman in this town, which was known to be suspicious of TV newcomers. My education and reporting experience had qualified me as a capable reporter in the eyes of management, but I knew none of that would mean anything to the audience unless I could convince them I knew their city,

Interviewing Chrysler Chairman, Lee Iacocca

their culture, and their issues. It was performance, not credentials or reputation, which ultimately counted. And slowly but
surely, calm and consistency were replacing chaos and uncertainty in the newsroom. We were getting to know each other,
trust each other, respect each other, and were working together
as a team. We still weren't garnering respect from the local press,
but Lynagh and Snyder urged patience.

"We just have to keep producing quality news, and stop
paying attention to the critics," Snyder often reminded us.

It was good advice, but with ratings languishing and columnists pounding us, it was difficult to follow.

As the station's front man I took much of the media heat,
and the columnists had been brutal. *Detroit Free Press* critic

Chris Stoehr was especially hard on me, once devoting a large portion of her column to comparing sweat on my upper lip to Richard Nixon's five-o'clock shadow.

And when we hired a young woman from San Francisco, Kai Maxwell, to be my co-anchor at five o'clock, Stoehr grabbed the opportunity to take another shot at me, describing my newscasting style as "overly formal" and "stiff," adding that "Mort Crim leads off each newscast…reading it as if his hand should be cupped over his ear, 1940s radio-style."

In another column she quipped,

"Watching Crim try to exchange quips with other anchors is nothing short of painful."

Unfortunately for my new newsroom team, Stoehr was as gushing and effusive about Channel Seven and Bill Bonds as she was derogatory about Channel Four and me.

The constant barrage of criticism and the perpetually low ratings were getting to me. One afternoon, I walked into Snyder's office, told him I felt terrible that after all our hard work we were still in the ratings cellar, and handed him an envelope.

"What's this?" Snyder said.

"It's my resignation, Jim. I can't hold you guys to my contract when it's obvious I'm not getting the job done."

It was a foolish act of bravado. I had signed a five-year, no-cut contract, and that letter would have given WDIV a legal out with no financial penalty if they had wanted to fire me. Ralph Mann, the agent who had spent weeks negotiating my deal, would have had apoplexy had he known what I was doing. Nicki wouldn't have been too thrilled, either. But I was thoroughly embarrassed and placed much of the blame for our poor performance on myself. Offering to resign seemed to be the honorable thing to do.

Jim never took the letter out of the envelope. He held it out toward me, tore it into two pieces, dropped it into his wastebasket, then said sternly, "Crim, get out of my office and don't ever pull a stunt like this again. We knew what we were getting when we hired you. We didn't expect overnight success. Post-Newsweek is in this game for the long haul. Now get back into the newsroom, stop reading the columnists, and just do your job."

In retrospect, it not only was a melodramatic move on my part, but arrogant—as though I alone was responsible for the news department's success or failure. But Jim Snyder gave me the vote of confidence from management that I needed—I went back to work with renewed determination to justify Post-Newsweek's faith in me.

* * *

With all the challenges I faced at WDIV, I confronted a more distressing one in my personal life.

About a year after we moved to Detroit, Dad's lung cancer turned aggressive, ravaging his body, sapping his energy, limiting his mobility, and dimming his usual sunny optimism. Doctors now measured his remaining time in months. He had to retire as Dean of Students at Gulf Coast Bible College in Houston and resign from the small church he had been pastoring on weekends. We brought Dad and Mother to our home in Grosse Pointe, where we turned our guest room into a hospice.

Nicki's oncologist, Dr. John Burrows, had become a good friend. He was a pilot who shared my love of airplanes, and along with his wife, Nancy, frequently flew with us on vacations or weekend jaunts. John agreed to take over Dad's care and we hired around-the-clock private nurses, although Mother rarely left Dad's bedside.

All of my life, I had been extremely close to my father. He was my hero, the kindest, finest man I had ever known. Despite my rejection of many church doctrines and rules, I never lost my respect for Dad, his unwavering faith, his sterling character, and his devotion to God and to his family. Looking back, I find it sad that I never discussed my religious doubts with Dad. I don't think he ever knew how much my departure from the ministry was because of troubling uncertainties about religious dogma. Dad believed I left simply because I decided that the ministry was not my calling and that's what he preferred to believe. I considered him so firmly fixed in his own views and so solid in his own faith that serious questioning on my part would have caused him pain. He would have blamed himself and considered my deviation from *the truth* to reflect his failure as a parent.

Not only was I reticent to cause Dad such anguish, I also worried that total honesty might create an emotional chasm between us. So I shared my doubts mostly with Nicki and sometimes with Steve Bell, my closest friend. Because we still attended church, said grace at meals whenever Mother and Dad visited, and because I continued to speak in churches from time to time, I don't think Dad ever suspected the spiritual turmoil that raged inside my brain. I have often regretted my failure to level with the most important man in my life.

Although I was still struggling for answers to life's big questions when we arrived in Detroit, I had not given up on faith. I considered myself a follower of Jesus despite the nagging questions that wouldn't go away. Nicki and I joined Grosse Pointe Memorial Church, just up the street from our home, and attended services most Sundays. We recognized that the Christian education we had received as children was the bedrock of our value system, and we wanted the same for Al and Carey. I continued to read the Bible, but no longer accepted all of it as divinely inspired or error-free. There were too many inconsistencies and too many assertions that plainly defied scientific and historical facts as we know them today. Even though I derived much inspiration from the Bible, I was convinced that some of its stories were human attempts to explain and understand God rather than God's word to humanity. After all, the Bible had been written by humans, edited by humans, and gone through numerous translations by humans. Even the process of deciding which texts should be included had been a human endeavor, and thus fraught with much controversy.

For Nicki and me, following Jesus did not demand that we live by all those rules we'd grown up with. By the time we moved to New York, we had been attending movies for years. We also learned to dance, signing up for lessons at Arthur Murray in anticipation of attending a formal affair. With my late start, I have to admit I never became very good at it. My initiation into social drinking had occurred one night after my eleven o'clock newscast on WNEW, just a few months after we'd moved to New York. It was customary for the news team— producer, writers, and reporters—to end the week with a visit to an Irish pub a few blocks from the station. It was my third Friday night with the gang. They all ordered their usual Irish coffee. I was about to ask for my usual Coke when something inside my head said:

What are you doing? You know you don't think it would be wrong to enjoy a drink with your friends.

So, I ordered an Irish coffee.

"I had a drink with the guys tonight," I told Nicki as we relaxed around the kitchen table.

She was not shocked. We had discussed the issue many times. Technically, we had broken the alcohol taboo a couple of years earlier when we had that glass of wine at Mike Eisgrau's. Of course we understood that drinking is not without risk; some people drink to excess. Some become alcoholics. We know the horrible statistics about drunk driving. Nicki and I each had at least one alcoholic in our families. Too much drinking can destroy a liver, a livelihood, or a marriage.

I often wonder if many people who oppose social drinking on religious grounds have ever actually read the Bible. Drinking is there, plain to see, in both the Old and the New testaments. Jesus himself must have loved a good party because the writer of Matthew says he was criticized as a glutton and a drunkard who often hung out with a pretty questionable crowd.

Mother and Dad would have been disappointed had they known that Nicki and I had alcohol in our home, so after setting up a bar behind a pull-down door on our living room book cases, I installed a lock on it. Whenever Nicki's parents or mine visited, that cabinet was locked. Our children found it quite amusing that even grown kids could sometimes feel it necessary to hide things from their parents.

Steve and Joyce Bell found a different solution. Her dad, a Quaker minister, was as opposed to drinking as my father. So, whenever Joyce's parents were coming for a visit, Joyce would haul all the wine and liquor up to the attic in a cardboard box. One time, as she was lifting the heavy box over her head, she threw her back out and was out of commission for the entire visit. I couldn't resist teasing Joyce that her back injury was God's punishment for their wickedness.

Whatever my evolving view of God, I had long ago decided that He didn't play favorites based upon a person's good or bad behavior. Even the Bible says that the rain falls on the just and the unjust. Bad things do happen to good people and evil people often seem to get away with it. So I couldn't ask, 'Why does Dad have lung cancer?' Intellectually, I accepted that life is random and that whatever the reality is, God is not some cosmic puppeteer, pulling the strings on our individual lives. There was no way I could make sense of it all based upon merit.

Dad had spent his life in the service of his God, preaching the gospel, ministering to the sick and the discouraged, counseling the bereaved, and seeking God's guidance and wisdom in every aspect of his life. By any scale of justice, it was unfair that such a good man and faithful servant would be struck with lung cancer on the very eve of his retirement. But my years as a reporter, covering all manner of terrible tragedies, already had taught me that life is not fair.

Dad was a true Renaissance man: gifted artist, musician, poet, teacher, and writer. If he had not responded to the ministerial call that he heard at the age of twelve, he could have found success in any number of creative professions.

"I could never be bored," he once told me.

"I've got so many paintings I want to paint, music to write, and a lot more fish to catch, once I'm retired."

He also looked forward to spending more time with his grandchildren. Now, just months before his sixty-sixth birthday, Dad was dying, and so were those dreams.

His faith never wavered, and a few days before his passing,

Dad, painting a portrait of our son

Dad told Mother that something very strange had happened.

"Honey, I sensed that Jesus was on the bed, right there, right beside me." he said. "It was so real. I knew then that everything would be alright."

I was still wrestling with my unanswered questions about God on a cool spring night when I pulled my car into our driveway after delivering the eleven o'clock news. The car parked in front of our house belonged to one of the special duty nurses we had hired to care for Dad. But she had a day shift, since Mother always tended to Dad at night. What was this nurse doing at our house at this hour?

I hurried up the stairs to the guest room where I found both the nurse and my mother sitting close to dad's bed. Mother was holding his hand. His eyes were shut. He was pale, drawn, and motionless. His breathing was heavy, labored, and irregular. There would be long periods when he didn't seem to breathe at all, followed by a gasp. I had sat on his bed and talked with Dad in the afternoon, just before leaving for the TV station. How could he have gone down so fast?

"We're losing him," the nurse said softly.

She had grown close to both Dad and Mother. There were tears in her eyes.

I moved close to the bed, put my hand on Dad's arm and looked at Mother. Dad was the light of her life. Her rock. Her everything. Married when she was a teenager, she always told people that he had raised her, and there was truth to that. Dad had always taken care of everything for her. I don't think she had ever written a check.

I expected that in those closing moments of Dad's life, Mother would break down. She had been so devoted during Dad's final months, hardly ever leaving his room. Instead of bursting into tears, Mother calmly squeezed Dad's hand, leaned over the bed, and looking at his closed eyes, began to sing, softly.

Have I told you lately that I love you,
Can I tell you once again somehow ...

Many times during my growing up years, I had heard Mother and Dad sing that song to each other—Dad in his clear tenor voice, and Mother harmonizing with her smooth alto. Tonight, the duet was a solo.

Have I told with all my heart and soul how I adore you? Well, darling I'm telling you now.

How Mother found the courage and composure to offer Dad that final gift of love, I will never know. Later, she would tell me it was God's grace. Perhaps that same grace was spilling over onto me, because as I held Dad's other hand and silently prayed for his peaceful passage, I felt strangely comforted.

For weeks, I had been angry, confused, and pissed off at God for not providing a miracle, even though I didn't believe in them. After all, Dad believed. I thought of all those retirement years he had counted on to do things he'd never had enough time to do. His death marked the cruel, tragic end to an unfinished life. At least, that's how it had seemed to me.

Now, as Dad was taking his last breaths, I began to see that his life was not unfinished at all, and what had felt like an unfair and untimely death was sad, but not a tragedy. The change in my perspective came as I looked around the room at shoe boxes crammed full of cards, letters, telegrams, and notes expressing appreciation for Dad's life of ministry. I had read many of them, but now their meaning took on a new poignancy.

"Thank you, Dr. Crim, for counseling with my daughter," someone had written. "You may have saved her life."

"Brother Crim, you'll never know how much your sermons have meant to me and my family," another card read.

"Reverend Crim, I'll never forget your visits when my mother was in the hospital. I don't know how we could have made it without you."

Since word of Dad's illness had gotten out, the messages of gratitude had poured in; evidence of the profound way he had affected people. Each note, each letter, each card, was a testimony to a life well lived in the service of others. Early in his youth, Dad had discovered something many never find in a lifetime: his purpose. For nearly half a century, he had lived that purpose, believed in it, and made those whose lives he touched better because of it. Saying goodbye was heart-breaking, and unbearably sad—but how could it be considered a tragedy when his beloved wife of forty-five years was there to escort his final departure with a tender love song?

Could it be a tragedy when, just a few days before closing his eyes for the last time, he believed that Jesus was beside him, ready to take his hand when Mother had to let it go? Was that vision real? Was it some hallucination triggered by medication? Was it an illusion generated by his deep faith? It didn't matter; it was real to Dad.

He wasn't with us as long as we would have liked, but measured by its depth rather than its length, Dad's life was complete. His life and his death brought home to me the truth that life is not measured by how many breaths we take, but by how many moments take our breath away. I continue to be inspired by Dad's simple but genuine faith; he walked steadfastly, and with total commitment in the truth as he understood it. Can anyone do more than that?

I've known people raised in a conservative and restrictive religious tradition such as mine who grow bitter and resentful of their past. Some become dismissive of what they consider the quaint views of their church and their childhood; in their disillusionment and cynicism, they may abandon altogether the whole idea of God.

I believe one reason I've continued to appreciate and respect my past, even while shedding much of it, is the unconditional love I received from my parents, their kindness toward everybody, and their absolute integrity. I could not agree with all of Dad's opinions, but I couldn't argue with the life I saw him live. He made Jesus look good. I smile as I write those words, because Dad would have corrected me. He would have said, "No, son. Jesus made *me* look good."

It became impossible for me to follow dad into the pulpit, but at the core of my being I follow him still.

Dad behind the pulpit in his church

Chapter Fifteen

GETTING DOWN TO BUSINESS

I report the news. That's what I do

—RON BURGUNDY

IT FELT LIKE ALL OF MY LIFE experiences had been leading me to this point: helping build a news operation from the ground up, and participating in the rebuilding of a once-great city. This dual challenge was exciting, and eventually would involve me in all kinds of projects in addition to reporting the news. At the outset, I couldn't have imagined how deeply the job would take me into the community, nor how far it would take me across the globe.

Detroit was the seventh-largest television market in the nation and a single ratings point was worth $770,000 in advertising to a TV station.

WDIV poured every resource into increasing our abysmal numbers. There was a two-page fold-out in the regional edition of *Newsweek* that traced my life in photographs all the way back to a baby picture of me wearing nothing but a smile and a straw hat.

One billboard featured a black-and-white photograph against a black background with only one word: *Mort*. It was dramatic, but someone in our promotions department didn't realize that *mort* is the French word for death. Several French-speaking Canadians from across the river called the TV station to find out who had died. "They must have seen our ratings," weatherman Sonny Eliot quipped.

The billboard that had French-Canadians asking, "Who died?"

The station set me up with a personal hair stylist at Saks Fifth Avenue in nearby Troy. They also flew me to Washington to meet with a clothing consultant who assisted in selecting fabrics for my tailor-made suits, along with shirts and ties. I think they wanted me to have that "Washington touch."

Frankly, I think this turned out to be a major problem during our first year of taking on Bonds and Company. Our management had been running Post-Newsweek's station in the nation's capital for so many years that they seemed slow to recognize that Washington is not the center of everybody's universe. Loading our newscasts with a preponderance of national and international news did not help to diminish our outsider image.

Less than two months after I arrived, there was an election. We brought in two nationally known political pundits from the Washington Post—Carl Rowan and James J. Kilpatrick—for analysis. It was an impressive display of media fire power that Channel 7 couldn't match. But the election results that mattered most to Detroiters were local and we were thinly equipped to explain those races. Bonds and his colleagues trounced us in the overnight ratings.

Our Washington focus unleashed a flood of stinging criticism from the local press. They chided us and mocked us for being a bunch of inside-the-beltway snobs. Even though I'd been imported from Chicago, not Washington, I was perceived to be one of those Capital elites who didn't know a Vernors from a Strohs, or a Lafayette Coney from a Hamtramck pierogi.

Two months after I arrived in town, *Monthly Detroit* magazine characterized Post-Newsweek's approach as "a philosophy that admires national and international stories on local news shows while heaping disdain on the blood-and-guts coverage that has been the staple in Detroit for so long."

There's no denying it: we were the smart-assed, know-it-all new kids on the block, and too often it showed. Everybody at the station recognized that if covering the news was job one, job two had to be breaking down that outsider image, and that process started with me. To kick off this new initiative I was teamed with a very talented producer, Simon Gribben, to create a month-long series of reports about ethnic diversity in Detroit.

Detroit is made up of a remarkable assortment of heritages and we devoted reports to each of the city's major immigrant populations, including Koreans, Hungarians, Italians, Russians, Armenians, Japanese, Irish, Polish, and a variety of Middle Easterners (Metro Detroit at that time had the largest concentration of Arabs in any city outside the Middle East). We counted at least seventy distinct ethnic groups, and it took us nearly three months to complete, but we delivered a smart and powerful show. Such a series was almost unheard of in television news, since it was believed audience interest in any subject would wane after a week. But we wanted to convince the city that we understood and cared about Detroit. We called the series *Detroit's New Americans* and followed it with two additional hourlong documentaries.

The normally hostile press gave it good marks, with a Detroit News columnist praising producer Gribben, and even tossing in the first positive line I'd seen in print about myself since arriving in Detroit: "Mort Crim, Channel Four's big-gun anchor, gets a big bravo for his 'Detroit's New Americans' series."

The project was good journalism and it also achieved the public relations goal. Just as importantly, it gave me a better feel for the people I would be covering. Detroit is very much a city of neighborhoods, and as I moved from place to place interviewing first-, second-, and third-generation immigrants, I developed a deeper understanding of the audience we served.

My work on this series also advanced my developing concept of God. In the lives of people who practiced religions other than my own Christianity, I witnessed a common thread, deeper and more universal than I had suspected. Many of those I interviewed—Buddhists, Muslims, Hindus, Taoists, Coptic

Christians—had spoken in various ways about how they felt a unity with creation. God was, for many of them, a relationship that developed through the practice of their faith. It seemed the people who were most devoted in observing the demands of their religion, whatever it was, had the strongest sense of God. I had already concluded that encountering God is an experience, not a mental exercise, and that no ladder of logic can reach that ultimate reality. We don't find God through formula or syllogism. What I saw in the practice of these various religions confirmed it.

It was growing increasingly clear to me that experiences of God are not produced by the words we say, the creeds we profess, or the doctrines we so tenaciously cling to. In this variety of cultures and beliefs, I was recognizing how encounters with the divine result from how we live and how we love. I was witnessing how people of any faith are drawn closer to the reality we call God as they are drawn closer to each other. I saw in this kaleidoscope of beliefs a profound truth: loving God and loving each other are two aspects of the same experience.

Preparing the series also provided me with a fresh lesson in the importance of humility: God is larger than our grandest perceptions and to find God requires that we transcend the influences of family, community, and tribe, and the boundaries those influences may impose. That sort of humility is especially challenging for those of us raised to believe that we not only have the absolute truth, but also the only way.

* * *

Some auto workers were about to take sledgehammers to a Honda in front of their union headquarters. It would be a dramatic, made-for-television event, and of course I wanted to cover it. John Baker knew I was eager to be out front on any story that improved my Detroit resume; the *New Americans* series was important for my credibility as a reporter, but it's the day-to-day coverage of stories in the community that earns an anchor credibility. And nothing in this auto-recession year was more Detroit than a group of angry UAW guys taking out their anti-import fury in such a theatrical fashion. This was before Japanese companies had established factories in the U.S., and every time an autoworker saw a foreign car driving down the street, he figured it represented lost American jobs. The rage was well-founded and ran so deep through the union that any member driving a foreign car was not allowed to park it in the UAW lot. Needless to say, nearly all Detroit auto workers drove American cars.

Before the Honda-smashing protest, we were aware of anti-foreign-car sentiment and "Buy American" bumper stickers were cropping up more and more. But none of us at WDIV fully appreciated just how intense the sentiment was. Some of our newly arrived employees innocently showed up in the WDIV parking lot driving imports, and unfortunately I was one of them.

As the recession deepened, so did the auto workers' loathing of foreign cars. I was driving a silver-blue Mercedes, purchased shortly before leaving Philadelphia. It was a classic 280SL sport convertible. I loved that car and hand-washed it, carefully polished its interior wood trim, buffed the leather seats, and hoped I could hold onto my man-toy for many years.

That thought ended on a Thursday afternoon after I'd given a speech before a group of auto executives' wives at the Edsel Ford estate in Grosse Pointe. The grand old estate on the shores of Lake St. Clair, with its massive stone buildings and expansive green lawns, was once home to Henry Ford's son Edsel and his wife Eleanor. Now it served as a conference center.

The women at the luncheon were a Who's Who of automotive spouses, and all of them members of Motown's elite: Mary Iacocca, wife of Chrysler boss Lee Iacocca; Jo Anne Peterson, whose husband Donald ran Ford Motor Company; Barbara Smith, wife of GM's CEO Roger Smith, and about three dozen other well-connected women.

It was one of my first public appearances in Detroit, and as we lined up on the front porch to retrieve our cars from the valet, I was beginning to feel increasingly uncomfortable.

Mary Iacocca took the keys to her navy blue Chrysler New Yorker. Jo Anne Peterson stepped into her Lincoln and Barbara Smith drove away in a cream-colored Cadillac. Thankfully, many of the women were gone before the valet brought up my Mercedes, apparently the only foreign car on the grounds.

When I got home that evening, I said, "Nicki, the 280 has to go."

Two weeks later, I reluctantly sold the car to a dentist in Bloomfield Hills and bought myself a Dodge.

Parting with the car proved to be the easiest step on my long road to acceptance as a true Detroiter. The toughest part was earning the trust and respect of the audience and convincing them that I cared about their problems and understood their issues. While it sometimes

Detroit anchormen don't drive foreign cars

214

felt like the full responsibility for the station's success fell on my shoulders, the truth is that any anchor is only one cog in the newsroom machine. From the fictional Ron Burgundy to the legendary Walter Cronkite, no news anchor ever succeeded without the support of a strong, solid team. It takes a visionary news director, talented and hard-working reporters, editors, writers, camera operators, technicians, and scores of others to make it all work. Jim Snyder understood this.

Among Jim's early hires was a young producer named Terry Oprea, who arrived the same week I did. Terry's judgment and eye for a good story were immediately evident. I was fortunate to have Terry as my producer on some of the biggest stories assigned to me, including Pope John Paul II's visit to Poland, a series on African-Americans who became Muslims, and national political conventions. Terry and I developed a close friendship, as well as a professional bond that has lasted throughout our lives.

With Terry Oprea at the 1980 GOP Convention

For the time being, I tabled troubling questions about God and Jesus. I believed in Jesus the man and tried to follow his teachings. But was he actually *God in the flesh* as I had been taught? Was he really a deity who emerged onto the planet from the womb of a virgin?

If years of intense searching still hadn't brought me satisfactory answers, maybe such answers simply couldn't be found. I focused my attention on being a good dad, a good husband, and a good journalist. I was still motivated by that desire to *"help an old, beat-up city find its way back."* For now, that was my calling. The truth is, I loved it all—the speech-making, the emceeing, the reporting, the documentaries and specials, the writing, and the anchoring. I was young, pumped by ambition and adrenaline, and happy to endure the long days, even when they stretched to twelve or fifteen hours.

One of Jim Snyder's first challenges was to find a compatible co-anchor to sit by me each evening. David Wittman had joined the exit parade of people left over from the station's previous owners, and several contenders moved through the news set before we finally found exactly the right replacement. She had been on staff all along, anchoring the station's weekend news. The first time she sat next to me in front of the camera, we all realized that we had stumbled onto a winner. Carmen Harlan and I clicked. There was an immediate chemistry between us. She was smart, attractive, and had a great television personality. Carmen knew how to *sell it* when she looked into the camera to deliver a report.

That Carmen had grown up in Detroit and had graduated from Mumford High School and the University of Michigan were all pluses as we worked to overcome our outsider image.

That she was African-American also didn't hurt in a predominantly black city. It was a successful and enduring pairing. Within five years, we had won the ratings battle with Channel Seven. We also remained an on-air team until my retirement nearly twenty years later.

Sharing a laugh with Carmen during a commercial break

Of course, there will be an occasional conflict of egos, even among the most compatible anchor team. Early in our relationship, Carmen and I got into a disagreement over the division of news copy. Competing for face time is not an uncommon issue between co-anchors, and as much as I wanted to believe that I was above that kind of vanity, sometimes I wasn't.

I don't remember which one of us was feeling on the short end of the deal, but the unhappiness was spilling into our performances and becoming noticeable on the air. Our colleagues were concerned and the audience could tell that things weren't quite right between us. During the newscasts, our conversations were minimal and a bit icy. In the newsroom, we barely spoke to each other.

Alan Frank, who had joined the station as program director, was now the station's general manager. He knew both of us well.

"Mort, can you and Carmen come up to my office after the show?"

It was a few minutes before five and Alan typically would not call us so close to airtime. Carmen and I knew immediately what this was about.

Alan was cordial, but he looked concerned as we walked into his glass-walled office on the second floor.

"Guys, I don't know what's going on between the two of you, but you've got to work it out. It's starting to show on the air. We've all got too much at stake."

He didn't have to spell it out. We knew that if the audience felt ill at ease and stopped watching, over time it could cost the station millions in advertising revenue.

Alan stepped toward the door.

"Now, I'm going to shut you both up in this office, and I don't want you to come out until you've resolved it."

Carmen and I were sitting together on Alan's couch, closer than we'd been to each other in days, except for our mandatory time at the anchor desk. It took only a few seconds for both of us to recognize the absurdity of our situation. Here we were, two highly paid, supposedly mature, and ostensibly intelligent professionals, acting like spoiled brats. In that awkward moment, I remembered a verse of Scripture:

"For everyone who makes himself great will be humbled, and everyone who humbles himself will be great."

Maybe I still had questions about God and religion, but I knew that my attitude and actions had not been consistent with my core values. Without a word we both started laughing. We laughed so hard we cried. I put my arms around Carmen, and said,

"Carmen, I'm so sorry. Let's promise that we'll never let ego come between us again."

Carmen returned my hug.

"I'm sorry, too. You and I are bigger than this," she said.

"Now let's get back downstairs and go to work."

A little humility and a willingness to admit when you're wrong can make any relationship work better. During nearly two decades of anchoring together, that was the only time Carmen and I ever had a serious falling out.

* * *

At home, life was good.

With each passing month, the possibility that Nicki's cancer might come back receded further into the background. I think we both were happier than we had ever been. Whatever had happened in Philadelphia, we were in this marriage for the long haul.

Nicki's faith in me and the strength of our bond was made evident one day in early August 1981, when she answered the phone.

"It's Jessica," she said, "and she sounds really upset."

After handing me the telephone, Nicki slipped out of the room. My conversation with Jess was brief. Afterward, I walked into the den where Nicki had picked up a magazine. She placed it on the coffee table, looked up, and waited for me to say something.

"Donald killed himself," I said.

"Jess found him in the basement of their condo, hanging from Chewy's leash. She's nearly hysterical."

Dr. Donald Payne was the society gynecologist whose patients included many of Washington's elite. Chewy was Jessica's beloved Siberian husky. Jess had married Payne shortly after her brief marriage to Philadelphia ad man Mel Korn fell apart. Payne's suicide came just five months after he and Jessica had wed.

"How is she? What's she going to do?" Nicki asked.

"I don't know. I think she's still in shock."

There was a brief pause.

Nicki got up from her chair, walked over to where I was standing, put her arm around me, and said, "If she needs a place to get away, please tell her she's welcome here."

I shouldn't have been surprised by Nicki's offer. She was one of the kindest, most compassionate, and selfless women I had ever known. In that moment of both generosity and self-confidence, I knew for sure that Nicki no longer harbored even a shred of doubt about my love for her, or the enduring strength of our relationship.

"Honey, I have no idea about her plans. But that's really kind. I think you should tell her," I said.

Later that evening, Nicki called Jessica, extended her deepest sympathies, and invited her to spend some time recuperating at our home in Grosse Pointe.

Jessica's weekend newscasts on NBC, along with her reporting and prime-time news updates, had made her very popular with viewers and network affiliates alike. Eager to escape Washington and the barrage of reporters and questions that she knew would follow Donald's suicide, she accepted Nicki's offer.

Jess spent several days in our home, joining Nicki and me for meals, but mostly staying in the guest room or taking solitary walks along the lake. Never once were Jess and I alone, and I never wanted us to be. Our relationship had evolved into the kind of platonic friendship it always should have been.

It was summertime, 1981. Al would be a sophomore in high school, and one evening he joined the three of us for dinner at Jim's Garage, one of our favorite Detroit restaurants.

"Al, I have a favor to ask," Jess said, as we looked over the dessert menu.

"You know that Jensen-Healey of mine?"

Al probably didn't remember it, but I certainly knew the car. It was a flashy yellow sports car Jess had acquired while we were in Philadelphia.

"I'm going to be in New York most of the time now, and the last thing I need in Manhattan is a car. Do you think you could take care of it for me?"

Al, still nearly four months away from getting his driver's license, looked stunned but ecstatic.

"What do you mean by 'take care of it'?" Nicki interjected.

"Oh, I mean drive it. Treat it like his own car," Jess said.

"It's not good for a car to sit around unused."

"Jess, that's a really generous offer, but Al doesn't have a license yet," Nicki objected.

"November twelfth," Al shot back.

Nicki was warm and gracious to Jessica during her time in our home and as supportive as anyone could be.

"You have been so great," Jess said, giving Nicki a big hug before we took her to the airport. Then she added, "I don't know how I could have made it without your love and generosity."

A week after Jess returned to Washington, the Jensen-Healey was delivered to Grosse Pointe. Three months later, Al got his driver's license. Today, Al remembers those three months of waiting as the longest of his life.

* * *

In late September 1984, I was invited to join President Reagan at a White House press luncheon. Out of town assignments were especially enjoyable, because they usually meant I could fly my own plane. Many of those assignments, including regular substi-

Flying to Washington for lunch with President Reagan

tutions for Martin Agronsky on *Agronsky & Company*, took me to Washington. I had parked my plane at the Dulles airport FBO so many times, I knew several of the linemen by name.

Deputy press secretary Lou Gerig, a fellow Anderson College alum, recognized my name when the guest list hit his desk. Lou placed me at Reagan's table, next to the president. Most of the visiting journalists were scattered around at other tables, each table hosted by a cabinet member.

It was my first time to meet Reagan, and I was immediately impressed by his charm and his wit, something attested to by most people who had met him, both Democrats and Republicans.

There were several topics that I wanted to discuss—things I knew would be of primary interest to our Michigan audience such as unemployment, the auto industry, gasoline prices, and education. We were only a month away from the election, so politics was also on my list.

Before we got into any serious discussion, it seemed Reagan mostly wanted to talk about his life in Hollywood, the actors he'd known, producers with whom he'd worked, and his years as head of the Screen Actors Guild. I thought maybe this was his technique for avoiding tough questions. Between his stories, some of them fascinating, I did manage to slip in my own agenda. At the end of the serious questions, I asked:

"Mr. President, do you ever miss acting?"

Reagan looked at me and, in that made-for-movies voice, said, "Why, Mort, this is the greatest role I've ever played."

Of course, everyone at the table laughed.

What I learned about Reagan from that statement helped me understand why he was so well liked, even by those who disagreed with him. Reagan was the ultimate optimist and he oozed enthusiasm for life. No matter what role he had played, whether he was performing in the movies, hosting a TV show, heading up a Hollywood union, serving as Governor of California, or being President of the United States, he viewed each job as the greatest. You might disagree vigorously with some of his policies, but as a person, you had to like the guy.

By 1985, WDIV was leading in both the early and late news

ratings, and by a wide margin. Much of the credit had to go to the Post-Newsweek management who often reminded us that we were in a marathon, not a sprint. It's easy in the heady rush

Listening to Reagan's stories about his Hollywood years

of success for a news anchor to experience a fit of Ron Burgundy ego. It is at these times that we need people in our lives to help keep our feet on the ground.

One evening, after I had received an Emmy for Best Local Newscast, I sat at home in our den, still in my tuxedo and smugly admiring the little gold statuette. I complimented myself on being such a fine newscaster and mused about how smart WDIV had been to hire me.

The moment of self-importance didn't last long. From the bedroom came a friendly reminder that I was, after all, a mere mortal.

"Honey, don't forget to set out the trash."

Chapter Sixteen

HERE AND ABROAD

The only way to do great work is to love what you do.

—STEVE JOBS

THE FAST-PACED, COMPETITIVE LIFE of television news kept me moving, but I couldn't outrun my anxieties about God. Sometimes in church, and sometimes in the quiet dark of a restless night, the questions would surface and trouble me.

After years of looking for answers, I still found it easier to say what God was not than what God might be. I had found no evidence to convince me that God choreographs the details of human life. To suppose that a supreme deity could be called upon to cure cancer, prevent grotesque birth defects, stop hurricanes, or win wars contradicted my observations as a journalist as well as my common sense. If God is involved in the affairs of people, then it must be by acting through people. That made sense to me and seemed consistent with the essential message of the Bible. From the Old Testament prophets to Jesus and his disciples, there was a continuous narrative of God—transcendent creative spirit and universal love—being manifest, experienced and working through people.

As a young preacher raised on Bible stories, I once had hoped for an instantaneous revelation of God—something like the blinding light that Scripture says struck down Saul while he was walking to Damascus. Saul, then renamed Paul, not only believed he met God in that dramatic encounter, but also that he heard the voice of Jesus.

I've known people who claimed to have experienced God in a sudden if less theatrical fashion; their revelation of the divine was like someone had flipped on the light switch. My awareness definitely was coming through a rheostat—slowly, tediously, and over a number of years. Now in my mid-forties, more light was starting to creep in.

Most importantly, I was beginning to understand God not as a riddle to be solved or a question to be answered, but as a presence to be accepted. God might be a reality beyond comprehension, but perhaps not beyond knowing. Could that *knowing* come through a relationship? I knew that the most meaningful realities in my own life and the things I held to be most true were not discovered intellectually; my love for my wife, my children, and my parents did not come through a rational, logical process but from my experiences with them. No one talked me into that love, and no amount of reasoning could ever persuade me to not love them. Furthermore, that love is beyond description. No matter how much I try, I cannot find words to adequately express it, even though it's the most real part of my life. Why had it taken me so long to grasp the obvious where God is concerned?

It was an important insight, but it left another, crucial question, unanswered: since it was clear to me that God does not direct the weather, protect those I love, guarantee health or career success, support my favorite ball team, or decide which country wins a war, does believing in God even matter? If I can only discover this reality through experience, does it make any difference what I believe, intellectually? Does prayer matter? I was still struggling with these questions.

*   *   *

Nicki used to say that the only thing Mort enjoys more than being on the air is being in the air. She was right. Flying was much more than a hobby; it was an obsession, and as you know by now, I used my plane extensively in covering the news.

Often the plane permitted me to travel hundreds of miles, report on a story, and still be back at the anchor desk in time for the 5 p.m. news. My airplane gave us a distinct advantage over our competition in many situations, but there was one story where it didn't quite work out as planned.

It was during President Jimmy Carter's campaign for reelection in 1979. He was flying into Flint and was scheduled to make a late afternoon speech at the Flint airport.

Perfect, I thought. This story was made for my plane.

I could fly to Flint with a camera crew, record Carter's speech, fly back to Detroit and have the report edited and on the air while our competitors were still fighting evening rush hour traffic. This was before satellite feeds were routine, and out-of-town stories were typically shuttled to the TV station on videotape.

After Carter's speech, we packed up our gear, strapped ourselves in, and I radioed for a clearance.

"Flint tower, November four, seven, five, seven, Charlie, on the ramp with tango, ready to taxi VFR Detroit City."

Instead of receiving the clearance, I heard these unsettling words:

"Five, seven, Charlie, hold on the ramp. No traffic moving until Air Force One has cleared the airport."

Whoops. I hadn't counted on that complication. Cameraman Bobby Stevens, sitting in the co-pilot's seat, looked out his window and said, "There goes Action News."

I turned in time to see the Channel Seven news van pulling off the tarmac and heading for the freeway. Now there was a good chance my competitors in their slow-moving ground vehicles would beat my airplane and beat us to the story.

"What do we do now?" grumbled sound engineer Pat Stratton in the back seat.

"Not a thing we can do," I replied. "We're stuck here until the president's plane is in the air."

President Carter and his entourage boarded the plane, and after a twenty minute wait that felt like two hours, Air Force One was on its way. Moments later, so were we. Back at Detroit City Airport, I wheeled the plane around in front of the hangar door as Bobby jumped out, grabbed his gear from the luggage compartment, and made a fast dash for my car.

As we squealed tires out of the airport, I glanced at my watch: it was twenty-two minutes before five. Twenty-two minutes until I was supposed to be in the studio, ready to open the five o'clock news, and we were in the middle of evening rush hour.

I bobbed and weaved down the freeway, trying to gain a car length here and there, but congested traffic moves at its own pace, no matter how important we think we are, or how hard we grip the steering wheel.

We raced into the station parking garage –wheels screeching like a teenager's hot rod—jumped out of the car and headed for the door. A frantic Bob Warfield, our assistant news director, was already holding it open for us. It was now one minute before five.

Bobby tossed the videotape to Bob. I knew there was no time to review the tape, let alone to edit it. "Tell the control room to cue this up to Carter's speech. I'll ad-lib around it," I said as I rushed straight for the studio.

There was no time for makeup, or even for me to comb my hair, which the airplane headphones had considerably flattened.

I sprinted through the studio door, pumping up my hair as much as possible, threw on my jacket en route, pulled my tie up tight without buttoning the top shirt button, ran breathlessly onto the news set, and then dropped into my chair at the anchor desk just in time to gasp,

"G o o o d evening."

It wasn't until the first commercial break that I finally got my breath back. But that close call was the exception—usually when I used the plane to cover a distant story, it worked out well.

When Terry Oprea proposed that he and I produce a series on the phenomenon of the Black Muslim movement, Jim Snyder's first response was, "Terry, you know this is sweeps month. We can't have Crim off the air."

Sweeps is that period of time when the ratings services calculate the audience size and demographic makeup of newscasts. News directors are absolutely paranoid about the absence of their star talent during this time. The standing joke about anchors is: The only way you can get off work during sweeps is for a funeral. And it has to be yours.

"Mort and I have already discussed it," Terry said, anticipating Snyder's objection. "With his plane, we've worked out an itinerary where he will miss only one day of shows."

Jim said if we could pull it off with me missing only one early and one late newscast, he would okay it.

The Black Muslim story was a logical one for us to do. Elijah Muhammad, founder of the movement, had grown up in the Detroit area, and the late Malcolm X was from Lansing. Most importantly, the Black Muslim organization was gaining ground in Detroit, winning converts and opening mosques, community centers, and various businesses.

So on a Monday, we flew my plane to Chicago, picked up a rental car, and started filming. We interviewed prominent Muslim leaders as well as rank-and-file members. We shot a lot of footage of gathering places for the faithful. I was back at WDIV by 4:30 p.m., in plenty of time to make my five o'clock newscast.

The next day we flew to Washington D.C., did more interviews, and shot some footage and on-camera reporting called *stand-ups* at B'nai B'rith headquarters, where seven dissident black Muslims had taken hostages a year or so earlier. We did the same at three buildings that had been taken over by Nation of Islam breakaway members on March 9, 1977. They had held one hundred forty-nine hostages and killed a radio journalist.

Then, we flew to White Plains, New York, and traveled to

Sing Sing prison for an interview with Talmadge Hayer, aka Thomas Hagan, one of the men convicted of assassinating Malcolm X. Our last stop was in Manhattan for some footage and a stand-up at the Audubon Ballroom in Washington Heights, where Malcolm X had been killed.

With some great advance planning, we did it; in a whirlwind tour of three major cities, using my airplane, we had managed to bring home enough material for a weeklong series of reports, plus an hour-long documentary. Incredibly, I had missed only one day at the anchor desk.

Of course, I couldn't always fly my plane on assignment. Sometimes I was dispatched overseas. In my dual role as WDIV-TV's senior anchor and national correspondent for our parent company, Post-Newsweek Television, my foreign datelines included Cairo, Tel Aviv, Rome, Berlin, London, Warsaw,

My plane allowed me to be both reporter and anchor on the same day

Moscow, Amsterdam, Toronto, and Guatemala City.

The goal always was to bring the local angle to an international story. One of those occurred in 1981, just three weeks after Egyptian President Anwar Sadat was assassinated. His murder had put new strains on the fragile Camp David Accords, which President Jimmy Carter had negotiated a few years earlier. Detroit has a sizeable Jewish population, and neighboring Dearborn is home to the largest number of Arabs in any city outside of the middle east, so turmoil in the region was of intense interest to Detroiters. We decided to produce an hour-long special on the situation called *Christmas in Crisis.* The plan was for me to spend a couple of weeks in Egypt and Israel with producer Harvey Ovshinsky, a brilliant young writer and filmmaker, and send back daily reports by satellite.

We arrived in Cairo just two weeks after Sadat's murder. The city was still under martial law. Even before disembarking from the plane we could see soldiers, guns slung over their shoulders, marching back and forth on the roofs of the airport terminals. When we arrived downtown, Harvey picked out what he felt was a suitable spot for me to record my stand-up. Just as I was about to speak my first lines into the camera, an official-looking car carrying four gun-toting policemen in white helmets screeched to a halt and we were ordered to "get in." At least that's what our driver, who was also our interpreter, told us they said. Their guns and gestures left no question.

We had been briefed on the challenges that a TV crew might expect to encounter under martial law, but the briefer failed to mention that filming on the streets required a special permit. Our detention didn't last long. Our interpreter-guide discovered that he had been a classmate of the police chief, so after a short interrogation and our guide's explanation, we were released.

That evening, from our room in the Mena House Hotel, Harvey placed a call to our news assignment desk back in Detroit. He wanted to let them know that we had failed to get an interview with the new president, Hosni Muburak, but Harvey was optimistic that we could interview the widow of the

In Cairo, Egypt, with Harvey Ovshinsky, just before our arrest

late President Sadat the next day.

"Well, guys," Harvey said over the phone, "We missed Muburak today, but I think we'll have a good shot at Mrs. Sadat tomorrow."

Immediately, there was a click and the phone went dead.

"Harvey, do you realize what you just said?" I asked.

Announcing that we should have a "good shot at Mrs. Sadat" is TV lingo for "I think we'll get the interview." But our intention, expressed in English, could easily be misinterpreted in a nation still reeling from an assassination. Was our telephone bugged? For the next few minutes we waited, wondering if there would be a knock on our door and another interrogation. It never came, and we concluded that our phone line had not been bugged and the lost connection must have been coincidental.

If Egyptians were tense, Israelis were no less edgy. The peace treaty Sadat had signed with Israel had become his death warrant. It was that treaty which infuriated the Muslim extremists who killed him, and now Israel had to wonder if their truce with the Arab world would hold.

Our focus would be the ongoing tension between the Israelis and the Palestinians, which the peace treaty with Egypt had done nothing to alleviate. We wanted to get inside the minds of people on both sides, ordinary citizens as well as government leaders, and I personally wanted to learn about the role of faith in the ongoing conflict.

After Harvey and I completed our assignment, Nicki flew to Cairo to meet me for a few days of vacation and sightseeing. We checked into the Mena House Hotel near the Great Pyramid, the same hotel where the crew and I had stayed. On our second night, the telephone rang. I glanced at my watch. It was three in the morning. I answered the phone still half asleep. It was our son. Hearing his voice, I suddenly bolted awake.

"Al, what's wrong?" I asked.

"What time is it there?" he wanted to know.

"It's three in the morning. What's the problem?"

"Gee, Dad, I'm sorry. I forgot about the time difference. I know you told me only to call if it was an emergency, but this is, sort of."

Al was still in high school. My mother had flown up to

Detroit from Florida to stay with him and his sister, Carey, while Nicki and I were out of the country.

"Is your grandmother all right?" I asked.

"Oh, yeah, Dad, it's not that kind of emergency."

By now I was fully awake.

"The Rolling Stones are coming to the Silverdome, and if I don't get my tickets tomorrow, the best seats will be gone."

What Al wanted was permission to attend, but more importantly, he wanted to know if I would pay for the tickets.

Nicki and I were so relieved to find out the house hadn't burned down, or my mother hadn't had a heart attack, that we ended up laughing about Al's view of what constituted "an emergency."

* * *

In late May 1981, my airplane again proved its value to the station when inmates at three Michigan prisons went on a rampage. Our challenge was to cover the riots in widely separated areas—Marquette, Jackson, and Ionia.

Producer Terry Oprea, along with a camera crew, jumped into my plane, and we took off to cover the story. The worst disturbance was at Marquette Branch Prison in Michigan's Upper Peninsula, an all-day trip by car but an easy two hours for our plane.

Although the riot was over by the time we arrived, the rage and fury were palpable as we walked through the newly secured cell block. Marquette is Michigan's maximum security prison, where the really bad dudes—the worst of the worst—are confined. The prison's high stone walls, topped with razor wire and roaming guards armed with automatic weapons, immediately convey the fact that this is no country club facility for embezzlers and crooked politicians. Marquette is the very definition of hard time, and it's home to killers, rapists, and other violent criminals.

After I interviewed the warden and a couple of guards who'd been taken hostage during the uprising, the warden took us on a tour. First stop: the prison yard.

It was exercise time, and a dozen or so inmates were playing softball. As soon as they spotted us, the pitcher dropped the ball onto the mound, the guy who was up at the plate tossed his bat, and everybody started running toward us. This might have been unnerving under the circumstances, but the inmates were all smiling and the warden didn't seem concerned.

"It's Mort!" one of the inmates yelled.

The warden explained that our WDIV newscasts were seen regularly in the prison via the same cable that brought our programs into many areas in the state that lacked regular TV service.

"Hey, I want my picture with Mort!" one big, burly inmate yelled at our cameraman.

"Put us on TV tonight, me and Mort," he said.

Then, looking straight into my eyes with a steely stare, he added, "I'm your biggest fan."

The other prisoners laughed. The guy who wanted his picture taken with me put a muscular arm around my neck and pulled me in close. His buddies jostled around us for a group shot. Paul Brinkerhof, our cameraman, dutifully took the picture while audio engineer Sue Dice recorded the sounds.

One after another the inmates shook my hand. There was a lot of excited talk and several of the guys asked for autographs amid yells of "How ya' doin' Mort?" and "Man, we love your show!" Then they went back to their ballgame, and I saw the warden smile. I wondered what was so funny, but before I could ask he volunteered.

"That guy who insisted on having his picture with you? The one who said he's your biggest fan? He's doing life for killing four people with an axe."

Terry, Paul, and Sue loved it, of course. On our way back to the plane, Terry said, "Well, Mort, you may not have won over all Detroiters yet, but at least you're number one with the axe murderers."

I wondered how many convicted killers Bill Bonds could count among his fans.

In 1989, another international story intersected with the interests of our local audience: the imminent demise of Soviet Communism. I was sent to Russia to cover it. Detroit had aligned itself as a sister city with Minsk, Belarus, under a program started in 1956 at President Dwight D. Eisenhower's White House conference on citizen diplomacy. With the Soviet Union's political structure clearly on the verge of collapse and talk of democracy in the air, Detroit's business leaders saw a potentially huge new market for Michigan-made goods and services.

A group of our city's entrepreneurs and corporate leaders organized a visit to Minsk, ready to lead the charge as Detroit's corporate community considered ways to tap into this new opportunity.

We saw this as a terrific news story, and WDIV promptly made plans to send me along with the business group, which also would be visiting Moscow and Leningrad. The station gave me a blue-ribbon crew: John Owens, an excellent videographer, editor, and producer, along with another first-rate cameraman, Jim Stanhope.

Our son Al was by then a graduate student at Vanderbilt, and since he was home for the summer I hired him as a grip to help the crew tote equipment around the Soviet Union. I knew it would be a unique opportunity for him to see history in the making.

We had been in Moscow only a few hours when Al observed, "Dad, we've always thought of the Soviet Union as a superpower. They're actually just a third world country with a bomb."

Al had succinctly summarized our early impressions. There was little about Moscow's dreary landscape that compared with the excitement and vitality of an American metropolis. Moscow's architecture was impressive, especially the Kremlin and the cathedrals, but just about everything else seemed shrouded in Communist drab. The few people on the streets seemed joyless. The one department store we saw was nearly devoid of both product and customers. So much for their socialist system creating a workers' paradise.

We took video of a small food store, the closest thing to a supermarket we saw. Patrons waited in a long line and hoped there might be some meat left by the time they reached the counter. Most canned goods were in jars that looked very much like the ones Mom Crim used to can produce from her garden, only many of these jars hadn't been sealed properly, and there was visible mold underneath the lids.

Under Mikhail Gorbachev the iron grip of communism was now starting to loosen. Near that grocery store was a church that the Soviets had converted into a museum and now had been restored as a church. I stopped a woman coming down the steps and, through our interpreter, asked her how she felt about the change. Tears welled up in her eyes.

"We Russians never lost our faith in God," she said.

"Now we can worship again, openly."

Russian food turned out to be much better than we had feared, although it was quite heavy on cucumbers. Each dinner was accompanied by vodka. Lots of vodka. It seemed every sentence uttered at the table became the occasion for a toast, and a toast meant a shot of vodka, taken right down the hatch. No sipping. We knew the folks in Belarus were putting on their best for the American journalists. That included inviting one of Minsk's most celebrated hometown heroes, gymnast Olga Korbut, to dine with us one evening.

Our official host was Oleg Morosov, a television news anchor in Minsk, but we discovered that wasn't his only job. One night he took us to dinner at a high-end restaurant in Minsk. There was a line of people waiting to be seated. Oleg moved to the head of the line, flashed an open wallet, and we were immediately given a table.

"Being on television does have its privileges," I laughed, thinking he had just played the celebrity card.

As we took our seats, Oleg smiled, pulled out the wallet, and opened it for me to see what he had flashed to the restaurant host. It was his KGB credential. While the idea of simultaneously being a journalist and an intelligence officer for the government is unthinkable in the U.S., under the old Soviet system there was no conflict between reporting and spying. And why not? The government owned all the media.

Oleg's attempts at being a good host included trying to set up my son, Al, with a prostitute. The offer was politely declined.

On the last day of our Minsk leg of the visit, we were scheduled to fly to Moscow on Aeroflot, the Soviet airline that was notorious for its poor safety record and shoddily maintained

Oleg's KGB card was our ticket to Minsk's finest restaurant

aircraft. We almost missed the flight.

Our driver, logically thinking we Americans were headed out of the country, had dropped us off at the airport's international terminal. By the time Gene Pyatenko, an attorney who also worked for us as an interpreter, realized the error, our driver was long gone. Gene got us a taxi, and we made it to the domestic side of the field just in time to dump our luggage and board a flatbed truck for the ride to the airplane. The truck bounced so hard that we hung on to the side panels for dear life.

As we approached our plane, a Tupolev Tu-134, one fellow passenger remarked, "Look at those tires."

I did, but immediately wished I hadn't. All the tires on the airliner were completely bald.

Once we had climbed the air stairs and entered the cabin, we found little to boost our confidence. When I told the captain that I was a pilot, he honored my request to look in at the cockpit, and I immediately regretted having done so. The instruments and radar looked like relics from an old World War II movie. In that moment, thinking back on all the Aeroflot plane crashes I'd reported in our newscasts, I was just grateful that it was a bright, sunny day.

I was proud of our documentary, which examined a nation where the old way of life was crumbling but the new way had not yet been born. Apparently, I wasn't the only one who thought we'd done a pretty good job: our documentary, *Parting the Curtain*, won an Emmy.

* * *

Frequently, the demands of anchoring and reporting required some serious juggling, and Fridays became especially challenging after I was given a Friday night talk show.

TV screen shot during my reporting from Russia

Mort Crim's Free for All was the brainchild of then Program Manager Alan Frank and Executive Producer Henry Maldanado. *The Oakland Press* described it as an electronic, eighteenth-century town meeting. Harvey Ovshinsky was assigned to produce.

Harvey knew how to find all the pieces needed for a live show and make them fit together.

Free for All ran for an hour in prime time in front of a live studio audience. I sat at a horseshoe-shaped desk, surrounded by a cast of panelists selected to give voice to various segments of our community: there was plain-spoken anti-tax crusader Mike Sessa, affectionately referred to as the Archie Bunker of our team; Joan Israel, a little loud and opinionated, but lovable, played a Maude-type role;

Suburban housewife and registered nurse Diane Trombley was our June Cleaver; and Urban League executive Larry Simmons served as a spokesman for the black community.

Rounding out the lineup were Janice Burnett, a mental health therapist, and Frieda Gorrecht, who rolled up to the set in a wheelchair. Frieda was an outspoken advocate for others with disabilities.

It was a no-holds-barred, raucous circus, and for sixty minutes each Friday night we managed to focus Detroit's attention on significant community issues such as abortion, taxes, sex education, corruption in government, gun control, capital punishment, school funding, and problems of the elderly. All of this, of course, years before political pundits and talking heads became a 24-hour-a-day reality on cable news channels.

One winter night during a huge snowstorm, director Bob Brooks walked into the studio about a half hour before airtime and to his horror discovered an audience of only six people. We needed at least fifty, and filling those seats was one of the director's jobs.

It was understandable that people preferred staying home by the fire to slipping and sliding their way to our studios in a blizzard. But you can't have an audience participation show without an audience, so Bob did what any good TV director would do—he yelled at his intern.

"Laura, get me an audience!" Bob demanded, although he was quite sure he was handing her Mission Impossible.

Five minutes before showtime the studio door opened and in walked fifty or sixty people, coats still on, many of them seeming a bit more animated than usual.

"Laura," Bob said, as the red camera light came on and we opened the show, "I never thought you could pull it off."

"It was easy," Laura said. "I walked across the street to the Anchor Bar and told Leo we needed a favor. Leo yelled out that anyone who wanted to be on TV should go across the street. It practically emptied out the bar."

Oh well, Leo owed us that much, since it was mostly WDIV and the neighboring *Detroit News* that kept his seedy joint in business.

Free for All proved to be a ratings winner for the station,

Cast and production crew for *Mort Crim's Free For All*

as well as a way to showcase different dimensions of their anchorman. The free-flowing banter of a talk show allowed my sense of humor to come through and eventually helped shake the "Grim Crim" title.

But despite the success of *Free For All* and our steady climb in the news ratings, there were always people around to keep me from becoming too full of myself. A couple of local radio DJs wrote and recorded a song called "Mort Crim's Hairspray." They played it over and over, day and night, much to the amusement of my Channel Four colleagues and especially my kids, Al and Carey, who thought the song was cool.

* * *

A newsroom will appear to the casual visitor as a place of utter chaos and confusion—police and fire radios blaring, reporters scurrying in and out of editing booths, producers and writers arguing over copy—but there is a rhythm to a well-functioning operation. Occasionally, however, some unexpected glitch throws a monkey wrench into everything. Of the more than nine thousand newscasts that I anchored during my nearly two decades at WDIV, the one I'm about to recount stands out for pure drama.

It happened before we had computers and electronic teleprompters. We typed news copy on multi-carbon sets of six pages, each a different color. Blue went to me, pink to Carmen, white to the prompter, and other colors to the producer, director, and T.D. (technical director).

When the copy was all assembled, a production assistant would pull each set apart and place the pages in order, upside down, in stacks on a long counter. On our way into the studio, each of us would walk by the counter and claim our designated color.

On this particular night, producer Al Berman was first to arrive at the counter.

"Where are the scripts?" he asked, looking around the newsroom, his voice expressing more puzzlement than concern.

There wasn't a script anywhere on the counter. Not a blue, pink, green—nothing.

"Where the hell are the scripts?" Al barked, recognizing that we were only minutes away from air.

A little earlier, I could have sworn that I'd seen all six stacks of copy, in perfect order, right there on that counter. Now the counter was completely bare.

Slowly, panic set in. We all looked at each other.

"Holy shit, we don't have any scripts," Berman shouted, clenching his fist, his face tightening.

Then somebody noticed the cleaning lady who was busy emptying waste baskets into a large, round trash container. We had not seen her before; this was her first night on the job. By now everyone in the room was looking at her.

"Ma'am, did you see some papers on this counter?" Assignment Editor Terry Oprea asked.

"I clean counter," she responded in broken English.

"Goddammit, she's thrown away our newscast," one of our writers screamed, as she and a sports reporter simultaneously rushed the big round can and began dumpster-diving for our eleven o'clock news.

With one grand sweep of the counter, the cleaning lady had consigned six hours of work to the trash, now topped with stale coffee residue, half- empty soda cans, sandwich and candy wrappers, partly eaten lunches, and other assorted nastiness from the various newsroom waste baskets.

A production assistant joined the frantic search, clawing through the trash in a desperate attempt to recover the words we were supposed to speak. It was now three minutes to air.

We did have our printed run-downs, which listed the stories in order of appearance, and how much time was allotted to each. I was accustomed to working under all kinds of pressure, but this was new. Trying to collect my thoughts, I waved the rundown in front of my co-anchor as we headed for the studio.

"Okay, Carmen," I said. "We've got to wing it. You and I know these stories forward and backward. We'll have to ad-lib our way through the first block. Let's just follow the run down."

The opening theme ended, the floor director pointed to me, and the red camera light came on.

"Good evening. Mayor Young's news conference is our lead story tonight."

I knew the details of the news conference and had written the story for our earlier newscast. This would be no different than anchoring an election where everything happens on the fly. I knew the biggest problem was that the technical crew had to follow what we did, blind, with no script and no cues prompting them when to roll the videotape.

"In a wide-ranging give-and-take with reporters, the mayor defended comments he made about Eight Mile Road," I ad-libbed. "He denied his remarks were intended as an insult to suburbanites. Let's get the full report now from News Four's Mike Wendland."

They were ready in the control room and the director, technical director, and sound engineer, all working in perfect harmony, got Mike's tape on the air as flawlessly as if they'd had scripts in front of them. This wasn't easy, as the technology of the time required rolling the tape four seconds in advance of air so it could get up to speed. Without scripts, the control room couldn't be certain when I was into the last four seconds of introduction. But they anticipated my words with perfection, providing a seamless transition.

For the next seven minutes, Carmen and I ad-libbed our way through the stories and the tape lead-ins, while the control room followed our improvised dance without missing a beat. By the end of the first commercial, somebody had managed to recover the scripts, put them in order, and distribute them around. Had Carmen and I been merely readers without a thorough knowledge of our stories, saving that newscast would have been impossible.

Solid journalism was the hallmark of our ratings battle against Channel Seven and the foundation of our success, but personality also played a role. Our friendly banter on the set, especially around weather and sports, was calculated to make the audience feel comfortable with us and rarely did it include anything of consequence. There was one night, however, when my words ran way ahead of my brain.

It was on September 4, 1989, that I made one of the most thoughtless statements I had ever uttered on live TV. "Did he just say that?" Carmen asked Chuck as we went into commercial break. Yes, I had, indeed, said it.

The Detroit Tigers (who had not been having a good year) had defeated Kansas City that afternoon. It was their fourth win in a row and our sportscaster, Bernie Smilovitz, waxed eloquent about the turnaround. The Tigers, he insisted, were now on a genuine winning streak. I challenged Bernie on how long they could keep it up, and he said they should be good for at least four more wins.

Then, apparently overcome by a moment of temporary insanity, I blurted out,

"Bernie, if the Tigers stretch this winning streak to eight, I'll shave my head."

Bernie laughed. Carmen gasped. I could only hope that some technical glitch had momentarily knocked my microphone off the air, and that nobody but Bernie and Carmen actually heard what I had said.

That hope was dashed the next morning when both newspapers prominently announced my pledge. In their next game that evening, the Tigers made it five in a row, once again taking down Kansas City. The next day they beat the Royals again. That was win number six.

This was getting serious. The *Detroit News* not only ran another article, reminding everyone of my pledge, but included a doctored photograph showing what I might look like without hair.

People would ask me on the street,

"Are you really going to do it?" Carmen asked me. Bernie asked me.

Nicki and our kids asked me.

On September 8, the Tigers beat the Chicago White Sox for their seventh win in a row. My scalp was now just one game away from looking like a honeydew melon. On our newscasts that evening, Bernie Smilovitz reminded our audience:

"Tomorrow is the big day, folks. Will Mort be bald, or won't he? Be sure to join us and find out."

It was great television, sure to build our audience, but for me it was like walking a wire across Niagara Falls.

The afternoon game started at 3 p.m. and was ending just as we went on the air with our five o'clock newscast.

Final score: White Sox 13, Tigers 3.

The next morning's *Free Press* headline: "That's Cutting It Close, Mort: Tigers Fall 13-3, Save His Hair."

The Detroit News included me in the stats column on the sports page:

Winning Pitcher—Perez

Losing Pitcher—Robinson

Saved—Mort Crim

If the Tigers had won game number eight, would I really have shaved my head?

We'll never know.

Sometimes, a co-anchor's quick response to a flub can save the day, like the night we ended our newscast with an animal story. We often closed the show with a light-hearted feature called a kicker, and this one happened to be about a rare white

Tim Allen joins in hosting the Thanksgiving Day Parade

rhinoceros at the Detroit Zoo. Only instead of 'rhino,' the words that came out of my mouth were,

"rare, white *wino*," to which Carmen immediately responded,

"Mort, they aren't that rare. There're lots of them down in the Cass Corridor."

The Cass Corridor was Detroit's skid row, and Carmen, sensitive lady that she is, probably wouldn't have made such a quip had she thought about it. But sportscaster Bernie Smilovitz, weatherman Chuck Gaidica, and I all broke up so completely that none of us was able to say goodnight.

The show ended with all of us, including Carmen, inappropriately howling with laughter.

Clowning around with *The Tonight Show's* Jay Leno

Interviewing Neil Armstrong on stage at Oshkosh

Chapter Seventeen

CAREER OR CALLING?

I believe there's a calling for all of us. I know that every human being has value and purpose.

—OPRAH WINFREY

GOOD JOURNALISTS should never allow themselves to be impressed by the people they interview. Throughout my career, I had tried to maintain a detached objectivity while covering the world's influential and famous—from U.S. presidents to sports superstars and Hollywood's elite. But this time, I was finding it difficult to be objective. Having read a lot about the South African clergyman seated in front of me, and researching his speeches and sermons, I had acquired a respect and admiration for him that made impartiality nearly impossible. Despite the priestly formality of his attire—white clerical collar and black suit, enlivened by a cherry red vest—he was *different*. It wasn't fame, money, power or professional achievements that distinguished this Anglican cleric from other renowned people I'd interviewed. It was his amazing attitude. His very persona exuded selflessness, grace, and an astonishing love.

Thousands of his fellow South Africans had been imprisoned, tortured, and burned alive. Desmond Tutu and his family had been demeaned, degraded, and threatened, and he had spent many years in prison. His response to this evil was to extend forgiveness.

South African Bishop Desmond Tutu: a most remarkable interview

It was January 1986, and bitterly cold when Tutu arrived in Detroit to raise money for his work back home in South Africa. My crew had set up for the interview in front of a fireplace at the historic Detroit Club.

"Too bad we can't be having this conversation in South Africa," Tutu said with a grin.

"We'd be a lot warmer."

The bishop was relaxed and seemed quite at ease in front of the camera.

As the crew set up lights and checked sound, I studied the pleasant face of this international icon. His rimless glasses, white hair and studious expression gave Tutu the distinguished look of a professor or diplomat. But he also seemed approachable, like a priest or pastor you could talk with about your deepest anxieties.

Tutu smiled as the cameraman adjusted his lapel microphone. There was not a hint of arrogance or self-importance.

His stand against Apartheid and his campaign for racial justice had earned him a Nobel Peace Prize just two years before our interview. But it was his approach to those who had ruthlessly inflicted so much pain that was most impressive to me; while many of his countrymen demanded retribution for the brutality they'd suffered, he advocated for reconciliation. It was his remarkable attitude that prompted my first question:

"How can you forgive people who've committed such atrocities?"

The twinkle in his eyes momentarily faded.

"Forgiveness doesn't mean you aren't angry," Bishop Tutu said.

"It means you refuse to let yourself be consumed by anger and hatred. That you won't allow yourself to be a perpetual victim."

He paused.

"By forgiving, you not only may become a better person—you may help the one who hurt you to become better."

"What role does faith play in your ability to forgive?" I asked.

He smiled.

"It's a crucial part of it. Remember, Jesus forgave the soldiers who were nailing Him to the cross, and they hadn't even asked for forgiveness. Love and forgiveness are at the heart of our Christian faith."

It was the same message my father had proclaimed from the pulpit Sunday after Sunday. It was that spirit of love and forgiveness that sustained my aunt during more than two decades of medical missionary service in Kenya. It was at the heart of my uncle's evangelism crusades. These familiar words took on a new force when spoken by this man who had lived out their power in the face of unspeakable persecution and death.

For Tutu, the Bible's assertion that 'God is love' was not a premise to be proved. It took on reality and depth for him in the compassion, the suffering, and the death of Jesus. His Jesus was a man born of flesh and blood who drank wine with his buddies, hung out with the deplorables of his day and enjoyed a good party. His Jesus got tired, was tempted by sin and had to use the bathroom just like the rest of us. This human Jesus was the prism through which the light of God, the love that is God, found practical expression.

As a preacher's kid I had been taught that Jesus was God come to earth, so I always imagined that God had descended to us from somewhere else. Somewhere higher. Maybe another planet. It seemed that Tutu had a different perspective on Jesus—not God coming down from somewhere in the galaxy to take on earthly form, but a man in whom the very essence of life, of consciousness, of love, had come so conclusively into focus that the mysterious ultimate could be seen, or witnessed and experienced through him.

* * *

"Crim, you never stopped being a minister, did you?"

The technician in the control room had just finished recording several of my *Second Thoughts* commentaries.

I laughed.

"Well, I hope they didn't come off as too preachy," I said.

Second Thoughts, the syndicated radio series that I developed in the early nineties, was not religious, but consisted of life-affirming, motivational, positive stories and observations about real people and how they went about solving everyday problems. It was a sequel to *One Moment Please*, the series I had launched in Louisville and continued in Philadelphia. When I first got the idea for such a feature, many program directors were skeptical.

"Those features will never make it in today's radio environment," one of them had told me.

"They aren't controversial enough."

I recognized that stations were looking for programming that pushed the listeners' hot buttons—like the bombastic Rush Limbaugh or the acerbic Dr. Laura.

"That's the stuff that sells," one station manager cautioned me.

I was willing to test my own theory that despite all the rancor and name-calling on radio, there just might be a market for civility and encouragement, a market for three minutes a day of hope.

The risk was rewarded with two national sponsors, Kmart and Chrysler, and we grew the *Second Thoughts* network to more than thirteen hundred stations in the U.S. We also had a sizable overseas audience through the Armed Forces Radio Network. Letters from both program directors and listeners confirmed that this was an idea whose time had come, although it certainly wasn't an overnight success. Initially launched as *One Moment Please* in Louisville, it took nearly twenty years of persistence and hard work for the feature to become fully developed as *Second Thoughts.* There may have been an element of truth in the technician's observation that I had never stopped being a minister. I never lost the desire to help people make sense of their lives, and while I felt that my journalistic work did that to an extent, there was a more spiritual dimension to *Second Thoughts* that didn't belong in the newsroom.

In all facets of my work, I wanted to know, 'Will anyone understand more, care more, or handle their life any better because of what I'm doing?' I won't pretend that my career has been based strictly on altruism. Television is fun. Performing in front of the camera is an ego-blast. A need for the spotlight is in my DNA. For me, the career also was quite rewarding, financially, although that isn't always the case. And, to be perfectly honest, early on, television gave me an excuse to cover my blemishes with makeup. As a teenager, and well into young adulthood, I had suffered from acne. I may have believed journalism was my calling, but not all of my motivations were high-minded.

For Dad, a calling was something you got directly from God. My calling didn't come in a dramatic revelation or grand vision. I simply figured out, eventually, that broadcast journalism was right for me. It was where my need for a stage, my interest in just about everything, and my desire to do something positive with my life all intersected. Broadcast news was where I could inform, educate, motivate, occasionally inspire, perform, and maybe, from time to time, help the audience get a handle on life.

Sometimes, while writing a news report or sitting in the

studio, I would hear my father's words: "None of us can do everything, but each of us can do something."

At the heart of Dad's calling was his belief that we are not to squander life selfishly. He took seriously the mandates of Jesus to feed the hungry, to care for the poor, to befriend life's losers and misfits, to love enemies as well as neighbors, and to turn the other cheek. These concepts are as radical now as they were two thousand years ago, and just as challenging to live out in the real world.

"Christianity hasn't failed," Dad once told me. "It's never really been tried."

In both my *Second Thoughts* radio series and my television commentaries, I employed stories from the news, or sometimes history, as a way of making a larger point. This was a technique I'd heard my father use in the pulpit. It was the teaching method used by Jesus in His parables and it's still effectively used by the best communicators today.

* * *

In 1987, I was handed an assignment that would allow me to look at another aspect of faith: what happens when it collides head-on with political ideology. The Vatican announced that Pope John Paul II would be making a visit to his native Poland, a country still under Communist control. This was a story tailor-made for Detroit with its huge populations of Catholics and Polish Americans.

We knew the Pope's visit was a delicate situation for the Polish government, which had declared martial law in order to quell Lech Walesa's Solidarity movement and its growing power. Protests, along with unauthorized newspapers demanding democratic reforms, were popping up everywhere. Because Poland is nearly one hundred percent Catholic, the regime had granted more religious freedom than was permitted in most Soviet satellite countries.

In some ways, the Polish Pope was more of a threat to the regime than Lech Walesa. John Paul II had been openly calling for human rights reform in his native land and Warsaw was helpless to stop him, since doing so would have resulted in mass revolt in an already unstable situation.   We were going to Poland to produce an hour-long documentary, as well as to send back daily live satellite reports on the Pope's visit. Detroit was on the Pope's itinerary during his U.S. visit, planned a few months later, and our documentary would be a good prelude.

We had set up several interviews in advance, including one with Poland's top prelate, Cardinal Jozef Glemp. We also hired a guide and interpreter, Grazyna Gorska, but she almost quit the first day over a program WDIV had produced called *Hamtramck*. It was supposed to be the pilot for a new sitcom, roughly based on a wedding in Detroit's Polish community, but the jokes backfired and the people of Hamtramck didn't think it was funny. They were especially incensed by depictions of elderly women wearing nylon stockings rolled below their knees and stealing floral centerpieces at the wedding. Adding to the insults were family members in garish outfits dancing the hokey-pokey to an accordion rendition of *Proud Mary*. The response was immediate. WDIV phone lines were jammed with angry calls, pickets showed up in front of our studios, and the station was forced to apologize. While it got phenomenal ratings, the show went down in the annals of local television as a disaster.

Unfortunately for our news team and me, the fiasco had

been widely reported beyond Detroit, including on CNN International. If Polish jokes weren't funny in Detroit, they were even less so in Poland. As we stepped off the plane, Grazyna met us with fire in her eyes.

"I heard about that terrible show!" she said, "and I'm not about to work for such rude people."

There was some serious cajoling by Terry Oprea, my producer, who explained that the show had been produced by WDIV's programming (entertainment) department, and not by the news people. That clarification and the promise of extra money, finally brought Grazyna around. And by the time our seventeen-day trip was over, she had become a good friend, often going above and beyond to help us get our story.

One morning, we climbed the stairs to the top floor of our hotel, and I held a heavy curtain back from the window just enough for Paul Brinkerhof, our camera man, to slip his camera lens through the opening. Paul then shot video of Polish army tanks in the street below, ready to move if things got out of hand. We had been warned against shooting anything military, and if we were caught, at best our tape would be confiscated and at worst, we might be kicked out of the country or end up in jail. Fortunately nobody noticed our covert filming, and this shot made it into our documentary so Detroiters could see the national unrest for themselves.

The most dramatic incident of the trip occurred after an outdoor Mass performed by the Pope before more than a million of the faithful who'd gathered at a park in Krakow. Hundreds of Lech Walesa's solidarity members were in the crowd and had planned a protest. The entire area was ringed with hundreds of Communist police.

Just as the Mass ended, all hell broke loose: demonstrators began throwing rocks and bottles at police, who responded with tear gas. I ran along with the crowd, microphone in hand, describing the melée while Paul kept the camera rolling.

"Here Mort, take this!" Paul yelled, as he thrust a heavy tripod my direction. "I can't shoot and carry this thing."

With the tripod in one hand and the wireless mic in the other, I continued reporting while running. It was pandemonium. Police were roughing up the protestors, and we later learned that at least one had been killed.

Covering the Pope in Poland, with cameraman Paul Brinkerhoff

Suddenly, I didn't see Paul or Terry—we had been separated by the thronging crowd. My passport, wallet, and hotel information were all in Paul's camera bag. I was now on my own in a foreign (and Communist) country, unable to speak the language, with no identification and no idea how to get back to the hotel.

After thirty or so harrowing minutes, as the crowd began to dissipate, I started asking passersby how to get to the Holiday Inn. They either shrugged or threw their hands into the air. Nobody understood me until finally I encountered an older gentleman who spoke English. He pointed me toward the hotel, which was about two miles away. When I finally arrived, exhausted and still toting the tripod, I found Terry and Paul in the hotel bar calmly sipping wine.

"What took you so long?" Paul chuckled.

Terry wasn't laughing, though. He had been frantically looking for me, having Grayzna ask everyone along the route if they had seen a lost American carrying a microphone and a tripod. As the station's executive producer Terry later joked, "I knew that if I lost our anchorman in Poland, I was in deep trouble." Our coverage of the confrontation must have been pretty good, though: that evening our report led *NBC Nightly News*.

But while that wild conflict grabbed the headlines, the real story for me was what went on quietly behind the scenes. Pope John Paul II deserves credit for "staring down the Communists," as one writer put it, but the real foot soldiers in the battle were the Polish people, and the Catholic Church that provided their bunkers. While reporting the story, I discovered an active underground network of artists, writers, and intellectuals meeting regularly in church basements throughout the country. There they found sanctuary to discuss issues, create newspapers, stage plays, and explore the outside world in ways strictly forbidden by the Communist regime. In effect, there were two societies living side by side: the Communists and the Church. Ultimately, the Church won.

* * *

To be effective as a television newsman, whether reporting on events of international importance or small-town interest, I tried to be an honest broker: objective and fair to all sides of an issue. Today, when many cable news anchors freely spout whatever they think and feel about any subject, the idea of trying to be objective may sound quaint. Fox News Channel may tout their coverage as "fair and balanced," but anyone who watches for five minutes knows it is neither. The same can be said for MSNBC on the other end of the political spectrum. But prior to 24-hour cable news, journalists at most networks and stations did try to adhere to standards of fairness.

Despite my commitment to journalistic integrity, there were times when a deeply held conviction may have pushed me over that line. Some of my fellow reporters thought so, and a few times I was taken to task in newspaper columns for risking my objectivity to support a cause about which I felt passionate.

One columnist questioned whether I violated journalistic ethics by speaking out against the missile defense system that President Reagan proposed. One newspaper headline, following a speech I'd delivered in a Port Huron church, proclaimed: "Faith Guides Crim on and off TV Set."

Fortunately for me, the front office at WDIV understood and respected that on those rare occasions when I did take a public stand on a controversial issue, I was speaking and acting from conscience (and doing so on my own time). As I look back on it, I wonder if I was still conflicted between an evangelistic urge to change the world and the journalistic role of explaining it.

While trying to follow my own conscience as a newsman, I also began to push back against the tide of irrelevancy and titil-lation that was eroding real reporting in America's newsrooms. Sometimes I raised my voice in a staff meeting, questioning why we were starting to care more about demographic appeal than pure news value. As a result, I took a few concrete steps toward improving the quality of our news. In retrospect, I wish I had done more.

One of those steps was to cancel a Friday night feature that I had created called *Tabloid Tales,* which aired in the final

Chimp's Head Put on Human Body!
Dolphin Grows Human Arms!
Farmer Shoots 25 pound Grasshopper!

You get the idea. Besides making fun of the tabloids, it was a light-hearted way to provide viewers with a few chuckles at the end of a weary week, and a way to offset some of the gloomy news. But one day, in 1992, it hit me that so much of our regular news had started to mimic that tabloid style that maybe *Tabloid Tales* wasn't so funny anymore. As the content of our newscasts began to incline more and more toward sensationalism—murders, rapes, gossip, and celebrities—there was less contrast between our hard news and our satire. Maybe blood-and-guts was what the audience wanted, but we also had an obligation to give them what they needed to know; what was happening in the public schools, city council meetings, nursing homes, public housing, rehab clinics and state government. Didn't voters need facts about taxes, roads, funding of police and fire departments, local businesses and the economy? It was particularly disappointing to many of us in the newsroom to see our State Capitol bureau in Lansing closed, and our fulltime reporter pulled out of City Hall. The night we dropped *Tabloid Tales*, I told the audience exactly why and pledged to replace it with a positive feature to be called *Above and Beyond*. Instead of poking fun at ridiculous "journalism," we would put some positive stories in that slot, highlighting something good that someone in the community had done. It was the same philosophy that had given birth to *One Moment Please* and *Second*

Thoughts. The new feature received positive viewer response and I don't recall a single complaint about deep-sixing Tabloid Tales.

As the trend toward tabloid content increased in local newscasts all over the country, my concern for our own product deepened. While WDIV was doing a better job than most at holding the line, I thought, "If this station, owned by the revered Washington Post Company, should slip into the journalistic mire, then the whole industry is in trouble."

Unable to stay quiet any longer, I began making public comments in my speeches about what many of us considered the deteriorating state of TV journalism. Many of my newsroom colleagues were equally worried about the trend, but as an anchorman with a high profile, I felt a special obligation to speak out. I wrote an article for the *Detroit News,* saying it was time to draw the line between real news and the frivolous stuff reported in the tabloids. The national media took notice.

First, I was invited to appear on NBC's *The Today Show,* and because WDIV was an NBC affiliate, my appearance and criticism was aired by my own station. In a live interview with Matt Lauer, I talked about the need for all news people at all TV stations to start bucking the trend toward sensationalism. Then, talk show host Phil Donahue invited me to come on his afternoon program, along with Dan Rather and media critic Howard Kurtz. Donahue challenged me by asking whether my newscasts had included the story of Lorena Bobbitt cutting off her abusive husband's penis, or the Menendez brothers murdering their parents. I had to admit, yes, we did, but in my view we didn't sensationalize them. We didn't allow these grotesque stories to crowd out other, more important information. While I believed that statement to be true, at the same time I was concerned that the balance in our news programs might be tipping.

The night before I flew to New York for the taping, the first story on our 11 p.m. news was about a woman who was raped and then stalked by a preacher. That story led into these: a shooting at a fast-food outlet; the bathtub drowning of two children; the charging of Detroit cops with arson; and the tracking of a serial rapist on the University of Michigan campus. Apparently I didn't have to look beyond our own newsroom to prove my point.

To be sure, stories of crime and corruption were important, but were we balancing our newscasts with the hard information that was vital to peoples' lives? Not once did management suggest that I tone down my criticisms and my colleagues in the newsroom urged me to keep it up.

In fairness, I believe our bosses were as concerned about the drift toward sensationalism as we were. But the competitive pressures were enormous, and today with the advent of twenty-four-hour cable channels, competition for viewers has only become more intense. TV newsroom budgets have been slashed everywhere and reporting staffs are required to do more and more with fewer resources. Journalism is a profession, but television is an industry, and big audiences mean big advertising money. Today, the proliferation of available news channels combined with an infinite variety of internet competition has cut substantially into station audiences and revenues. Managements do have a responsibility to shareholders and to the bottom line. The danger for journalism comes when the bottom line becomes the only line.

Given all the pressures on today's broadcast journalists, both financial and political, I can only hope they are finding the same satisfaction, thrill, and sense of purpose that I experienced during four decades in the business.

Paul Harvey was right when he told me early in my career, "Mort, when you find a job that you enjoy, you will never have to work a day in your life."

Speaking of Paul Harvey—well, let's save that for the next chapter.

Chapter Eighteen

THE REST OF THE STORY

Things turn out best for those who make the best of the way things turn out.
—JOHN WOODEN

"YOU HAVE A CALL," Ruthie said, pressing my door open slightly.

"Sorry, Ruthie. Too close to deadline."

I could count on Ruthie to protect me from distractions in the important minutes preceding a newscast.

It was 4:45 p.m. and I was making final edits on the lead story for our 5 p.m. news. Seconds later, Ruthie opened the door wider.

"He says it's important," she insisted.

With slight irritation in my voice, I said, "Take a message." I turned back to the typewriter.

A moment later, Ruthie was back.

"This guy is calling from New York. He says his name is Pete Flannery and that if you don't take his call, he'll come to Detroit and break both your legs."

Pete Flannery! It had been more than ten years since I'd talked to Pete, back when I was an ABC radio correspondent and he was a producer.

"Pete, great to hear from you, but you caught me on deadline. What's up?"

"I'll get right to the point. You may not be aware that I'm now Vice President of radio news."

"That's great, Pete. Congratulations!"

"I've just come from a meeting of the news brass. We've decided we need to be thinking about a replacement for Paul Harvey, and everybody's agreed you should be the guy."

I was beyond stunned. Paul's shows were ABC Radio's top moneymakers, bringing in more advertising revenue than the rest of the network's schedule combined. There were no rumors about an imminent Harvey retirement. And what about all the radio talent in New York? Why me?

"First of all, nobody knows when or if Paul will finally hang it up," Pete said, anticipating my next question.

"Paul is sixty-one, he's in good health, and obviously could go on for years. On the other hand, he could decide to retire or even drop dead tomorrow. The fact is we don't have any backup plans, and as you know, he *is* the ABC radio franchise." I knew Paul well enough to know that his retirement wasn't likely, at least not anytime soon. He loved his work.

"You're a good storyteller, and we think your style would be a complement to Paul's. And Paul is totally on board with this," Pete said.

Pete was familiar with my *One Moment Please* radio series, which station program managers sometimes compared to Paul's *The Rest of the Story*. Many ABC affiliates were airing my series as well as Paul's.

"So," I asked, "just what would it mean being on the bench as his successor?"

"It means we'd start to get his audience familiar with you by having you fill in for him whenever he's on vacation or off making a speech. Paul is now away from his microphone around four or five weeks a year, and we know he'd like to take even more time off."

"Pete, it's a flattering offer. As you know, Paul's been helpful to me over the years. Of course, I'd be honored to fill in for the nation's most famous commentator. But I don't see how that could work. I've got a fulltime TV job here in Detroit."

Paul originated his broadcasts from ABC's studios in Chicago.

"We've thought of that," Pete said. "We're estimating there'll be about six weeks of work a year—8:30 a.m. and noon shows, five days a week, and whenever Paul's gone, we'll send his producer over to Detroit. You can originate the broadcasts from wherever you want. Do them from your living room if that would work best."

I was feeling exhilaration, but also pressure to finish writing my newscast.

"Pete, I really have to go. Let's leave it this way: I like the idea, but obviously I have to look at my WDIV contract and talk this over with management. I'll get back to you."

"Great!" Pete said. "Once you give me the green light, I'll have our attorney get in touch with Ralph [Mann] to negotiate a contract. I think it's a terrific opportunity for you, and we're excited about it at our end."

For now I had to focus on the upcoming newscast, but that would be a challenge; I had just been offered a backup position, and potential succession, to the dean of America's radio commentators. It was a stunning and totally unexpected opportunity. After the newscast I relayed the offer to Jim Lynagh and Jim Snyder. Their immediate response was positive, as long as the substitutions didn't interfere with my television work. They saw promotional value in my selection. I accepted the offer, and the day before my premier Harvey broadcast WDIV ran a full-page ad in the Detroit News. It featured a large photograph of me, which ran under the headline: "Of all the Famous Newscasters, Guess Who ABC Picked to Fill in for Paul Harvey?"

Bill Bonds had worked briefly for ABC's television stations in New York and Los Angeles, and because WXYZ was owned by ABC, Bill was an ABC employee. Yet the network had chosen his professional arch-rival to sub for their national radio star.

The word from inside Billy's newsroom was that he took one look at that ad and kicked a waste can so hard it could have shot across the river into Canada.

For the better part of five years, I took over the Paul Harvey franchise whenever he was away, except for his afternoon feature, *The Rest of The Story*, which Paul recorded in advance.

It was satisfying to be back on network radio. At the time, Paul had the largest and most loyal audience of any radio personality. From my first broadcast, I began receiving mail from listeners all across the nation, most of it positive. After my first two-week substitution, I received a letter from Paul saying how pleased he was with my performance, how much positive feedback he was getting from his audience, and how my work made him feel a lot more comfortable about taking "time away from the microphone."

My substitutions were stretching over about six weeks a year, and during those weeks the schedule was grueling. After arriving home after midnight following the eleven o'clock TV news, I had to arise by 4 a.m. for the thirty-minute ride back to WDIV. ABC provided me with a limousine, so at least I could enjoy a cup of coffee, read the paper, and relax a bit on my way to the studio.

When I arrived, producer Ron Gorski would already be there, having sorted through reams of wire copy and organized the various story topics into neat stacks on my desk. Ron was willing to write the shows for me, which would have allowed me nearly two more hours of sleep. But I knew Paul wrote his own newscasts, I had always written all my own radio copy, and I was determined to do no less now.

After feeding the five-minute, 8:30 a.m. show to Chicago, Ron and I would walk down the street for breakfast at a local diner, then return to my office to immediately begin work on the fifteen-minute noon show. We fed the noon show to Chicago at 11:35 a.m., and by twelve o'clock, I was back in the limo and on my way home for a brief catnap. Then, it was back to the station to work on the evening television shows.

It was a brutal schedule, but I was young and propelled by adrenaline, ambition, and the certain knowledge that I was on track to succeed the best radio talent in the business. Paul's enormous audience would give me an additional opportunity to inspire and encourage, as I had tried to do with my *One Moment Please* series.

Broadcasting *Paul Harvey News* on ABC

Days after my selection as his substitute, Paul called me.

"Mort, when I'm away, the microphone is yours. I don't expect you to reflect my views. Feel free to say whatever you want."

This was important, because my view of the world, like my theology, had liberalized considerably from the staunchly conservative influences of my youth. I knew that while Paul and I shared certain basic values, there was a significant gap between our political philosophies. And while Paul told me he had no expectation that I reflect his views, somebody forgot to tell his audience. That audience, like Paul, was staunchly conservative.

Taking him at his word, I would on occasion use the terrific megaphone he'd provided me to promote civil rights, workers' rights, gay rights, and larger issues of U.S.-Soviet relations.

More than once, I criticized the policies of Paul's good friend, President Reagan. I called out Interior Secretary James Watt for telling what many considered to be an inappropriate story, only to learn that Watt was one of Paul Harvey's golfing buddies. Paul's audience was not amused, and I imagine that Paul didn't much care for that commentary either.

My mail, which had been overwhelmingly favorable when I stuck with straight news, now took a nasty turn. Newspapers across the country published letters to the editor asking such questions as, "Who is this left-wing radical they've got filling in for Paul Harvey?"

Ron Gorski had warned me to be careful, but I had taken Paul at his word. In retrospect my brash advocacy, though sincere, was naive. The final straw was when I came out strongly against the deployment of intermediate-range missiles in Germany, Italy, and England, a move many believed would be a serious escalation of the Cold War. Reagan and his advisers were solidly in support of deployment, so once again I was on the wrong side of Harvey's audience. Whether or not I was on the right side of history didn't matter.

I soon discovered that my commentary had put me at crosshairs not only with conservative radio listeners but, more importantly, with the real power behind Paul Harvey—his wife, Angel. Nicki and I were invited to join the two of them for lunch at the Club International in Chicago's Drake Hotel. We flew our plane to Chicago, landed at Meigs Field, the downtown airport (since closed), and climbed into a limousine that the Harveys had sent for us.

Paul and Angel were both waiting at the head of the short stairway leading up to the restaurant. It's an old-school, luxury dining room where everything is gilded, waiters speak in French accents and walk around in tuxedos with napkins draped over their arms. If the Harveys were upset with me about my attack on the president's missile policies, there was nothing to indicate it, at least not yet.

Paul was gracious, as always, motioning us to a table for four. Angel was polite but reserved. Paul ordered an iced tea, Nicki and I settled for Perrier, and Angel asked for a glass of chardonnay. Wine wasn't an option for me, as I had a plane to fly after lunch.

We made small talk for a few minutes. Then Angel looked straight at me and asked, "Why are you against putting our missiles in Europe?"

I wasn't prepared for such a sudden challenge, but tried to explain, as diplomatically as I could, why I had taken that position and why I thought the President's decision inched us closer to a nuclear confrontation with the Russians.

Then came the bombshell.

"Mort, do you believe the Bible?"

I had no idea where Angel was going with this question. My views on Scripture had evolved so much, my thinking about the Bible had become so nuanced, that it was impossible for me to give her a simple yes or no answer. Clearly, a yes or no answer was what she wanted.

I looked at Paul. He had a faint smile on his face but said nothing. I learned during that luncheon that when the two of them were together, she took the lead. Paul had always credited her with being the brains of the family, and referred to her on the air as his executive producer.

"Do you believe Bible prophecy?" Angel pressed on before

I could answer her first question.

"I'm not sure I follow you," I said as Nicki gently nudged my leg with her knee as if to say, 'Be careful. You're talking to the boss.'

"Well, if you believe the Bible and you believe the prophecies," Angel went on, "then we know the whole world is going to be destroyed by fire. That probably means there'll be a nuclear war. Do you think we can stop a prophecy?"

It was the most incredible interpretation I had ever heard, even from fundamentalist preachers, and I was stunned.

"Well, Angel, I know some people interpret the Bible as prophesying that we'll all go up in flames. But Angel, with all due respect, I don't think prophecy is my business as a Christian. I can't do anything about that. I do think it's my business as a Christian to carry out Jesus' mandate to be a peacemaker."

Nicki didn't even bother to nudge my leg. She knew, even if I didn't, that I had just committed professional suicide as far as the Harveys were concerned. We didn't talk about the lunch on our way back to Meigs Field, not with Paul's personal driver at the wheel. But as we walked across the tarmac toward our plane, Nicki said, "You know it's all over for you on the Paul Harvey shows. I'll bet you never do another substitution."

"I can't believe that," I said.

"Just because I don't agree with Angel on the meaning of some Scripture?"

"It's a lot more than that," Nicki said.

"You challenged her, and you did it in front of Paul. I think you're done."

"Well, we'll see. Paul's scheduled to take a week off next month, and I'm on tap to fill in."

Two days later, Pete Flannery called to tell me that Paul had cancelled his vacation. Paul did not take off another day until my contract with ABC expired some three months later. A few days before the end of the contract, Pete called to tell me they wouldn't be renewing. They had decided to go a "different direction."

"Why?" I asked.

"Well, Mort, sending Ron back and forth to Detroit, putting him up in a hotel, providing you with a limousine, the remote broadcast charges, wire services—they just decided it was all too much."

I knew that was a cover story, so I didn't bother to ask any more questions. Knowing how much money ABC made on the Harvey shows, and how little it cost, comparatively, to do those remotes from Detroit, Pete's reasoning didn't make sense.

And what about ABC's plan for me to succeed Harvey down the line? It seemed clear that removing me as Paul's sub and successor had not been ABC's decision. It was Paul's. (More precisely, it was Angel's.) Would ABC really skimp on a few thousand dollars a year in expense money while protecting a franchise that brought in fifty million dollars or more each year? Maybe, to be totally fair, it was ultimately Paul's audience that made the decision.

Filling in for Paul had been an honor and it had been fun. To this day, I run into people all across the country who remember me from those years of broadcasting *Paul Harvey News* at 8:30 a.m. and noon. While losing the assignment in 1985 was a blow to my ego, it turned out to be the best thing that could have happened; had ABC renewed my Paul Harvey contract, I never would have created *Second Thoughts* six years later.

...and now you know the REST of the story

Furthermore, I would have waited on that backup bench for a very long time, because Paul never did retire. In 2000, at the age of eighty-two, he signed a new ten-year contract with ABC. He died at the age of ninety, still broadcasting. By then, I was seventy-three. *Paul Harvey News* died with Paul, and with its demise, ABC radio virtually vanished.

A few years ago at an ABC radio reunion in New York, I had an opportunity to speak briefly with Pete Flannery, by then long retired from ABC.

"Pete, I have to ask you. It's always bugged me. I think I know the answer, but it was the Harveys and not ABC who made the decision, wasn't it?"

Pete seemed uncomfortable with the question. It was clear he didn't care to talk about it in the presence of so many ABC radio people. But he did give me a brief, affirmative nod.

"Call me sometime, Mort, and we'll talk about it," he said.

I never did.

Pete's nod confirmed what Nicki had intuited, and what I already knew.

Chapter Nineteen

FADE TO BLACK

It's so much darker when a light goes out than it would have been if it had never shone.

—JOHN STEINBECK, *THE WINTER OF OUR DISCONTENT*

THE SERVICE ENDED.

The funeral director walked toward Herman Dale's casket. We all stood. Nicki was between her mother and me. I clasped her hand. At the foot of the bier, the funeral director took ahold of a handle on the light brown oak casket, and pushed it slowly forward. The rubber wheels on the aluminum dolly began their silent roll down the aisle, toward the open doors at the rear of the chapel.

Nicki released my hand, stepped into the aisle behind her daddy's casket, and began to sing:

Oh Lord, my God, when I in awesome wonder...

Her beautiful voice was clear and strong, and seemed to transcend her grief. She had not planned to do this. But when the organist started playing Pop's favorite hymn, Nicki had responded spontaneously to the song as though unable not to.

Consider all the things thy hands have made...

The casket had just rolled past the second row of pews, right behind the family section, when Kathryn moved out and joined Nicki, adding harmony to the old Swedish hymn.

I see the stars, I hear the rolling thunder...

Almost simultaneously, their older sister Smiley joined the recessional, her fifty-eight-year-old soprano voice as beautiful as when she had sung with her evangelist husband, Bernie Smith, two decades earlier. It was all spontaneous, but so flawless that it sounded as though the trio had spent hours practicing for this moment.

When siblings merge their voices, the sum is greater than the parts. Like the McGuires and the Andrews Sisters, these Dale sisters had that divine harmonic gift that only genetics can grant. Even though it had been many years since the three had sung together, the fusion of their mellow three-part harmony was almost mystical.

Thy power throughout the universe displayed...

Nicki's sweet, clear alto, Smiley's flawless soprano, and Kathryn's mezzo merged into a sound that angels would have envied. Pop would have loved it. When they reached the black hearse, the three daughters stopped walking but continued singing while Pop's casket was slowly eased onto the track just beyond the coach's open door.

Then sings my soul, my savior God to thee...

As the mourners began filing out of the Dawkins Funeral home in Harrisburg, Illinois, they were mesmerized by the Dale sisters' tender show of love. Those who hadn't wept during the funeral were shedding tears now. Somewhere, Pop must have been smiling.

It was a profile in courage that the three Dale sisters found the strength to rise above their heartache and give the performance of their lives. Love can be stronger than our deepest pain.

With tears trickling down my own cheeks, I walked over to Nicki, and embraced her trembling body as the hearse's door latched shut. I shouldn't have been surprised by Nicki's singing or by her bravery. From the moment we had fallen in love twenty-nine years earlier, I had recognized in Naomi Ruth Dale a strength of character, an inner toughness, and a resilience that would serve her well throughout her lifetime. She also believed that death was not the end—she would see her Pop again.

And singing? That was so organically Nicki that every time you thought of her, you thought of her voice. Singing was as much a part of this adorable lady as her gorgeous blue eyes, her infectious laugh, and her almost perpetual smile.

She sang in good times and found refuge in song when times were difficult. She sang in church and in private recitals. She sang in the car and while doing housework.

She even sang on the day the doctor told her she was dying.

* * *

October, 1983. I was in a remote, wooded area in northern Ontario, covering a story about Canadian mining. The location was unreachable by airline, so my producer and camera crew were happy to have me fly us there in my plane.

We had completed most of our interviews and stand-ups, and planned to spend this final day shooting B-roll—generic footage to run while my voice told the story. I was still in the hotel room and had just finished shaving when I heard an urgent rap on the door.

"Mort, Nicki wants you to call her."

It was Deborah Johnson, my producer.

"She tried to call your room, but you must have been in the shower."

This was before cellphones, and our routine was for me to always call Nicki in the evening before going to bed, so the early call from her was concerning.

"Honey, anything wrong?" I said, trying not to sound worried.

"Mort, I've got some really bad news."

Nicki's voice was trembling. "I hate so much to tell you this, but Jessica is gone."

The words didn't immediately register.

"Gone?" I said.

For a moment, there was silence.

"Mort, she was in an accident. She's dead. I don't know anything else, but it's on the news."

It's difficult to describe my feelings in that moment. Shock. Disbelief. Numbness.

"I'm sure there'll be more information by the time you get home. When are you coming home?"

"I'm coming tonight," I responded, not quite sure how I would manage that since the crew was dependent upon my airplane for their own transportation back to Detroit.

"Please don't take any chances," Nicki said, obviously

concerned about me flying at night, especially in an emotionally distraught state, and after a long and tiring day. In retrospect, my decision to fly under such circumstances was risky and perhaps foolish.

I knocked on Bobby Stevens' door. He was our cameraman.

"Bobby, Jessica Savitch has been killed in an accident," I announced, my voice shaky.

I didn't have to tell him who Jessica Savitch was. WDIV was the NBC station in Detroit, and Jessica's weekend newscasts were on our air every Saturday and Sunday. I explained that she was a former colleague and close friend.

"I've got to get back to Detroit, but I can't leave you guys up here."

"Don't worry about it," Bobby assured me.

"We'll finish your stand-ups and shooting B-roll, and then we can rent a car. We can make it back to Detroit in one day. You go on back this evening and do what you have to do."

It was a very black night, moon and stars hidden by a thick overcast. Flying between broken layers of clouds, I saw only a few lights from an occasional town, and even they were spread far apart in this mostly uninhabited part of Canada.

With the autopilot activated, there was little to do during the two-hour flight except watch the soft yellow glow of the instrument panel, and listen to the monotonous hum of the two Continental engines as they powered my Cessna through the night.

There was lots of time to think. To reflect. To remember.

Was this real? How could it be? Was this all a terrible dream? A nightmare? Am I really flying or am I still in my bed, about to wake up and realize I've never left the hotel?

Sitting in my plane, being whisked through the blackness, added to the sense of unreality.

Was it only ten years ago that Jessica and I had met?

Was it only a year ago that she was at our house, recuperating from the trauma of her husband's suicide?

This is crazy. This just can't be. Jessica, dead?

By the time I got home, Nicki had more details.

Jess and the man she was dating, Martin Fischbein, were leaving a restaurant in Bucks County, Pennsylvania, when he backed his car over an embankment in rain and fog. The car flipped, landing upside down in a canal. Fischbein, Jessica, and her beloved husky, Chewy, had all drowned.

I knew about Fischbein, a Vice President at the *New York Post*. Jess and I talked by telephone with some regularity, mostly about work, but also about our lives and what had happened to us since Philadelphia. We had spoken just four days before the accident.

"I'm dating this really great guy," she told me, her voice sounding more upbeat than I'd heard it in some time.

"He's an executive with the *New York Post*, and I really like him."

I told her how pleased I was that she was getting her life together since Donald Payne's suicide. She didn't mention the drug rumors about her that had been rampant in the tabloids, but said she thought things were going a lot better at NBC.

"One more thing," she said, before we hung up. "I went to Marble Collegiate Church last Sunday. I had heard you talk so much about your regard for Norman Vincent Peale, so I decided to try his church. His sermon was wonderful. I plan to go back."

"That's good, Jess," I said.

It was an acknowledgment that she was continuing her search for meaning. She and I had often talked philosophy, about the different concepts people have of God, and of our own search for truth. We agreed that finding something bigger than ourselves is perhaps life's most important and daunting challenge. Following one of these discussions, Jess had given me *The Prophet* by Kahlil Gibran, a Lebanese philosopher. It was one of her favorite books.

The next morning, I received a call from Jessica's older sister, Stephanie.

"Mom and I want you to deliver the eulogy," she said.

"The funeral will be day after tomorrow in Margate [New Jersey].

It'll just be a small, private affair for family and closest friends. Can you come?"

"Stephanie, you know I'll be there."

Giving the eulogy would be very difficult, I thought. But how could I say no?

"We're sure that's what Jess would have wanted," Stephanie said.

I wondered how much Jess had told them. Did Stephanie, and perhaps their mother, know that we had been more than friends? If so, they never said.

The next day I roughed out a few thoughts but was still working on the eulogy as Nicki and I flew to Philadelphia. We rented a car for the short ride to the Roth Memorial Chapel in Margate, New Jersey.

Jess's family and a handful of her closest colleagues from KYW were there. Ed Bradley, CBS correspondent for *Sixty Minutes*, had flown down from New York. Jess had worked as an intern for Ed when she was first out of college. There'd been rumors of a romance between them, but Jess insisted it never happened.

My attorney friend Don Hamburg, who had represented both Jess and me, put his arm around my shoulder as we walked into the chapel.

"Well, Mort, I guess all of us who knew Jess never expected her to die of old age."

I wondered if his comment referred to Jessica's widely reported drug problems, or if it was simply a recognition of how our brightest stars often streak across the sky and flame out early.

* * *

It was early July, 1987. I walked into the basement. I could hear Nicki singing in the laundry room. I turned the corner and saw her at the ironing board, pressing clothes for our daughter, Carey. She would turn 16 in a few days and was scheduled to leave the next day for the Interlochen Arts Camp near Traverse City, Michigan. Nicki was singing the Rodgers and Hammerstein tune "Younger than Springtime." It was one of the songs she had been practicing for an upcoming benefit concert.

When Nicki saw me, she placed the iron on its end, and said,

"Honey, I don't think we need to tell the children just yet. It would only ruin Carey's summer, and nothing is going to happen to me right away."

Hours earlier, we had learned that Nicki might not live to see Carey graduate from high school the following year. Her breast cancer was back. Yet through the heaviness and the sadness of that reality, Nicki was singing—singing of life, love, youth, and hope.

I had been fighting back tears ever since we had received the shocking news in Dr. Burrow's office. John Burrows was more than our oncologist; he was our close, personal friend, and I knew that delivering Nicki's prognosis had to be one of the hardest things he had ever done.

"I agree, babe," I said.

"No reason to tell Carey yet."

"And we shouldn't tell Al until we're able to sit down and explain everything to both of them," Nicki added.

Al was about to begin his final year at the College of William and Mary.

Driving home from John's office after receiving the terrible news earlier in the day, my eyes still smarting, I felt like I'd been sucker punched. It wasn't the first time I had wondered, *where are you, God?*

It was a question I had pondered so many times since my first crisis of faith at the age of fifteen. Now it took on a new urgency. I had spent a lifetime searching for answers, doubting, questioning, challenging, and finally coming to believe, as I once heard a minister say, that doubt isn't the opposite of faith; it's a component of faith. But at this moment, the doubt was all I could see.

For ten years, Nicki and I had lived under a cloud of uncertainty, aware that the malignancy might come back. Doctors in Chicago had found traces of cancer in her lymph nodes at the time of her surgery. Now, ten years later, anxiety had turned to alarm. How much comfort and reassurance would we find in our faith? Even though we both had shed many of the religious taboos from childlhood, I don't believe Nicki's core beliefs ever changed much. Her keen, analytical mind didn't seem to prevent her from easily accepting God as a given in her life. I envied the simplicity of her faith and her ability to trust, and if she was frightened by the prospect of death, I never once heard her express it. There was no doubting the sadness she felt at the prospect of leaving the children and me—of giving up the life she so dearly cherished, but she never once indicated that death itself held any terror for her.

Of course, the recurrence of Nicki's cancer changed our lives.

In the early months after the diagnosis, we didn't use the word 'terminal.' We didn't discuss how much time she might have. But the reality was an ominous, ever-present fog, over-shadowing all attempts at normalcy.

Regular bouts of chemotherapy were a continuing reminder that things would never be the way they were. John had told us that Nicki would require chemo once a month. For how long? Until it stopped working, he said. We did not ask when that might be.

One day at a time, one treatment at a time—that's how we determined to deal with it.

We would think of it as living with cancer, not dying from it.

The present moment was what we had; our future together was happening now.

The side effects from the chemo were awful. Nausea. Headaches. Two or three days of feeling so terrible that bed was Nicki's only option. But she had at least two fairly good weeks out of every month, and we took full advantage of those: lunch or dinner out, black-tie charity events, visits with friends, time with family, church on Sundays, and flights in our plane to Sawgrass for some long Florida weekends. The WDIV man-agement was both understanding and generous. They allowed me extra time, and could there be any greater gift than time?

Carey would be starting her junior year in high school, and Al was about to graduate from college. Nicki was adamant that we not tell them the seriousness of her condition nor the inevitable outcome. She would protect Al and Carey from the pain for as long as possible. I'm not sure how much the children instinctively knew, but they understood that their mother was not well. Carey, especially, must have sensed it, because she was living at home and saw her mom every day. She saw her on those sickest of sick days, watched her hair come out, and saw the collection of wigs.

For more than a year, drugs held the cancer at bay. But by the twentieth month, it was evident that the treatments were no longer effective. We were quite certain that Christmas 1988 would be our last holiday with Nicki.

Now, she was mostly confined to bed. I hired around-the-clock nursing care so she could remain at home. Our home was about halfway between John Burrows' house and his office. He stopped in to check on Nicki every morning on his way to work, and every evening on his way home.

"How much time?" I finally worked up the courage to ask.

"Not much, Mort. She's failing."

I called Al. He was in Switzerland with his fiancée and wasn't scheduled to come home for several days.

"Al, I think you had better come now. And I think you should take the Concorde."

Nicki's older sister, Smiley, had come from Hamilton, Ohio, to help take care of Nicki and Carey, and to assist me in keeping the household operating. The next day, John and I flew Smiley home in our plane so she could check her mail, pick up fresh clothing and take care of some business before returning to Detroit. That evening, as the three of us entered the front door, we were met at the foot of the stairs by Edie Burkhardt, the nurse on duty.

"Nicki doesn't want to go on," Edie said.

"What do you mean, doesn't want to go on?" I responded.

Edie was now weeping.

"She told me it's just too hard. She's tired. She's ready. She doesn't want to fight anymore. She wants to stop her meds." I knew it was only the medicines that were keeping her alive, and that if she stopped, all of her systems would shut down.

John put his arm around me.

"Mort, she's looking for your permission to go. And you have to give it to her."

"I don't know if I can do that."

"Well, it's the most compassionate thing you can do. Mort, she's dying. You've both put up an incredible fight. Now it's time to let go. Yes, it will be the toughest thing you've ever had to do, but you must do it. For Nicki. If we keep fighting, we won't be extending her life. We'll only be extending her suffering."

I broke down. I knew John was right. But where could I find the strength to tell the love of my life, "It's okay to die?"

I tried to pull myself together before walking into our bedroom. The lights were dimmed. Nicki was awake. I whispered a silent prayer and sat down next to her on the bed.

"It's alright, honey," I said, as I took her hand in both of mine. "You've fought long enough." I choked on the words.

"You have been such a wonderful wife. Such a terrific mother. You do know how much the kids and I love you."

"I know," she said. Tears were forming in her tired eyes.

I remembered a conversation John told me he had with Nicki a few days earlier. She had wanted to know what it's like to die. Is it painful?

No, John had assured her. When the time was right, he would place her on a morphine drip. She would simply fall asleep and not wake up again. He said she seemed comforted by this.

"Bugs, I love you so much," I blurted out before collapsing onto the bed beside her.

Bugs was the private and affectionate nickname I had given her at a church picnic in Portageville during our first year of marriage. It was an endearing term, one she understood was something only I could call her. It was how she signed birthday, anniversary and Christmas cards to me.

"You know our love will never end."

"I know that," she said.

As I sobbed and stroked her arm, Nicki had one more thing she wanted to say.

"Mort, I know you are going to be sad. But don't make a career of it. We've had a really good life together. More than anything, I want you to build a new life for yourself and for the children."

In that moment, perhaps without knowing it, Nicki was giving me love's greatest gift: If I had granted her permission to die, she had just given me permission to live. For Nicki, the children and I had always come first. This was her final, unselfish act.

I could not possibly imagine life without her. I could not fathom the possibility of building a new life. What did that even mean? But as searing grief slowly gave way to the healing power of time and beautiful memories, those words would become my deliverance from self-pity and chronic sadness, and my key to a new future. Nicki's thoughtfulness, her concern for others, her selfless love, had been the hallmarks of her life. Now, in death, they would be her legacy. Her wise and compassionate admonition, "I know you will be sad, but don't make a career of it," eventually helped me find the courage and the will to move on.

The next day, Nicki seemed a little stronger. She asked to have all the family together in her room. She wanted an opportunity to tell them—especially our children—a personal farewell.

"I think I'd like Smiley to make some orange roughy," she said.

Her appetite had waned in recent days, and I was pleased to hear her ask for a dish that had always been one of her favorites. Smiley was an excellent cook, and knew how to prepare the fish exactly the way Nicki liked it.

Nicki's brother, Chuck, his wife Sandy, and my mother were there. Carey was there, too, and Al was on his way home from Switzerland. Nicki's sister, Kathryn, was unable to leave California where her husband was on a waiting list for a liver transplant.

So, at lunchtime, with the family gathered around her bed and Nicki looking more radiant than I had seen her in days, Smiley walked into the room carrying a food tray and placed it on Nicki's bed.

The fish was broiled to perfection, accompanied by cooked cauliflower, a small salad, and some fruit. We told Nicki we would all eat later. Right now, we just wanted to enjoy her company while she had lunch.

Propped up in her adjustable bed, pale and drawn, a tan

turban covering her bald head, Nicki managed a faint smile. She was beautiful.

"Thanks, Smiley," she said as she finished most of the fish.

"You're such a good cook. And thanks to all of you for being here." Her eyes seemed brighter as they swept around the room.

"I love you all so very much."

As Smiley took the tray, Nicki said,

"What a wonderful way to spend a last . . . "

She paused. Then she changed her sentence: "What a wonderful way to spend a day with the family I love."

As Smiley removed her tray, Nicki asked for a private moment with each person; Chuck, Sandy, my mother, Smiley, and of course, Carey.

We all walked out of her bedroom, and then each of the people who mattered most to her walked back in, alone, to sit on the edge of her bed and share their love. Al arrived later that evening, jetlagged but eager to see his mom. He was the last to visit her room.

I don't know what was said. I've never asked either of my children. It was Nicki's time to say goodbye in her own way. Everyone knew it was the final conversation they would have with her.

That night, her kidneys began shutting down, and her lungs began to fill with fluid. John inserted the morphine drip into Nicki's IV port.

I kissed her, lay down beside her, and held her hand until she was asleep. A folding screen at the foot of the bed provided us a modicum of privacy, and I had slept next to her every night during those difficult weeks. Edie, the nurse on duty that night, sat as she always did, on a chair just beyond the screen. I lay there, staring at the ceiling, unable to think, my mind numbing itself to the reality that this was our last night together. At some point, fatigue finally overpowered the sadness and I drifted off to sleep.

The next morning, Sunday, January 8, 1989, I slipped out of bed and for a moment gazed at Nicki as she slept. She looked so peaceful. I exchanged nods with Edie, then went into the bathroom for my morning routine. After brushing my teeth, I walked out. Edie met me at the door.

"We're losing her, Mort," Edie said.

She hugged me, and silently we wept.

I awakened both the children and summoned them to our bedroom. Al, still exhausted from the flight home from Europe, had fallen asleep on the couch in the den.

The three of us huddled around the bed. I held Nicki's hand and whispered, "Thank you, babe. Thank you for being part of my life." And then I said what I'd always told her at bedtime: "See you in the morning, Bugs."

I had a few final moments before the undertaker came to take her away. As I held her, I remembered a particularly tender moment from our wedding. It was not in the rehearsal. Nicki had saved it as a complete surprise for me.

Taking both of my hands in hers, she had looked up at me with those big, blue eyes, and in a sweet, gentle voice, sang this promise:

With these hands, I will cling to you
I'm yours forever and a day
With these hands, I will bring to you
A tender love as warm as May
With this heart, I will sing to you

Long after stars have lost their glow
And with these hands, I'll provide for you
Should there be a stormy sea
I'll turn the tide for you,
And I'll never
No, I'll never
Let you go.

Nicki

Chapter Twenty

BUILDING A NEW LIFE

There is no distance on this earth as far away as yesterday.

—ROBERT NATHAN

SUNLIGHT FILTERED through a stained-glass window, adding soft pastels to the gun-metal gray casket. Neither the refracted rainbow nor the casket's blanket of bright yellow roses could lighten the sadness. Yellow roses were her favorite flower, what she always wanted for our anniversary, her birthday, and Valentine's Day.

"We know Nicki is not gone," the minister declared from his neo-Gothic, carved-oak pulpit just above the casket.

How many times had I heard such reassuring words at a funeral? How many times, as a young pastor, had I delivered similar promises of hope?

"Our faith tells us she is with God," he assured the hundreds of mourners who had turned out for Nicki's funeral.

I squeezed Carey's hand. She raised a tissue to her teary eyes. Al, whose tears were too deep to reach the surface, stared blankly at his mother's casket, his clenched but stoic face barely masking an unspeakable pain.

The Reverend Doctor Bruce Rigdon, senior pastor at Grosse Pointe Memorial Church, was also a personal friend who had often visited with us during Nicki's illness. His bedside words of comfort were always reassuring as he tried to prepare us for her final journey. Bruce never attempted to give us false hope that she would recover from the cancer.

Now, Bruce *was* offering the ancient Christian hope always expressed at times like these and supported by the reading of Scripture.

"Mort, we know you will see Nicki again," Bruce declared, looking directly at the children and me.

"As Christians, we have the promise of the resurrection."

I was certain that Nicki was with God—a God I had come to believe was the very essence of love itself—but I still had more questions than answers. To believe Nicki was with God brought comfort, but what, in any sense that I could understand, did that actually mean? Nicki and I had talked about death in our final days together and had promised each other that our goodbye would be only temporary. Most days, I believed that.

I gazed at her casket with an uneasy sense of both hope and doubt. Was it reality or fantasy to believe that individual consciousness continues beyond death? Is there a soul that survives our mortal bodies? The Bible tells us there is, and physical resurrection is a fundamental part of traditional Christian dogma.

During one of Nicki's last hospital stays, as she lay sedated following a difficult procedure, I sat by her bed and wrote a prayer for her. It included these lines. Did they spring more from hope? Or conviction?

We know our last goodbye on earth will be but a preamble to our joyous reunion in that existence beyond human understanding, beyond scientific proof.

We've discovered that not all truth comes to us through the intellect; that cold and calculating reason alone, no matter how thorough or logical, is insufficient to understand that truth . . .

When I left the ministry, I was determined that my faith would be built on a rational foundation and be intellectually defensible. But I also recognized that if the word 'faith' has any meaning at all, it must move us beyond logic and carry us to realities unreachable by reason alone. Yet staring at the casket that soon would take my beloved Nicki into the earth, doubt cast a shadow over my hope of seeing her again.

When I was growing up, our church didn't question such fundamental tenets as Heaven, Hell, or the afterlife. Believing the right doctrines was critical to inheriting eternal life. Belief meant total acceptance of everything the Bible said, even if that required some tortured logic. You had to convince yourself that improbable stories were historically factual; you were expected to rationalize away the Old Testament's fiendish characterizations of God as a vengeful baby-killer. You also had to pretend that the Bible's many inconsistencies were not there.

As a young man, skeptical about this kind of faith, I would say many of the required words the way a hostage is forced to make statements: under duress. I'd been taught that failure to declare unequivocal faith meant the threat of eternal damnation. But belief can't be reduced to a commodity, something to be picked up like a loaf of bread. How do you make yourself *believe* something if you don't? Eventually I decided that if there is a "personal" God, he must respect honest doubt more than forced belief.

All descriptions of Heaven in Scripture, song, art, and poetry are imaginative metaphor, created by humans to explain the unexplainable. If taken literally, many of them paint images of an afterlife no rational person would be eager to experience. Who wants to spend a week, let alone eternity, strolling over gold-paved streets, dressed in white robes, waving palm branches or playing harps in a place where the only meaningful activity is glorifying God, night and day, as He sits on His throne, basking in all that praise while His voice thunders throughout the heavens. Surely most sane people would rather stay dead than to end up forever in such a sterile environment. I can only appreciate such descriptions when I understand them as allegory, not as images meant to be taken literally.

So, I trusted that whatever part of Nicki had survived was now one with the creative power, the mysterious force and the very essence of love. Her death was real. The pain we were feeling was real. So were my questions, my fears, and my doubts. But somewhere within all of that was a tiny grain of faith that gave me some assurance: Nicki is with God. If that was all I could say, for now it would have to be enough.

In his eulogy, our longtime friend Steve Bell brought a moment of relief with a happy reminiscence. His story reminded us of why so many people admired Nicki:

She saw an elderly man, at wits end, unable to get his car going in the snow. She pulled behind him in her new Cadillac, gave a push, and ran under his bumper to the tune of nine-hundred dollars in repairs. As Mort told Nicki, "I can't get mad at somebody for being a Good Samaritan, but next time hire a tow truck and rent him a hotel room. We'll still save money."

To know Nicki was to love her, and the large sanctuary of Grosse Pointe Memorial Church was packed with family and friends who had come from all over the United States to honor her. Even the balcony in the huge, cathedral-like church was filled.

After the funeral, we returned home to host a reception. My agent, Ralph Mann, had flown in from New York. Over the years, Ralph had become a close friend to both Nicki and me.

"Mort, I sure wish I could have your faith," he told me.

"I don't understand it, personally, but it must be of great comfort to believe so firmly that you will see Nicki again."

I didn't want to admit to my Jewish friend that there were times when my faith wasn't all that firm. I raised my wine glass to Ralph's.

"I guess we'll all know, eventually," I smiled.

"To Nicki," Ralph said as our glasses clinked.

* * *

The best thing the kids and I could do was to get away from the house and its memories for a few days.

While anchoring the news on ABC's *Good Morning America*, Steve Bell had filmed some underwater diving stories in the Cayman Islands. Through his contacts there, he arranged accommodations for us at a condominium on Grand Cayman. He also set up some diving excursions for Al and Carey.

It was a mostly silent flight to Georgetown. None of us felt like talking. Only someone who has lost a spouse can understand the empty, hollow feeling that death leaves in the pit of the survivor's stomach. Everything had a sense of unreality to it. In nearly thirty-five years of marriage, I had never taken a vacation apart from Nicki.

While Al and Carey were getting settled into their rooms, I opened my suitcase and took out a framed photo of Nicki. She had signed it, "With all my love, Bugs."

I placed it on top of the dresser and began to weep uncontrollably. Through my sobs, I spoke to the picture.

"I don't know how I'll do it, honey, but for the sake of Al and Carey, I will get through this."

The fun we had on that trip was pleasure without joy. We raced each other on wave runners, sailed a small catamaran just offshore, took a submarine ride, and fed stingrays. I snorkeled while the kids went scuba diving and we all tried as best we could to have a good time. Looking at photographs taken during that trip, the sadness was palpable. The pain was in our eyes.

The trip was "pleasure without joy"

Silence at the dinner table each evening testified to the emptiness we all felt. My Nicki was gone. Al and Carey's mom was not coming back. This was our new reality. In recounting the trip recently, Carey said, "Dad, it was the strangest vacation ever. In fact, it was completely surreal. It was just awful."

At the end of the week, Al went back to Nashville for graduate studies at Vanderbilt and Carey returned to Star of the Sea High School to complete her senior year. Nicki had not realized her dream of living long enough to see Carey graduate, but on commencement day it seemed every relative on both sides of our family converged on Grosse Pointe—Nicki's brother, her sister, aunts, uncles, nieces, nephews, a great aunt, and a grandmother. All of them came for Carey and for Nicki. Despite the outpouring of family support, all Carey could think about was her mother's request:

I just want to live long enough to see Carey graduate.

Carey's emotions reached the breaking point when her trio stood to sing, "When you walk through a storm, hold your head up high."

"Dad, I couldn't finish it," she told me.

I went back to work, sustained by a wonderful group of newsroom colleagues. WDIV would have given me more time off, but I needed to work for my own mental health. I craved the company of other people and wondered how long it would take for the raw pain to go away. The funeral director who handled Nicki's arrangements answered that question for me about a month after her death. We were both filling up our cars at the neighborhood gas station.

"How're you doing, my friend?" he inquired.

"It's tough," I responded.

"Well, Mort," the funeral director said, "I've seen a lot of people in your situation over the years, and this is what I've learned. If you go to grief counseling, read all the books about losing a spouse, and do everything exactly right, it will take you about a year to start recovering.

And if you don't do any of those things, it will take about twelve months."

I got the point. Time, he was telling me, was the only healer and no matter what a person did, the process couldn't be rushed.

Because of my high profile in the community and the press coverage of Nicki's passing, it wasn't long before I started hearing from single women. There were letters, phone calls, and invitations to lunch or dinner. Usually they included photographs. A couple of the pictures were, shall we say, quite provocative. One woman sent me flowers, twice. I was not yet interested in female companionship. Nicki's loss was too recent, the wound still too raw. So, I tried to fill the void in my life with work and friends. Many days, I came into the newsroom hours ahead of schedule just to be with people.

I also welcomed opportunities to join our news team after work. One Friday night each month, we all went bowling. Twice, I invited the news team to my house after the show for a midnight swim. These pool parties allowed me, at least temporarily, to escape the loneliness. One memorable night, I brought my accordion down from the attic and dusted it off, the same accordion I had played at my revival meetings. Sitting on the rim of the pool and dangling my legs in the water, I treated my news colleagues to a rousing polka, *Roll out the Barrel*. When I asked if anyone had a request, there was only one: "Take that damn thing back to the attic!" (It has been said that the definition of a gentleman is a man who owns an accordion but doesn't play it.)

Our late newscast was called the *Night Beat,* and after the show we often retreated to the Anchor Bar across the street to dissect the newscast, trade some newsroom gossip, and share a drink.

After Nicki's death, I started hitting the Anchor more than one night a week. Sometimes I would go two, three, or four nights, and without realizing it, my one drink became two, three, or four. It was a dangerous attempt to mask the grief. Instead of getting home at 1 a.m., sometimes I closed the bar at 2:30. I was treating my emotional pain in the worst and most self-destructive way.

Carey had always been a very responsible child and an unusually mature teenager. Now at seventeen, the loss of her mother seemed to propel her even faster into adulthood. No matter what time I got home, Carey would have completed her homework, tidied up the kitchen, and gone to bed. I made it a point most mornings to be up with her for breakfast before she headed off to school, no matter how late I had gotten home. I don't think Carey was ever aware of the self-destructive way I was dealing with my despondency, nor of the many long nights I was spending at the bar. I was not proud of it.

* * *

In September, nine months after Nicki's death, Carey and I loaded her belongings onto our plane and headed for Chicago. Carey had been accepted at Northwestern University where she planned to study drama. Her single-minded ambition since third grade had been to become an actor.

It was a busy weekend, getting her settled into the dorm and showing her Medill's Fisk Hall, where I had earned my master's degree. I kidded her about attending the drama school, pointing out that I had studied a *real* subject, journalism. The truth is, I was enormously proud of Carey, and I think also a bit envious that she had grown up with the freedom to follow her dream. The church's disdain for show business had made me feel as though my own ambition to become an actor was out of reach.

We hugged and exchanged our goodbyes. Then Carey paused, looked at me and said, "Dad, I think it's time you started to have a social life."

"You mean, time I started dating," I said.

"Well, I don't like thinking about you sitting at home all alone. Mom wouldn't like it. You need to start seeing people."

"Carey, I don't know if I'm ready yet. It hasn't been a full year. I think I'll know when it's time."

Flying back to Detroit alone in the plane, I thought about Carey's words. Like her mother, she had given me permission to move on with my life, letting me know that dating would not dishonor Nicki nor blemish the memories of the life we had shared.

I had married at nineteen. Now, at fifty-four, the whole notion of dating was intimidating. I wasn't interested in pursuing any of the women who had sent letters or called me; these women knew me only as a face on TV. Perhaps for a first date, I should ask somebody I already knew and could feel comfortable with. I called Sylvia Glover. Sylvia was our entertainment reporter with a great personality and a good sense of humor. She had been married to Joe Glover, anchorman at Channel Two. Working with her in the newsroom, I considered Sylvia a good friend.

"Sylvia, you know if we go to any restaurant in Detroit, it's going to be in the papers. What do you say we fly to Chicago for dinner?"

Sylvia's divorce from Joe had been grist for the columnists, and she knew they were just waiting to see whom I would start dating, and when. We flew to Chicago, landed downtown at Meigs Field, and took a taxi to dinner.

We engaged in some newsroom talk, but also discussed what it's like to lose the love of your life. Both divorce and death are experiences of profound loss and I think we both found some common ground in what had happened to us.

After dinner, we strolled Chicago's Magnificent Mile, took a walk out onto Navy Pier, and then flew back to Detroit City Airport. "See you in the newsroom," I said, as we kissed politely and parted company.

I had a few more dinner dates with women in the Detroit area before beginning a longer relationship with someone I had known for several years, Paula Blanchard. Paula and I first met when she was married to Michigan's governor, Jim Blanchard. Since their divorce, she had moved out of Jim's shadow and gone into the public relations business. Her name popped up in the newspapers from time to time, usually linked to a charity or cause that she supported.

One of those articles, with a photo of Paula, caught my eye. We had first met when Jim had asked me to emcee his inaugural ball following his second election as governor. Paula seemed like an interesting, fun person. I knew she was smart, and I had not heard that she was romantically involved with anyone. We were both Democrats. I called her.

By this time, I was comfortable enough with dating that I didn't bother suggesting that we slip out of town. Even though we both were easily recognized in the community, we went out together openly, dining often in Birmingham, the trendy suburb where Paula lived, and on occasion at the London Chop House, Detroit's number-one place to be seen and a favorite of both media and political types. One Sunday, we took my plane to Toronto for brunch, spending the afternoon strolling through a park. Paula was a wonderful conversationalist and she shared my keen interest in politics. I confided in her that earlier in my life, I had considered a political career.

It didn't take long for our names to be linked in the columns. The *Detroit News* conducted a poll to determine which of the city's eligible bachelors would be most compatible with the governor's ex-wife. My name topped the list, but for some reason our relationship didn't materialize. I've never known for sure why it didn't work out—we enjoyed each other's company and had a deep mutual respect. We remained on friendly terms, but sometimes these things just happen.

The last sort of date I ever expected to go on was a blind date, but Dr. Gary Jeffers and his wife, Nancy, thought they knew someone I should meet: Irene Miller.

Irene Bowman Miller's father, like mine, had been a minister in the Church of God. Both of us had attended Anderson University, though she was five years younger than I, so we had never met. Irene's former husband, Dr. Eugene Miller, from whom she had been divorced about six years, had taught music at Anderson. I knew Gene from my years on the university's Board of Trustees but had never met Irene.

"You two need to get together," Nancy had insisted.

Before marrying Gary Jeffers, a dentist, and moving to Michigan, Nancy had attended Anderson University and baby-sat for Irene and Gene. The Jeffers knew me only through television but they were aware of my Anderson University connections and Church of God heritage.

Irene lived in Indianapolis and the Jeffers lived in Northville, a Detroit suburb. They arranged for us to meet at their condo on a Sunday afternoon after one of Irene's visits with her father, who was retired in nearby Hudson. I had just purchased a new Chrysler-Maserati TC, a cardinal red sports roadster with tan leather interior and tan folding top. I couldn't believe that my first night out in this new hot toy was to pick up a blind date. But the moment I saw Irene, the idea didn't seem so crazy. She was gorgeous.

"I've made reservations at the Whitney," I said. "It's an old mansion, built in the 1800s."

Our table was in a cozy corner of the *Library*, a small, quaint room with book-lined shelves, probably appearing much as it did when lumber baron David Whitney and his wife, Flora Ann, lived there.

"Did you know my son was one of the graduates you spoke to at Anderson?" Irene informed me as we relaxed over cocktails.

"Really? Did he like the speech?" She laughed.

I had delivered the commencement address at Anderson University's graduation a few weeks earlier, but was unaware that Irene's son, Jeff, was among those receiving a degree that night. That was only the first of many connections I discovered that Irene and I shared as a result of our Church of God roots.

I was instantly smitten by Irene. Not only was she stunningly beautiful, but also smart, sophisticated, and obviously well-informed. She was a Republican, but one of the rare moderates who still existed in the GOP at that time.

"Would you like to meet my dogs?" I said, after paying the check. I'm sure it sounded like a clumsy come-on line, comparable to "Would you like to visit my apartment and see my etchings?" The truth is, my Doberman, Golum, and miniature Dachshund, Bogey, had been sources of comfort and companionship ever since Nicki's death. I loved those dogs, and I suppose it was a sign of my attraction to Irene that I immediately wanted her to meet them.

A new light enters the darkness

"Sure," she said—and to her credit, she managed to say it without laughing.

We drove to my home in Grosse Pointe, where Golum and Bogey met us at the door. After appropriate introductions, lots of tail wagging (by the dogs), and a few licks on the face (by the dogs), Irene and I sat on the couch and talked for about an hour.

"Would you like to spend the night?" I offered, hastening to add, "We have a guest room."

"No, I'd better not do that," she said with a smile.

We drove back to the Jeffers' condo in Northville, kissed and said goodnight.

After that, I had a couple of casual dates in Detroit but my heart wasn't in them. I kept thinking about Irene. That one evening with her had turned out to be quite special. Not long afterward, I got a call from Nicki's brother, Chuck, who lived just south of Detroit in Findlay, Ohio. Chuck and I had been close for years and had made some business investments together.

"Mort, Sandy and I are bringing a client and his wife to Detroit to see *Les Miz* at the Fisher Theater. We'll be having dinner before the show. Why don't you get a date and join us?"

"Sounds good," I said, thinking of Irene even before I had hung up the phone. I invited her to Detroit for the weekend.

Chuck and his party arrived at the Pegasus restaurant in the Fisher Building ahead of us. Walking up to their table, I said, "I'd like you to meet Irene."

Chuck stood up, looked a bit startled, held out his hand and said, "Irene Bowman. You're Irene Bowman."

"Chuck? Chuck Dale?" she said, smiling broadly.

"Mort just told me his brother-in-law was named Chuck. He didn't mention your last name."

"Mort, Irene and I were in college together at Anderson," Chuck said.

Was this a sign? I wondered.

After that, Irene and I began a long-distance romance made possible by my airplane and Southwest Airlines. Irene was an administrator with Social Security, so our jobs meant dating was limited to weekends. One weekend I would fly the Seneca to Indianapolis, and the next weekend she would catch a Southwest flight to Detroit.

I knew that Irene planned to be in Hudson, Michigan to visit her dad on Father's Day, so I suggested that we meet that afternoon as she was on her way back to Indianapolis. Coldwater seemed a good midpoint. I flew the Seneca there and she picked me up at the airport. Our first stop was an ice cream parlor, and as the girl behind the counter handed us our cones, she looked intently at me and said, "Sir, I have to ask you a question."

Coldwater was within our TV coverage area and I was certain that this girl recognized me. I also presumed she was about to ask for an autograph. That would be good. It would impress Irene.

"Yes?" I said, preparing to pull out my pen.

"Well sir, I just have to ask if you're a dad, because it's Father's Day and if you are, your ice cream is free."

A teenage girl had just reduced a Ron Burgundy-sized ego to pulp.

Irene and I took a walk through a lovely riverfront park, eating ice cream, holding hands, and talking in general about our lives and the future. I don't remember the details of our conversation, but it must have been somewhat specific because when I called her that evening, she said, "Mort, I have to ask you something. Did you propose to me today? Because if you did, I want to make sure I didn't miss it."

"Honey, when I *do* propose to you, there won't be any question about it," I laughed. She laughed. We said goodnight.

I had not asked her to marry me in so many words, but I could understand why she was confused about it. We had talked about what a future together might mean. We discussed our grown children and their possible reactions. My specific phrasing, "When I *do* propose to you," could have left no doubt about my intentions. But it's my nature to want important occasions to be well planned and properly executed, not casually stumbled into.

One Sunday afternoon while I was visiting her in

Indianapolis, Irene said, "Mort, I have something really important to tell you."

I didn't have a clue what was coming but her expression told me it was serious.

"I know what you went through with Nicki, and I have to tell you this. A few years ago, I had breast cancer. They performed a lumpectomy and treated me with radiation. The doctors think I'm cured, but I can't let you move ahead in this relationship without knowing that. And if that changes anything for you, I'll understand."

My response was immediate.

"Irene, it doesn't change anything. Life is uncertain. I could be hit by a truck tomorrow, or have a heart attack, or develop cancer.

Don't give this another thought," I said, "because I don't intend to."

On a clear night in July, we flew to Nashville to spend some time with Al. By now I had started calling Irene by her nickname, Renee (pronounced REE-nee). Both Al and Carey knew that my relationship with her was becoming serious and they seemed fine with it, as did her two sons, Jeff and Randy.

The plane was flying on autopilot as Renee and I relaxed, drank coffee, and enjoyed the lights of cities as they passed beneath our wings. The only sound was the soft purr of the engines and occasional radio chatter from a flight controller. As we flew over the last town before the blackness of Kentucky Lake, I pulled a bag from the back seat.

"I brought you back a little something from Russia," I said.

I had recently returned from filming a documentary about life after Communism in the Soviet Union.

"Oh, I love it," she said, as she removed a brightly painted red and yellow Matryoshka, the traditional Russian nesting doll, from the bag.

"Well, why don't you open it up," I suggested.

"I know, there's just another doll in it, and another inside that."

"Of course. But go ahead and check it out. We've got nothing up here but time."

Renee began to open the dolls, pulling a slightly smaller one from the main doll, then a smaller one from that, and still a smaller one, spreading all of them out over the airplane floor until she was down to the tiniest doll of all. It was no bigger than a finger. Around that doll's neck was a diamond ring.

"I told you that when I proposed, you would know it," I smiled. "That didn't come from Russia, I bought it in Amsterdam on our way back. Carey helped me pick it out."

Al had worked for me as an equipment grip a year earlier on my first visit to Russia, so this time I'd given the job to my daughter. The fact that she had helped me select an engagement ring and suggested the nesting-doll surprise signaled to Renee that Carey was totally okay with the woman I had chosen to marry.

"So, Renee," I said into my microphone, "will you marry me?"

We embraced across the console that separates the pilot and co-pilot seats, and, tilting the headset microphones out of the way, we kissed.

Then Renee said the words I had been waiting for:

"Yes, Mort, I will marry you."

I made an X on my chart, marking the exact spot over Kentucky Lake where Renee and I had become engaged.

* * *

"We're doing a story on your engagement," the reporter said as he shoved a microphone toward Renee's face.

She was nearly blinded by the bright television light atop the camera. It was Renee's first visit to Detroit since our engagement had been announced. Columnists had already run the story along with her photograph, but as she stepped off the jetway at Detroit City Airport, she had not expected this.

"How do you feel about marrying the city's top anchorman?" the reporter asked. Finding herself in the spotlight was just one of many adjustments Renee would face as a result of becoming Mrs. Mort Crim. She would be giving up her job, moving to a new city, and leaving her two sons and closest friends back in Indiana.

After our July engagement, we settled on January 5 as our wedding date. It was to be a small private affair, family and close friends, with Renee's brother, the Reverend Ed Bowman, conducting the ceremony. By September, both of us were tiring of the long-distance relationship and the weekend trips. We were eager to be together full-time but the idea of Renee moving in with me prior to the wedding did not seem like an option. None of our religious relatives would have condoned such an arrangement, and for Renee's father and my mother, our living together unmarried would have been deeply hurtful. So, I proposed a solution:

"Renee, let's elope."

"What? We can't do that," she said.

"Everybody's already been told that the wedding is January 5."

"We don't have to change that," I said.

"We can get married secretly in Florida. That will keep it out of the Detroit papers.

Once we're married, we can tell your dad, my mom, and your brother so they will know that we aren't living in sin. They will keep our secret, you can move in with me and," I added with a chuckle, "Our kids might even think we're cool for living together."

We both laughed at that thought.

After considering it for a couple of days, Renee agreed, and we began planning to pull it off during the last weekend in October. We invited Renee's son, Randy, and his college buddy, Jon Abbey, to fly with us to Florida. I flew the Seneca to Metropolitan Airport, a small field north of Indianapolis, where Renee, Randy, and Jon were waiting. The boys had no clue that this was to be a wedding trip. We had agreed that our children were not to be let in on the secret elopement.

Sunday, the day we were scheduled to fly home, Renee and I exchanged our shorts and flip flops for some dressier clothes and told Randy and Jon we were off to have a meeting with our realtor. The boys then motored away from the condo in our bass boat, *Gator Hunter*, for some fishing. We had told them the truth, just not all of it. We *were* meeting our realtor, who was a notary public, and in Florida notaries can perform weddings. We had arranged for another friend, also a realtor, to accompany us as a witness.

We drove to Craig Field, met the realtors at our hangar, and along with a photographer, boarded the plane. Renee and I had become engaged in the Seneca so why not get married in it?

Climbing to an altitude of fifty-five-hundred feet, I headed for our condominium and proceeded to circle it. I radioed

Jacksonville approach control.

"Jax approach, this is Seneca One One Hotel Romeo with a request."

For the record, Renee had asked me early on if *Hotel Romeo* was a vanity call sign. I assured her that the letters, H-R, had come with the plane.

"Go ahead, One Hotel Romeo."

"Sir, we are about to have a wedding aboard this aircraft, and I'm requesting radar surveillance."

"Roger, Hotel Romeo. Who's the groom?"

I paused.

"Jax Approach, I am the groom."

There were several seconds of silence.

"Hotel Romeo, would you repeat your last transmission? We've never had a wedding before, and I want to put you on the speaker so everybody in the control room can hear it."

I complied.

"Okay, Hotel Romeo, proceed with the wedding. We'll keep a good eye on you. Advise when you've finished the *I do's.*"

"Roger that," I responded, then switched on the autopilot, turned to Renee, and asked for my copy of the wedding vows that she and I had written.

As we continued to circle one mile above our condominium, we exchanged our vows while photographer Carl Miller clicked away from the back of the plane. Then Gloria Thompson pronounced us husband and wife with Lynn Sickinger watching as our official witness. There were no rings. We wouldn't wear those until the real wedding in January.

"Mission accomplished," I radioed to Jax Approach.

"One Hotel Romeo, returning to Craig."

I landed more than the airplane that day

"Roger, Hotel Romeo. And congratulations."

We landed, kissed again for the photographer, thanked our wedding party, and drove back to Ponte Vedra. The boys had just returned from a successful fishing jaunt.

"Caught the nicest bass I've ever gotten," Randy said.

I squelched the urge to say, *Yeah, son, you wouldn't believe the nice catch I got.*

Later that afternoon, we were back at the airport, ready to fly home. Randy and Jon had no clue that Renee and I had been at that same airport, in the same airplane, only hours earlier.

"Here are a couple of headsets for you guys," I said, handing one to each of them in the back seat.

"Craig Ground, November One One Hotel Romeo, Craig Air Center with Zulu, ready to taxi, IFR, to Kilo Uniform Mike Papa."

"Roger, Hotel Romeo, cleared to runway three two via Alpha."

Then, after a brief pause,

"Hotel Romeo, am I talking to the happy newlyweds?"

I gasped. I glanced at Renee. Her look was just north of terror. If Randy or Jon had heard that transmission from the controller, our cover was blown, our secret elopement exposed.

"Uh, Ground, that information you just transmitted is confidential," I halfway whispered into the microphone.

Another pause.

"Oh, sorry about that, One Hotel Romeo. Cleared to taxi as requested."

Finally, I worked up the courage to turn around. To my relief, both Randy and Jon were chatting away, oblivious to the radio talk. Neither had yet put on his headset.

When she got home, Renee filed her resignation papers with Social Security and two weeks later moved in with me. We knew our parents and her brother were comforted by knowledge that the two of us were not living in sin.

On January 5, almost exactly two years after Nicki's death, Renee and I exchanged vows at the Grosse Pointe War Memorial, a community center on the Lake, adjacent to Memorial Church, with her brother Ed officiating. My longtime friend Steve Bell shared Best Man duties with John Burrows, the physician who had cared so wonderfully for Dad and for Nicki.

It was a small event—fewer than fifty family members and close friends. Out of respect for our families, we served only non-alcoholic beverages and made our toasts with sparkling grape juice. The marriage ceremony marked the closing of important life chapters for both Renee and me, and the beginning of a new one. At one point during the reception, I made a silent toast of my own:

"Thank you, Nicki, for encouraging me to build a new life."

In our wedding album, we have copies of two marriage certificates: one from Florida, one from Michigan, both of them signed and legal. Which raises a question I'm nervous about putting to our attorney: does marrying the same woman twice in two different states make me a bigamist?

Through divorce and death, both Renee and I had suffered and survived. We had evolved and matured. We understood, I believe, the nature and the demands of true love in ways that no younger person possibly can. Our similar backgrounds, and especially the religious culture from which we came, helped create a bond that may be difficult for people who weren't raised in such a tradition to appreciate. Today, when we are singing a hymn in church, sometimes we laugh and say, "How many other married couples know all the verses to this one!"

Not only did I hit the jackpot when I found Renee, but I've come to love and cherish her children—and now, our five grandchildren. We long ago stopped referencing *your kids* or *my kids*. Today, they're all simply *our* kids.

In a world where you're fortunate to find true love once in a lifetime, how lucky I was to find it twice.

Chapter Twenty-One

SOME SECOND THOUGHTS

The sole aim of journalism should be service.

—MAHATMA GANDHI

"HEY, CRIM, why don't you and I trade jobs?"

I had just taped an interview with the Michigan governor in an adjoining studio, and as we walked past the news set, he slid into my anchor chair.

Folding his hands on the desk, he looked solemnly into the camera.

"Good evening. This is Jim Blanchard."

His voice playfully mocked anchorman sincerity. The governor had no idea of the irony in his good-natured suggestion. Trading my job in journalism for a political career was something I had seriously thought about more than once. When we left Louisville, I believed the door to politics was closed, but three times in Detroit the door cracked open again. In the mid nineteen eighties, some influential Democrats suggested I run for Congress, and in the same year a major GOP donor approached me at a cocktail party and asked if I would consider running as a Republican. I always took it as a compliment to my fairness as a journalist that neither party seemed aware of my political views.

Governor Jim Blanchard joked that we should "trade jobs"

In the early nineties, two prominent representatives for the Democratic party approached me about running for Governor of Michigan. They claimed that nearly a million dollars were already available to my campaign if I would say yes. As I've noted, there were times during my career when I envied the politicians I covered. I thought that perhaps we reporters were only bystanders while the elected officials were the ones actually changing society. However, by the time a run for governor was on the table, I had long been convinced that nothing is more crucial to a functioning democracy than a free and honest press. As Thomas Jefferson said, "Were it left to me to decide whether we should have a government without newspapers or newspapers without a government, I should not hesitate a moment to prefer the latter."

Rarely has there been a time in our history when the need

for a free press to protect the public interest has been greater than it is today. Our social media is saturated with partisan propaganda, from posts by Russian bots to purposefully fake news. Anyone with a Facebook or a Twitter account has potential access to millions of people, no matter how bizarre, dangerous, distorted or false their opinions. Sadly, assaults on the press are also at historic levels while public confidence in media is at an all-time low. Unfortunately, the profession in which I invested my professional life must bear some of the blame for current audience skepticism.

Television has blurred the distinction between the opinionators who dominate news channels and honest, objective reporters who go about the business of uncovering and presenting facts. Such reporters still exist, but because news channels have fuzzied the lines between news and commentary, the public has become distrustful of *all* media.

Although the internet is gaining as a prime source of information, television remains the place where a majority of Americans get their news. As Fox News and MSNBC have staked out positions on opposite ends of the ideological spectrum, it has become increasingly difficult for viewers to sort out fact from opinion, or even to recognize the difference between the two. At times these channels use important information merely as a script for entertainment; they've learned that pushing agendas and hot buttons is a sure way to increase ratings and boost income.

There are still solid, professional journalists working at all the news channels, many of whom I know personally. They are as committed to truth as the best journalists were during my years in media, but because there's no clear line today between news and commentary, these honest reporters suffer from the widespread perception that all media is biased. The partisan channels tend to drown out the clear, fair, and objective reporting that goes on every day in hundreds of newsrooms around the country—TV, radio, and print. This plays directly into the dangerous narrative that none of the media can be trusted and that it all traffics in 'fake news.'

Attacks on the press are nothing new and there has always been tension between the watched and the watchers. Many presidents have feuded with individual columnists or reporters; President Nixon's infamous enemies list had several reporters on it. One biographer writes that President Kennedy regarded newspapers as his natural enemy. During the George W. Bush presidency, some journalists were threatened with jail, and Vice President Cheney once kicked reporters off his airplane.

But no President before Donald Trump has ever publicly described the entire journalism profession as the enemy of the people. Such words, normally associated with dictators and despots, are an attack not only on a fundamental foundation of democracy, but they further erode the capacity of Americans to respect and work with each other. When we view those with whom we disagree as disloyal, unpatriotic, or un-American, cooperation becomes impossible. It may be fun for viewers to see the people they don't like being bashed by their favorite commentators and pundits, but the 24/7 drumbeat of hyper-partisanship and parochialism further divides our highly polarized society. Unless the gap can somehow be narrowed, it could prove disastrous for the nation. As Lincoln reminded us, a house divided cannot stand. Closing the gap has to begin with a common acceptance of what is true.

We all have a right to our own opinions, but when we no longer can agree on facts, then democracy is in trouble. Determining the facts is not easy these days. Mix in the cacophony of cable news with unrestrained rants on talk radio, unverified diatribes and outright lies on the internet and from the White House, and you have a kind of media mayhem that can confuse even the most sophisticated seeker of information.

During my four decades of reporting, it became clear to me that most Americans, regardless of their politics, generally want the same things for themselves and for our country: fair treatment; equal opportunity; good schools; clean air and water; good jobs; honest and efficient government; and strong national and personal security. Most of our differences are not about these shared goals, but about how best to achieve them, and what the government's role should be. Democrats tend to emphasize the communal or government approach to problem-solving while Republicans rely more heavily upon private or individual effort. History teaches that success requires both.

At the dedication of his Presidential library, Bill Clinton observed that America needs conservatives to hold the lines that should never be crossed, and liberals to erase the lines that never should have been drawn. It has always been in the middle—between the two philosophies, in the dynamic tension of competing viewpoints—that America has made its greatest progress.

I saw a dramatic demonstration of this teamwork while covering the Apollo moon flights. When President Kennedy pledged to put Americans on the moon within a decade, we possessed neither the equipment nor the know-how to do it. Designing, building, and testing the complex rocketry and associated systems needed for space flight demanded a massive commitment and investment by government and business. It was a collective effort. To borrow a now-famous line, it took a village.

But it also required the initiative, training, and bravery of individual astronauts to ultimately make the whole enterprise work. Neither government nor private initiative can resolve our most serious problems alone. Our greatest successes come when Americans and their institutions work together. There may appear to be short-term political gains to be had by exploiting our differences, stirring racial and regional bigotry, and purposely seeking to divide. But in the long run, Martin Luther King, Jr., will be proved correct:

"I believe that unarmed truth and unconditional love will have the final word."

There are some ominous signs that after fifty years of civil rights progress, our nation may be slipping backwards, and that we are now losing what we've gained in the battle against racism, religious bigotry, homophobia, xenophobia, sexism, and other forms of intolerance. Overcoming these evils has never been a sure thing, and any incremental victories are never final. But the long arc of our history bends toward justice and fairness. Today's journalists have a clear obligation and an exciting opportunity to help America build on its unique heritage and progress. We do that first by telling the truth.

Over the course of my life, I've witnessed breathtaking changes in the means for delivering news, and those changes seem to continue at warp speed. But the reporter's main responsibility has not changed. Whether working for a newspaper, magazine, television station, writing a blog, podcasting, or communicating through new platforms yet to be imagined, the essential job of the journalist remains constant: Shed light into dark places. Report the facts with honesty and integrity. Speak truth to power.

When journalists do these things, they facilitate positive change; telling the truth is a powerful way to destroy the assumptions underlying prejudice and narrow mindedness. My good friend, Ted Koppel, believes our profession has veered seriously off track by sacrificing objectivity for advocacy. I'm afraid there are more than enough examples to justify his concern across all types of media. Redrawing that important line between fact and opinion is one way we can restore audience confidence in journalism and begin rebuilding public trust in journalistic institutions. Whenever someone asks if I wish I were still reporting the news, I usually answer with a smile, "I think I got into the business, and out of it, at the right time."

The truth is, if I had it to do all over again, I would. How many jobs come with a window on the world, pay you to watch the greatest show on earth every day, and give you the opportunity to make a difference? Admittedly, practicing journalism was simpler before there was cable news and social media, and when the line between news and commentary was clear and mostly observed. Add to that the financial realities that are squeezing the life out of newspapers and forcing TV reporters to do more with less, and it's clear that today's journalists face far more daunting challenges than my colleagues and I did.

But the best reporters have never ducked a challenge, whether digging into backroom dealings at City Hall, dodging bullets in a warzone, or risking their own safety to cover the coronavirus pandemic. We should all be inspired as we watch a new generation of television and newspaper journalists who refuse to be discouraged by the critics, intimidated by the

President's threats, or discouraged by the media's failings. Many of our best reporters go largely unnoticed as they work at small-town newspapers and television stations. But their persistent search for the facts often is more relevant to the health and well-being of their communities than is all of the Washington punditry combined.

It should be encouraging that amidst all the chaos, the commotion and the changes, there are still young men and women who are committed, above all, to telling the truth—reporters for whom journalism is not a job, but a calling.

Chapter Twenty-Two

ANCHORED AT LAST

I always get to where I'm going by walking away from where I've been.
—WINNIE THE POOH

EVERY NEWS STORY should include the five w's: *who, what, when, where,* and *why.* We learn that in our first journalism class.

Well, frankly, when it comes to my own story, I've struggled a lot with the *why.*

Why are we here? Is there any ultimate truth we can absolutely depend upon in this rapidly changing world?

Is there a fixed point? A foundation? Some solid place to stand?

Is there an anchor to hold us secure in life's storms?

For my parents, that anchor was their faith that God exists,

Jesus is his son, and the Bible is God's word. End of question.

For me, that was only the beginning of the question.

In the gospel song "Old-Time Religion," Buck Owens sings, "It was good enough for Mama, it was good enough for Papa . . . and it's good enough for me." But my inherited faith was *not* good enough for me. Early in life I began to be uneasy about many of the things Mother and Dad held as absolute truth.

Why did they believe? Had they only accepted what their parents told them about God? And had their parents simply believed what their parents had taught, and so on and so on? In many ways, the faith they handed down to me had the comfortable, easy, familiar feel of a well-worn shoe. But could their faith stand up to honest scrutiny? Was it anchored solidly to anything other than tradition and their own will to believe?

I recognized that truth can stretch us beyond the strictly rational, and that faith can take us deep into realities that intellect alone can never reach. If this weren't true, then the word faith would have no meaning. But moving beyond empirical evidence and pushing past the boundaries of known facts is not the same as denying facts. I simply could not accept a faith that, in some ways, contradicted the obvious, defied logic, and demanded a betrayal of reason.

Renaissance historian Bernard Berenson said, "Consistency requires you to be as ignorant today as you were a year ago." The faith that I claim today is alive, dynamic, still growing, and full of surprises. It is a faith that finds its focus in Jesus. I am unashamedly a follower, not always a good one, but constantly drawn toward the Jesus I've come to know as an experience. But to find this Jesus, I had to dig through layers of church lore, myth, fantasy, fairy tale, and misconception. The Jesus I eventually discovered is an engaging cosmic force that breaks through both my self-centeredness and my logic.

This Jesus is love itself, a love that revolutionizes life, a universal energy so powerful that it bursts through the constrictions of any name or belief system designed to contain it. What I believe about Jesus is not as important as my belief in him. In studying Jesus' words as recorded in the Bible, I don't find him saying, "Believe that I was born to a virgin, and you can be my disciple.

Believe that I turned water into wine, or that I walked on water, or that I raised Lazarus from the dead, and you can be my follower."

In making discipleship contingent upon declarations of such dogma, Jesus' simple invitation to *follow me* can be put out of reach for those of us whose minds stumble over tales of the supernatural. At its essence, his call was to love God and to love each other. He said his disciples would be known by their attitudes and their actions—love, kindness, humility, grace, forgiveness, generosity—not by passing a litmus test of beliefs. For me faith is a verb. At its core, it is about what we do, how we relate to each other, and how responsibly we care for creation.

Jesus may have been talking about people like me when he said we shouldn't try to store new wine in old wine skins, because when the juice begins to ferment, those skins will burst under the pressure. When profound questions about God, Jesus and the Bible began to ferment in my mind, my old belief systems could no longer contain these troubling views. I simply had to have some new skins.

I no longer view God through my parents' lens, but I believe I experience the same reality that sustained and guided their lives.

I don't read the Bible in the literalistic way that they did, but I still find within its pages the living water and bread of life that Jesus promised. My faith is not shaken by scientific revelations; I find each new discovery exciting, and it leaves me as much in awe of this complex universe as the ancient writer of Psalm 19: "The heavens declare the glory of God; the skies proclaim the work of His hands." (Psalm 19:1 NIV) With a fresh and less literal interpretation, the Bible has become a wonderful periscope through which I view aspects of human existence that are beyond the range of the quantifiable. Reading it now lets me share the experiences of other people who have struggled with the great questions even as I have struggled, and who have wrestled with the same frailties, weaknesses, and sins.

Now that I no longer take the Bible literally, I am able to take it seriously. Imperfect as they are, the Scriptures carry such power, such truth, such life-changing and dynamic force, that they have survived every attempt over the generations to eradicate them. Yet, at last count, there are more than thirty thousand Christian denominations, most of them believing their truth just as adamantly as the church I grew up in believed its truth. Countless other religions make similar claims, and within all religions there are splinter groups convinced that only their narrow interpretation of the faith is correct.

We have seen how claims of exclusive truth can lead to dangerous extremism. Not all who believe they know the true pathway to God are a threat to others, but we have learned, painfully, the potential danger that lurks in the dark recesses of any belief system that refuses to respect other viewpoints.

Religion by its very nature can be contentious, dividing people between believers and infidels, the saved and the lost, those who are in and those who are out. For all the good that's been accomplished in the name of religion, bad religion has been responsible for much evil and suffering.

Truth is especially hard to handle when it calls into question things we've always believed. Any challenge to the status quo can be unsettling; when I began scrutinizing the beliefs upon which my family had built their lives, and in some cases their careers, it was painful. Common beliefs and assumptions are the glue that holds families, ethnic groups, and societies together. Defying the tribe's assumptions risks disapproval of the people we love most.

In order to attend her senior prom, Renee arranged to spend the night with a friend. The friend's mother had no idea that Renee was not permitted to attend dances. The next morning, Renee overheard her on the phone talking to Renee's father about what a wonderful time the girls had at the dance. When he came to pick her up, her father said nothing until they were almost home. Then, without raising his voice, he said, "I'm so disappointed in you."

Renee still remembers, decades later, how those words cut like a knife. (If fear of Hell isn't sufficient to keep the faithful in line, there's always shame.) To me, challenging the rules sometimes felt like betrayal, but once honesty became more important than my own charade of certainty or the approval of others, there was no turning back. It was the beginning of an exciting, lifelong adventure of discovery.

I have in my library a book by David Dark entitled *The Sacredness of Questioning Everything*. Dark is a Christian thinker who believes that to seriously and honestly question is our only hope for escaping the closed-minded narrowness that perpetuates divisions and conflict. I share this view. I also think that any unexamined faith is not worth believing.

I have experienced in my own life the revolutionary power of love. It is my personal witness to this transformational power that has brought me to some conclusions in my long search for truth, a search that never took me very far from the heart of my parents' faith: Jesus.

He was their simple explanation for the dynamic and unconditional love that I saw demonstrated in their lives. It was example, not exhortation, that brought me back to Jesus as the cornerstone of my faith.

So what does it mean when I say that that Jesus is a living reality and presence in my life? When I expressed to a friend my skepticism about an angelic being showing up to roll away a big stone so a resuscitated body could emerge, she said, "Why, Mort, the resurrection is so much more real than merely a resuscitated body."

Her answer was bigger than my doubts. I sensed in her wise words an acknowledgement that the presence of a living Jesus in my life is more important than whether I interpret the resurrection story literally. My logical brain wrestles with the concept of a dead body coming back to life and eventually flying up into the sky where ancient people believed God lived. Nevertheless, on Easter Sunday, I can still enthusiastically sing, "He Lives!"

You see, I believe it was the spirit of unconditional love for all humanity that survived the grave; it was hope, meaning, and confidence that there is an ultimate purpose to my life and to yours. The true miracle of the Resurrection for me is the reality of a living Jesus, present with us in spirit. I no longer am concerned with the literalness of how it happened. I only know that the more I try to follow Jesus and his teachings, the more

I sense the reality of God.

The God I can believe in is the God who becomes real in relationships. God only becomes personal as I discover Him in service to others; the poor, the weak, the marginalized and the forgotten ("Whatever you did not do for one of the least of these, you did not do for me"[Matthew 25:45 NIV]).

As I review my life and career, I realize that every story I reported, every documentary we produced, and every commentary I wrote was a call to live my faith. So was that moment when I took time to listen to a discouraged or distraught friend, or made an extra effort to speak to that colleague who was unpopular, even shunned by his coworkers.

Looking back, I realize that God was right there, working through me, even in times of despair and emptiness when I didn't recognize it, or my logical brain prevented me from acknowledging it. Jim Snyder's challenge to 'help a broken old city find its way back' was a perpetual test of my faith, even while I was unsure of what I believed. It is not easy following the revolutionary and counter-cultural teachings of Jesus; every value he stood for is contradictory to society's norms and to human nature. To a world of greed, he preached generosity. To the proud and self-centered, he called for humility and service. To the ambitious, he said that the first should put themselves last. Grace, forgiveness, and self-sacrifice are not the natural way, but they are Jesus' way.

I sense God's acceptance and love each time I share the bread and the wine in the remembering ceremony we followers of Jesus call communion or Eucharist. The concept may baffle my mind, but the reality of Jesus' love and sacrifice touches my heart.

Prayer also remains a deep mystery to me, but I have experienced its power to see me through my darkest hours. CBS anchor Dan Rather once asked Mother Teresa what she said during her prayers.

She answered, "Nothing. I listen."

Rather then asked, "Well then, what does God say when you pray?"

To that Mother Teresa smiled and responded, "He listens."

What a beautiful description of the mysterious communication we call prayer.

Since I no longer believe in a deity who redirects storms, cures cancer, or decrees that some children be born with severe deformities, why do I continue to pray? I've never found a better answer to that question than the following words by pastor and writer John Pavlovitz:

"I still ask for people to pray and I still pray, but I try to reorient my prayers these days.

I no longer believe in prayer as a cause-and-effect endeavor.

I don't believe in a supernatural Santa Claus who dispenses life and death based on the conduct or heart of the recipients.

I don't believe in a God who withholds miraculous healing or compassionate care—until sufficiently begged by us to do so.

I believe prayer works by unlocking our empathy for others.

I believe it binds us together in relationship.

I believe it to be a beautiful expression of love for people who are suffering.

I believe it connects us personally to God in ways that cannot be quantified.

I believe it is a sacred act of kindness.

But I don't believe prayer can change God's mind about

healing people we love—nor do I want it to."

As for life after death, my faith gives me a calm assurance that whatever comes next will be okay, and any thought I might give to the hereafter would be mere speculation. All of the art, music, poetry, and biblical accounts of heaven are no more than metaphor and analogy. I believe that my life and personality will continue in some form after death, but that's as much as I feel comfortable saying, and even this is a matter of faith. It is certainly not provable. However, it is here, at the edge of the unknown and the unknowable, that my faith bridges the gap between hope and certainty. I believe that a creative force started the entire cosmos and in death, as in life, I'm willing to trust the God I experience through Jesus. To say that when this life ends I will be with God is all that I can say, and that's enough for now.

Since I don't voice the right words, embrace the formulas, believe all of the orthodoxies, or subscribe to all the doctrines, do I have a right to call myself a Christian? Some will say no, and I'm okay with that. Jesus' first followers weren't known as Christians. He simply called them *friends*. That works for me: A friend of Jesus. Throughout his ministry, it seems to me that he was more accepting of honest, even skeptical, sinners than of hypocrites who professed a faith they didn't live or didn't believe.

Today, my life is anchored not in creeds or affirmations, but in love. I hope each day to come closer to Jesus' ideal of nonjudgmental acceptance of others and gratitude in all circumstances. I will continue trying to follow him as a flawed seeker. I still haven't found all the answers to those questions that haunted me on the banks of an Oklahoma lake nearly 70 years ago. But I have found, in the living Jesus, the source of love and a personal connection to God. Whatever else I've left behind,

I do believe my parents and our church were right about that.

I'm as far from living a perfect life as I am from understanding the ultimate truth. But light chases away darkness, and the more of Jesus' spirit I let into my life, the less room there is for anger, hatred, jealously, covetousness, lust, false pride, ill will toward others, and all those other private failings that are always trying to find a home in my psyche.

This brief excursion we call life continues to be, for me, a wonderful, exciting, and beautiful journey. After eighty-five years, every day my pilgrimage of discovery provides new insights, fresh challenges, and ever-deeper experiences of love. And so I face the future with hope and with confidence:

> "For I am convinced that neither death nor life, neither angels nor principalities, neither the present nor the future, nor any powers, neither height nor depth, nor anything else in all creation, will be able to separate us from the love of God that is in Christ Jesus our Lord."
>
> (Romans 8:38 Berean Study Bible)

Epilogue

Retirement at sixty-five is ridiculous. When I was sixty-five I still had pimples.

—GEORGE BURNS

I BELIEVE THAT RETIREMENT should be a beginning as well as an ending. A friend once told me, "If you run fast enough, old age can't catch you," and since leaving the anchor desk nearly two decades ago, I've been running as fast as I can.

Of course old Father Time eventually will catch us, but trying to outrun him can be both healthy and a lot of fun.

It was never my intention to put the brakes on life. I was inspired by people who refused to let the calendar slow them down—legends such as Paul Harvey, Art Linkletter, George Burns, and my old friend, Colonel Sanders. All of them continued active and productive lives decades past the traditional retirement age.

The last time I saw the late Harland Sanders, the Colonel was in his mid-eighties and still flying around the world promoting his Kentucky Fried Chicken with the vim and vigor of a banty-rooster. Sanders had enough money that he didn't need to work, so I asked what kept him pushing so hard.

"Mort, I think a fella will rust out long before he wears out," he said.

The Colonel did not intend to rust, and neither did I.

When I stepped away from fulltime journalism at the age of 65, I was eager to create more radio commentaries, deliver more speeches, write more books, travel, and grow our fledgling production company. I also looked forward to spending more time with our children and grandchildren, and devoting more time to causes I felt were important.

Renee and I had launched Mort Crim Communications (MCCI), primarily to syndicate my radio series, *Second Thoughts*. By the time I left TV, the series was airing on more than 1,300 U.S. radio stations and overseas on the Armed Forces Radio Network. I knew that leaving the anchor desk would give me more time for those broadcasts.

We began our retirement filled with dreams, goals, travel plans and bucket lists. But, as the bumper sticker says "stuff happens" (that's the sanitized version). And happen it did.

Over the next few years, we experienced a lot that had not been scribbled into our day planners. Some of these serendipities were fun and exciting; some were ominous and scary. All of them reminded us that whatever road we were traveling into our sunset years, there definitely would be no rut to get stuck in.

* * *

I hung up the phone, turned to Renee, and proudly declared,

"Honey, did you ever in your wildest dreams think I would be performing at Carnegie Hall?"

"Mort," she responded with a smile,

"You were never in my *wildest* dreams."

Okay. Feet back on the ground. Renee's sense of humor never disappointed and I'm sure she thought I was joking (I think she was too).

We both knew there was no way my piano playing ever could earn me a spot on that venerable stage, but I was headed there nonetheless. Bill Gaither had just invited me to perform with his Homecoming cast at a musical tribute to the 9/11 First Responders.

Shortly after terrorists attacked the World Trade Center, I wrote an essay called *The Survivor*. America was in shock and mourning in the days following 9/11; there was a cloud of gloom over the nation. In my essay I predicted that Uncle Sam would emerge from the tragedy stronger than ever. Bill had heard a version from my *Second Thoughts* radio broadcast and invited me to perform it with musical backup at his Carnegie Hall concert.

In my own wildest dreams, I could imagine Bill backstage asking me to take a seat at the Steinway and bang out a gospel song from my days on the road with Uncle Alvah. Alas, Bill had heard me play and no surprise—that invitation never came.

The concert turned out to be one of the most moving musical experiences of my life, made especially so when members of the New York City Fire Department joined in singing "A Few Good Men." Tears mixed with wild applause as a packed house remembered and honored those brave firefighters, police officers, Salvation Army troops, and scores more who had risked their lives to save others on that fateful day.

My retirement was off to a beautiful start, and already it seemed my years in television were a lifetime away.

On stage at Carnegie Hall

*   *   *

The receptionist at MCCI buzzed my office.

"You have a call from Jack White."

Having about as much familiarity with contemporary pop music as I did astrophysics, the name Jack White meant nothing to me. But the young receptionist knew, and I'm sure she wondered what Jack White would have to talk about with an old newscaster whose favorite pop songs were written before 1950.

"I heard one of your commentaries," Jack said.

"I want to write a song around it and use some of your words in it."

"You mean write some of the words into your lyrics?" I said.

"No, no, I mean put you in the song. Your voice. Reading your own words."

"Jack, let me get back to you. I'll have to do some checking."

I immediately called my son Al, my go-to person when it comes to the contemporary noise they now call music.

"I can't believe Jack White called you," was Al's immediate response.

Not only was Al a fan, he had known Jack when the pop superstar was growing up in Detroit and Al was part of another local band, Goober and the Peas. (Al was one of the Peas. He played drums.)

"Dad, he's big. Jack White's band is at the top of the charts in England, and he's headed that way in the U.S. You should do it."

"You don't think he simply wants to spoof my commentaries or make fun of them," I asked Al. My motivational *Second Thoughts* features were not the kind of material associated with rock music. It was one thing for my friend Bill Gaither to find my words of wisdom worthy of an audience, but a rock star?

"No, dad, I'm sure he's sincere. But ask him."

I called Jack's agent.

"What's the deal?" I asked.

"Which commentary does Jack intend to use, and how will he use it?"

"It's the one you did about a woman who'd just gone through a painful divorce. She was overwhelmed, but when she saw a squirrel carrying acorns and burying them, one acorn at a time, she decided that's how she could handle her situation."

It didn't sound like a spoof to me. I could have called

my agent in New York, but what the heck—this was a small potatoes deal. No need bothering him. So, I negotiated a contract with Jack's agent—$5,000, which I thought was pretty good. I mean, the work was already done. No additional writing on my part. This would be bonus money.

The White Stripes and a platinum record

When the album *Elephant* with my voice on it went platinum, I realized what a truly lousy deal I'd made. Eventually, it went double platinum: it had sold well over 2 million albums.

"Dad, too bad you didn't just cut yourself in for a few cents per album," my daughter Carey laughed.

There is an old proverb that says: He who is his own lawyer has a fool for a client. This also would seem to be true for he who tries to be his own talent agent.

* * *

"It's definitely cancer," the Mayo Clinic surgeon said as he studied my pathology report.

The diagnosis came as no surprise. A month earlier, the doctor who had removed the polyp during my routine colonoscopy said it looked suspicious. I was immediately put on the surgery schedule.

"It's stage three," the surgeon responded when I asked the

extent of the cancer.

I had read enough to know that, statistically, my chances of living another five years were slightly more than 50-50. Oh well, I'd already lived five years longer than my dad. I figured I was already past my expiration date.

"Don't get hung up on the numbers," the doctor cautioned.

"Remember, they are only averages. Some people do a lot better."

Reassuring, but I also knew that some people did much worse.

During the months of chemotherapy that followed, my determination to beat the odds grew. I knew Renee loved me, but the support and encouragement I got from her and from our children was remarkable.

I've always believed that a positive attitude is an important component of the healing process, and my faith helped me to be calm despite an uncertain outcome. I knew that whatever happened, live or die, I was in God's hands.

It wasn't my first personal encounter with the C word; two years earlier, I had undergone surgery to remove a cancerous prostate. Statistically, my chances of beating that one were considerably better. But no matter what the odds, a diagnosis of cancer is life-changing. It brings a new appreciation for small things, a new understanding of both the preciousness and the precariousness of life. A heightened desire to make every moment count, and a deeper appreciation for relationships—especially with family and close friends.

Intellectually, we all know we have a date with death. But once you've stared squarely down the barrel of your own mortality, the concept of death becomes a lot more personal. It's no longer something theoretical that can be brushed aside by refusing to think about it.

This awareness also prompted serious reflection about my life. How wisely had I lived it? Did my contributions outweigh my mistakes? Had I helped more people than I had hurt?

Most importantly, how did I intend to spend whatever remaining days or years I might have? The calendar took on a new poignancy, and I felt a pressing need to telescope some of my bucket list goals into a shorter timeframe.

One thing was for sure: whatever time I had left would not be wasted. I would put everything I had into making these the best years of my life, investing time and energy into those people and causes that meant the most to me, and squeezing out of life all the joy, happiness, meaning, and satisfaction possible.

I would switch a few priorities.

And I definitely would live with a greater sense of urgency.

* * *

The steady purr of the airplane's single engine provided reassuring background to the voice of Mahalia Jackson. Her rousing rendition of *I'll Fly Away* echoed in stereo through my Bose headphones. I eased my feet off the rudder peddles to tap out the beat.

A light blanket of broken clouds below opened onto brief glimpses of Georgia's Okefenokee swamp. Sunlight from the clear blue sky above danced around the cockpit as it filtered its way through the plexiglass windshield. Surely, this was as close to heaven as a mortal could be.

A pilot flying alone experiences a unique kind of solitude and I was alone—as alone as Charles Lindbergh in the Spirit of

St. Louis, Chuck Yeager in his X-1 rocket plane, or John Glenn aboard the Friendship Seven space capsule.

But I didn't feel alone. Mahalia's joyful proclamation of great things to come matched my own mood of anticipation. After all, I was winging my way toward one of the greatest adventures of my life: an hour earlier I had taken off in an airplane that weighed about the same as the one flown by the Wright Brothers at Kitty Hawk. I called it my Teeny Weeny Airliner. Carey, our daughter, noted that the initials spelled TWA. So, TWA it would be. Now, TWA and I were heading out on a month-long coast-to-coast adventure to prove that even old age and cancer don't have to mean the end of a dream.

A few years ago, I interviewed an instructor pilot who had grown up in Dayton, Ohio, home of the Wright Brothers. He had seen Orville and Wilbur several times in his dad's drug store.

"You know, with the wonderful experiences you've had, why don't you write a book?"

The instructor looked at me with a twinkle in his eye.

'Oh, I plan to one of these days. When I find the time." (It's not likely that instructor ever found the time. When I interviewed him, he was 93.)

A diagnosis of cancer has a way of pulling *someday* right up to your doorstep. You look at your bucket list with a now-or-never perspective.

One dream I had nurtured since I began flying as a teenager was to make a solo cross-country flight, camping along the way next to my airplane. Reading articles by pilots who had done it heightened my desire.

I was approaching my 74th birthday. It had been nearly four years since my colon cancer surgery. Statistically, I had about a fifty-fifty chance of making it to my 75th. If I *really* wanted to live this dream, I shouldn't put it off.

"I think I'll set a goal of flying 7400 miles to celebrate my 74th birthday," I announced to Renee one evening.

She was aware that I had been considering such a flight, and encouraged me to do it.

A few years earlier, I had sold our larger twin-engine business aircraft and purchased a small, two seat, light sport plane. It had less room than the average sports car, but by removing the passenger seat, I could stash a tent, a folding bike, and all the camping gear needed for a month-long flight.

A video taken from a Piper Cub flying from the Midwest to California along the fabled Route 66 had inspired me to take a camera along and produce my own home video for other pilots.

The Experimental Aircraft Association holds its annual Fly-In at Oshkosh, Wisconsin, each July, and for a dozen years, Renee and I had flown there in our larger plane, pitching our tent and camping for a week. This summer, my birthday would come right in the middle of the Fly-In. I decided to make Oshkosh my first stop.

On a clear July morning, in my tiny Skylark loaded to its maximum takeoff weight, I lifted off the runway at Jacksonville's Craig Field and headed north to Wisconsin. Take-offs were always fun, no matter the destination, but the realization of the great adventure that lay beyond the horizon made this one especially exhilarating.

After an overnight stop in Illinois, I arrived at Oshkosh. During the week-long convention, the airport becomes the busiest in the world, with more takeoffs and landings than O'Hare, Kennedy, or Heathrow.

As I approached Wittman Field, there were airplanes behind me, in front of me, and landing on an adjacent runway beside me. During the convention, the FAA suspends normal aircraft separation rules, and we pilots descend on the field from all directions like a storm of determined bees. Cockpit discipline and an exceptional crew of controllers on the ground results every year in a remarkable safety record.

Camping in the midst of several hundred other airplanes was old hat to me, and the convention—the world's largest aviation event—seemed like an appropriate way to kick off my adventure. *Oshkosh,* as the event is referred to by the 30,000 or so pilots and their families who attend, attracts every imaginable kind of airplane, civilian and military, and the superstars of aviation.

Camping at Oshkosh on the eve of my great adventure

By the end of my stay, I had rubbed shoulders or shared meals with famous pilots from General Chuck Yeager to airline hero Sully Sullenberger and media stars from David Hartman to Harrison Ford. The real stars of Oshkosh are the thousands of aircraft from restored World War II fighters and bombers to modern jets and private and home-built airplanes.

I could happily have spent the entire week looking at airplanes, but I had thousands of miles ahead of me, so after three days in this aviation Mecca, I climbed aboard TWA and headed southwestward toward Lake of the Ozarks.

A phone call to the Osage, Missouri, airport was all it took for permission to camp. The airport manager even kept the office unlocked so I could use the bathroom and shower facilities. Most small airports are friendly to pilots that way.

The next morning as the aroma of brewing coffee wafted from the propane camp stove, mixing with the faint smell of new tent canvas, I pulled my bike from the baggage area and unfolded it for travel. After a hearty breakfast of powdered eggs and slightly burned toast, I headed for the lake and a day of fishing—my second-favorite sport after flying.

It wasn't to be my day for catching anything, but that hardly mattered. Sprawled out on the bank watching the water, the families laughing and splashing on the nearby beach, and letting my mind drift with the clouds as their reflection floated past me made it a perfect day. Besides, no catch meant no fish to clean. Hot dogs on the grill tonight would be just fine.

One of the benefits of visual flying in a small airplane is the ability to make up your schedule as you go along. Although I had a rough idea of airports I planned to visit, with Eugene, Oregon, my farthest destination, each day I let weather and my own fatigue level determine how far I would fly.

From Lake of the Ozarks, I traveled west across Oklahoma City, landing in Tucumcari, New Mexico. There I picked up Route 66 and followed it all the way to the Nevada border. Today most of the old 66 is an expressway, I-40, but remnants of the legendary road are still visible from the air.

Flying low, usually between 1,500 and 2,000 feet above the terrain, the scenery was awesome. Mountains towered on either side, and flying over deserts pumped so much hot, dry air into my un-airconditioned cockpit, it was at times hard to breathe.

But I loved every minute of it, and after decades of flying larger, more sophisticated aircraft at higher altitudes, TWA became a time machine, taking me back to my teen years; flying

Flying TWA over Arizona

Piper Cubs, Aeroncas, Ercoupes, and Cessna 140's. My TWA had autopilot, radar, traffic alert, and many other modern electronics that were non-existent for small planes when I started flying in 1950. Still, the feel on the controls, the fun of slow flight, and the incredible view from low altitude brought back all the adolescent emotions that had turned my fascination with flying into an incurable lifelong passion.

At the Tucumcari airport, I ran into a couple on their way back to California from Oshkosh in their Great Lakes biplane. We decided to fly in formation until our paths would part at the Colorado River where I would turn north toward Las Vegas and they would continue west to California. Besides making new friendships, Danny Matthews and I got some excellent photographs of each other's airplanes in flight.

After parting company with the obligatory rocking wing salutes, I headed to Las Vegas to visit two of my dearest friends, Vince Leonard and his wife, Frankie. Besides co-anchoring the news in Philadelphia, Vince and I had been partners in a couple of airplanes. The Leonards met me at the North Las Vegas airport and expressed some amazement that I'd made such a long trip in such a tiny airplane.

At their house in Sun City, Vince's office was lined with memories—photos from our newsroom days together. Sadly, two of our team had passed on: Jessica Savitch and our weatherman, Bill Kuster. Vince and I mugged for my video camera, pretending to do a newscast, just for old time's sake.

From Las Vegas I flew to the California coast, then north to Eugene, Oregon, to visit our son Al, who laughed at TWA, saying he was impressed by my 7,000 mile journey but volunteered that he wouldn't fly seven miles in "that thing." I countered that I would feel less safe going seven blocks on his Harley. It was clearly a stand-off.

The flight back to Jacksonville took me over California wine country, Texas farms, and an overnight stop in New Orleans. In the famed French Quarter, I enjoyed some great jazz music and took a riverboat cruise with one of my favorite bands, the Dukes of Dixieland. I guess my news instincts were still alive and well, because I couldn't resist renting a car for a day and surveying the damage left from hurricane Katrina. I even interviewed a few of the survivors. Why? I don't know. Just because it's what journalists do. I actually did use one short clip of a survivor in my video.

By the time I returned to Jacksonville, I had exceeded my goal of 7400 miles. In 31 days I had logged 8,772 statute miles at an average ground speed of 121 miles per hour, landed and taken off 72 times from 31 airports, shot more than 15 hours of video, and collected enough memories to last a lifetime.

The video, which I thought might be of interest only to flying fanatics like myself, evolved into an hour-long television special that was shown in several cities, including my own TV alma maters: Detroit and Philadelphia.

If there's anything I'm as passionate about as flying airplanes, it's my belief that we start dying as soon as we stop living. As I complete this book, I have survived fifteen years beyond my first cancer diagnosis, and today I remain cancer-free. For that I am deeply grateful.

Someday it will all come to an end. Maybe the coronavirus won't get me this year, but we all have an expiration date. I'm rather certain that when mine comes up, I won't have too many regrets over things I might wish I had done.

* * *

Perhaps it was inevitable that having been the archetype for Ron Burgundy, a sitcom would provide my next gig.

"Mort, they want you to play yourself on the new Comedy Central show *The Detroiters*," Kathy Mooney said.

Kathy was a well-known Detroit agent and casting director. I had read about the new show, produced by *Saturday Night Live* Executive Producer Lorne Michaels and featuring a hometown cast and crew. The entire series was to be shot in Detroit.

"It's a cameo role," Kathy said, "but you'll be on most of the episodes."

Well, why not. A show about Detroit has to be good for the city. Besides, I've never been on a sitcom. (There goes my ham gene, acting up again).

The show did well, and my brief appearances as the local anchorman, showing up on a TV in a local bar, must have been well received.

"Mort, this is Steven Yell."

The call was coming from Hollywood.

"I'm producer on *The Detroiters*. Happy to let you know the show has been renewed for a second season."

"Great," I responded. Before I could say anything else, Steven said,

"We want you back in an expanded role. In fact, we plan to give you the major guest role in one of the episodes."

It didn't take long for me to say yes, and within a few days a new contract was on my desk.

It called for me to continue with my cameos—each one longer than during the first season—plus a lead role in one episode they cleverly titled "Mort Crim."

I had been on many TV sets and a few movie sets, but it's different when they give you your own trailer, director's chair, personal hair stylist, and make-up artist, plus a car and chauffeur.

I had a rather busy summer schedule, so they agreed to compress all of my shooting into a couple of days. The crew was quite deferential to me, partly because of my status as the city's former anchorman, but mostly I'm sure it was because I was old enough to be their grandfather. It took me most of the first day to convince them they really didn't have to call me "Mr. Crim."

The premise was that a local furniture store wanted to hire me as their television spokesman. In the episode I finally agree, but while filming the first commercial I go off-script and launch into a rant about North Korea, ISIS, and a lot of other irrelevant stuff.

But one of the funniest moments, at least for the crew, was completely unscripted. They were creating a montage of me as a superhero that would open my newscast: I was to burst into a burning building, microphone in hand, cover a story while dangling from a helicopter ladder, and race off to cover breaking news on a motorcycle.

So when it came time for the motorcycle scene, an associate producer walked over to explain how it would work.

"We have bungee cords holding the motorcycle up. All you have to do is sort of sway it back and forth. We'll put in the background later so it looks like you're cruising down a highway."

"Got it," I said.

I had done some of this Hollywood make-believe stuff at promo shoots for the news station, so this would be no sweat.

"And, Mr. Crim, would you like for us to get you a box? That might make it easier to mount the motorcycle."

"No, definitely won't need that," I said with a chuckle.

How dare that young upstart suggest that I needed help mounting that bike. Did he think I was some decrepit old geezer?

My make-up artist, a delightful young woman (young enough to be my granddaughter!) was seated next to me and heard the whole insulting thing.

"Can you believe that guy?" I said to her. "He must think I'm as old as Methuselah."

A couple of minutes later,

"Okay, Mr. Crim, we're ready for the motorcycle scene."

I swaggered up to the Harley, which seemed to grow in size as I got closer.

Gee, this beast is tall, I thought, as I attempted to hoist my leg over the seat.

I tried. Believe me, I tried. With every ounce of strength I could muster, I commanded my leg to lift itself over the seat, but my leg wasn't listening. I grunted and strained but couldn't convince that leg to make it up the last few inches needed to clear the saddle. Totally humiliated, I refused to look over at the young make-up artist who, I was pretty sure, must be stifling laughter.

Without a word, the smart-ass associate producer slipped over and quietly set a box in front of me.

I've always hated motorcycles.

*　*　*

Certain birthdays I remember:

16—when I got my driver's license.

21—the year I could vote.

50—when I started cashing in on those AARP discounts.

65—the age at which I retired from TV.

80 was also memorable. That's when I officially became an octogenarian. Unfortunately, that didn't come with any additional discounts.

But it was a landmark year simply because Renee and I were still alive. That either of us would be had not been a certainty.

For me, there had been two cancer diagnoses and two heart stents installed since retirement, and for Renee, a heart attack, one stent, and a second bout with breast cancer.

The doctors continued to assure both of us that we were in good health, but of course always adding that familiar little caveat, "for your age."

Just being on the top side of the grass for another year was cause for celebration and we shared our joy with the family by taking everybody on a cruise to Bermuda.

But turning eighty called for more than celebration. It was a year for serious reflection, and I shared some of my thoughts with our children, as our daughter recently reminded me.

"Dad, do you remember the letter you wrote to Al and me when you turned 80," Carey asked. "I've kept that letter in a drawer next to our bed. Let me send you a copy. Maybe you could use some of it in your book."

Dear Al and Carey,

For some of us who are on a rather *short string,* the prospect of death becomes increasingly real.

I am sobered by the realization that most of the sand in my hourglass already has trickled to the bottom. This does not depress me, as I'm fully reconciled to the reality that my life will come to an end. But it does make me more thoughtful about priorities, core values, and the importance of making the remaining grains of sand count for something.

During my long career as a journalist, I encountered people at all levels of society during their final days—interviewed many, talked with survivors of others—and have come to the conclusion that how we die and how we face death is the end result of how we have lived. If we've been generous, giving, kind, thinking always of others, living as though we were placed upon this earth for the purpose of serving others, then I believe we are prepared for death. The thought of it may make us sad, but it holds no terror.

Whatever questions I have (and no doubt will always have) about some specifics of my personal faith, I do have a certainty that existence is meaningful and that we are much more than the accidental co-location of atoms.

And so, I still go to church, not because I fear some kind of eternal punishment; to be sure, I've often found more inspiration at a symphony or watching a play or in a boat, fishing, than in some church services. But I go because I need to be reminded each week that life isn't just about me and that I'm here for a purpose. I need to be challenged, inspired, and re-focus my recognition that life itself does, ultimately, matter.

This faith inspires a sense of obligation to the rest of creation that has guided and motivated me as I've stumbled and bungled and, with all my flaws and inadequacies, tried to make some difference in the world.

I hope that somewhere along the way I've shown a little kindness, enlightened and informed a few folks, guided a few young people and maybe will leave things around my little corner of the world just a bit better than I found them.

My prayer now is that your lives will be used to enrich our world, to touch and help heal the brokenness in our world and to use the enormous talents you both have in a way that will allow you, when you come to the end, to say:

I lived for something bigger than myself.

What that looks like, what form it takes, how it plays out for each of you, I certainly can't say, but it is my constant prayer that as you navigate the many intersections of life and make so many important decisions, you keep that *something bigger* always in mind.

Both of you, in your own, individualistic and unique ways, are sensitive, caring people. I see that. I know that. And while each of you faces different challenges, know that you have a Dad who loves you more than life itself, who will always have your back, and who never ends a day without offering a new prayer for you both.

I love you dearly,

Dad

Acknowledgements

WORDS ARE SUPPOSED TO FLOW EASILY for a writer, but when it comes to thanking those who have in some way contributed to this book, finding adequate words is difficult.

First, I thank you, Renee, for your remarkable patience during the five years I was preoccupied with research and writing. I am more grateful than I can express for your support, encouragement, and suggestions. Mostly, thank you for coming into my life. I love you.

Carey Crim, my daughter, a talented and successful play-wright who took time to review and critique the final work even as she juggled her own demanding personal and professional schedule, much of it amid the coronavirus crisis.

George DeFotis, Carey's wonderful husband, and the guy I would have picked for her—if she had asked me.

Albert Crim, my son, and a gifted screenwriter who, like Carey, is a far better writer than his dad. Al, your suggestions along the journey, including the book's title, were both welcomed and respected.

Alanna Nash, who began this journey as my editor and completes it as a dear friend. A successful author in her own right, Alanna was invaluable in helping me structure the memoir as well as eliminating extraneous material.

Lita Robinson, the manuscript's final editor, whose careful scrutiny and helpful suggestions definitely have made this a better book.

Susanna Einstein, my literary agent, for encouragement, for belief in my memoir, and for helping me successfully navigate the ever-changing world of publishing.

Mary Bisbee-Beek, a late-comer to the party, but whose skillfull handling of the final publishing and promotion processes was crucial.

I am grateful for a close and loving extended family, whose influence upon my life is quietly, sometimes noisily, evident in these pages:

Barbara Crim, my sister, and her children, Anne, Bryan and Naomi. You all have my enduring love and respect for the way you have handled everything life has dealt.

Alvah Crim, the evangelist uncle who was both mentor and 'big brother.'

Vera Martin, the missionary aunt who never married and

who considered Barbara and me *her kids.*

Chuck and Sandy Dale, Kathryn McElrath, Louise (Smiley) and Jayne Smith, the in-laws I inherited when I married Nicki, who soon became great friends. Our shared history and our love has created a forever-bond.

Jeff and Carolyn Miller, Randy and Jamie Miller—the sons and daughters-in-law who came into my life when I married Renee. The love, respect and affection that developed between my children and Renee's is a text-book example of a successful blending of families. We love you guys.

The Reverend Ed Bowman, Renee's brother, who officiated at our wedding, and his wife, Gloria. Ed's deep faith and his commitment to ministry inspire me, and Renee's devotion to her older brother never ceases to amaze me. "He's absolutely perfect," she insists.

I have been blessed with a multitude of wonderful friends, but one, the late Steve Bell, was so special we always called each other *the brother we never had.* My friendship with Steve and Joyce began at Northwestern in graduate school, flourished during our time as colleagues at ABC, and deepened over the years.

Their children, Allison and Hilary (my godchild), are like my own. Steve's generosity of time in reviewing parts of my manuscript made me think seriously about my beliefs, and his critiques and challenges forced me to sharpen the way I expressed those beliefs. Sadly, Steve and Joyce both passed away within a few weeks of each other and shortly before the publication of this book.

Other friends who have been especially important in my life: Bill and Gloria Gaither, Vince and Frankie Leonard, Frank and JonAnna Reidinger, Terry and Barbara Oprea, Tony and

Peggy Campolo, Al and Beverly Meltzer, Bill and Sheila Norris, and Lloyd and Vera Abel.

Many clergy have had special influence upon my life and thought, some as personal friends, others through their writings. A partial but important list includes:

Tom Walker, Carol DiGiusto, Holly Ingles, Laurie Furr-Vancini, Bruce Rigdon, R. Eugene Sterner, Denzel Lovely, Richard Rohr, Harvey Cox, Leslie Weatherhead and John Shelby Spong.

For both personal and professional reasons, I am also grateful to the following:

Betty Ash; Ruthie Amies; Paul Brinkerhof; Bob Brooks; Bob Clinkingbeard; Mack Combs; Mike Eisgrau; Silvia Fiondo; Alan Frank; Nick George; Bob and Elaine Goll; Ron Gorski; John Halbert; Donald Hamburg; Carmen Harlan; Sara Hassinger; Lisa Hubbs; Daphne Hughes; Jim Lynagh; Henry Maldonado; Paul Manzella; Amy McCombs; Dick and Alissa Mertz; Bob Morse; Tom O'Brien; Harvey Ovshinsky; John Owens; Carol Rueppel; Marciarose Shestack; Jim Snyder; Jim Stanhope; Pat Stratton; Ron Thayer; Anne Thompson; Bob Warfield.

Finally, I want to acknowledge the people who give me great hope for tomorrow when the future feels bleak: our five grandchildren. I list them from oldest to youngest, since they all are number one to us:

Zachary, Emily, Riley, Gabriel, and Eliana.

I am in awe of their accomplishments, inspired by their potential, and confident each will take seriously a fundamental lesson modeled by their parents to make a positive difference in the world.

Mother and Dad, for unconditional love and their positive example.

Finally, my late wife, Nicki—childhood sweetheart, fantastic mom, and a true partner with me throughout our 34 years together. The measure of her selfless love was her deathbed request that I "not make a career" of mourning her, and that I would promise to build a new life.